FAITH-BASED MANAGEMENT

WILEY NONPROFIT LAW, FINANCE, AND MANAGEMENT SERIES

The Art of Planned Giving: Understanding Donors and the Culture of Giving by Douglas E. White

Beyond Fund Raising: New Strategies for Nonprofit Investment and Innovation by Kay Grace

Budgeting for Not-for-Profit Organizations by David Maddox

Charity, Advocacy, and the Law by Bruce R. Hopkins

The Complete Guide to Fund Raising Management by Stanley Weinstein

The Complete Guide to Nonprofit Management by Smith, Bucklin & Associates

Critical Issues in Fund Raising edited by Dwight Burlingame

Developing Affordable Housing: A Practical Guide for Nonprofit Organizations, Second Edition by Bennett L. Hecht

Financial and Accounting Guide for Not-for-Profit Organizations, Fifth Edition by Malvern J. Gross, Jr., Richard F. Larkin, Roger S. Bruttomesso, John J. McNally, PricewaterhouseCoopers LLP

Financial Management for Nonprofit Organizations by Jo Ann Hankin, Alan Seidner and John Zietlow

Financial Planning for Nonprofit Organizations by Jody Blazek

The Fund Raiser's Guide to the Internet by Michael Johnston

Fund-Raising: Evaluating and Managing the Fund Development Process, Second Edition by James M. Greenfield

Fund-Raising Fundamentals: A Guide to Annual Giving for Professionals and Volunteers by James M. Greenfield

Fund-Raising Regulation: A State-by-State Handbook of Registration Forms, Requirements, and Procedures by Seth Perlman and Betsy Hills Bush

Grantseeker's Toolkit: A Comprehensive Guide to Finding Funding by Cheryl S. New and James Quick

High Performance Nonprofit Organizations: Managing Upstream for Greater Impact by Christine Letts, William Ryan, and Allen Grossman

Intermediate Sanctions: Curbing Nonprofit Abuse by Bruce R. Hopkins and D. Benson Tesdahl

International Fund Raising for Nonprofits by Thomas Harris

International Guide to Nonprofit Law by Lester A. Salamon and Stefan Toepler & Associates

The Law of Fund-Raising, Second Edition by Bruce R. Hopkins

The Law of Tax-Exempt Healthcare Organizations by Thomas K. Hyatt and Bruce R. Hopkins

The Law of Tax-Exempt Organizations, Sixth Edition by Bruce R. Hopkins

The Legal Answer Book for Nonprofit Organizations by Bruce R. Hopkins

A Legal Guide to Starting and Managing a Nonprofit Organization, Second Edition by Bruce R. Hopkins

Managing Affordable Housing: A Practical Guide to Creating Stable Communities by Bennett L. Hecht, Local Initiatives Support Corporation, and James Stockard

Managing Upstream: Creating High-Performance Nonprofit Organizations by Christine W. Letts, William P. Ryan, and Allan Grossman

Nonprofit Boards: Roles, Responsibilities, and Performance by Diane J. Duca

Nonprofit Compensation and Benefits Practices by Applied Research and Development Institute International, Inc.

The Nonprofit Counsel by Bruce R. Hopkins

The Nonprofit Guide to the Internet, Second Edition by Michael Johnston

Nonprofit Investment Policies: A Practical Guide to Creation and Implementation by Robert Fry, Jr.

The Nonprofit Law Dictionary by Bruce R. Hopkins

Nonprofit Compensation, Benefits, and Employment Law by David G. Samuels and Howard Pianko

Nonprofit Litigation: A Practical Guide with Forms and Checklists by Steve Bachmann

The Nonprofit Handbook, Second Edition: Volume I-Management by Tracy Daniel Connors

The Nonprofit Handbook, Second Edition: Volume II-Fund Raising by Jim Greenfield

The Nonprofit Manager's Resource Dictionary by Ronald A. Landskroner

Nonprofit Organizations' Business Forms: Disk Edition by John Wiley & Sons, Inc.

Partnerships and Joint Ventures Involving Tax-Exempt Organizations by Michael I. Sanders

Planned Giving: Management, Marketing, and Law by Ronald R. Jordan and Katelyn L. Quynn

Private Foundations: Tax Law and Compliance by Bruce R. Hopkins and Jody Blazek

Program Related Investments: A Technical Manual for Foundations by Christie I. Baxter

Reengineering Your Nonprofit Organization: A Guide to Strategic Transformation by Alceste T. Pappas

Reinventing the University: Managing and Financing Institutions of Higher Education by Sandra L. Johnson and Sean C. Rush, PricewaterhouseCoopers LLP

The Second Legal Answer Book for Nonprofit Organizations by Bruce R. Hopkins

Special Events: Proven Strategies for Nonprofit Fund Raising by Alan Wendroff

Strategic Communications for Nonprofit Organizations: Seven Steps to Creating a Successful Plan by Janel Radtke

Strategic Planning for Nonprofit Organizations: A Practical Guide and Workbook by Michael Allison and Jude Kaye, Support Center for Nonprofit Management

Streetsmart Financial Basics for Nonprofit Managers by Thomas A. McLaughlin

A Streetsmart Guide to Nonprofit Mergers and Networks by Thomas A. McLaughlin

Successful Marketing Strategies for Nonprofit Organizations by Barry J. McLeish

The Tax Law of Charitable Giving by Bruce R. Hopkins

The Tax Law of Colleges and Universities by Bertrand M. Harding

Tax Planning and Compliance for Tax-Exempt Organizations: Forms, Checklists, Procedures, Third Edition by Jody Blazek

The Universal Benefits of Volunteering: A Practical Workbook for Nonprofit Organizations, Volunteers and Corporations by Walter P. Pidgeon, Jr.

The Volunteer Management Handbook by Tracy Daniel Connors

OTHER TITLES IN THE *Mission-Based Management™ Series* by Peter C. Brinckerhoff

Financial Empowerment: More Money for More Mission by Peter C. Brinckerhoff

Mission-Based Management: Leading Your Not-for-Profit Into the 21st Century by Peter C. Brinckerhoff

Mission-Based Marketing: How Your Not-for-Profit Can Succeed in a More Competitive World by Peter C. Brinckerhoff

FAITH-BASED MANAGEMENT

LEADING ORGANIZATIONS THAT ARE BASED ON MORE THAN JUST MISSION

Peter C. Brinckerhoff

JOHN WILEY & SONS. INC.

New York • Chichester • Weinheim • Brisbane • Singapore • Toronto

Copyright © 1999 by John Wiley & Sons, Inc. All rights reserved.

Published simultaneously in Canada.

Library of Congress Cataloging-in-Publication Data:

Brinckerhoff, Peter C., 1952–
    Faith-based management : leading organizations that are based on
more than just mission / Peter C. Brinckerhoff.
        p.   cm.
    Includes bibliographical references and index.
    ISBN 0-471-31544-3 (cloth : alk. paper)
    1. Religious institutions—Management.   I. Title.
    BL632.B75   1999   99-22087
    291.6'5—dc21   CIP

Printed in the United States of America.

10 9 8 7 6 5 4 3 2 1

For Ben, Adam, and Caitlin.
You three give me faith.

About the Author

Peter Brinckerhoff is an internationally acclaimed consultant, author, and lecturer. He is President of Corporate Alternatives, inc., the consulting firm that he founded in 1982. He is a former staff member, executive director, board member, and volunteer for local, state, and national not-for-profit organizations.

Peter is the author of over 70 articles in the nonprofit press, as well as three previous books, which are used in over 50 undergraduate and graduate programs as core texts. His first two books, *Mission-Based Management* and *Financial Empowerment*, each won the Nonprofit Management Association's prestigious Terry McAdam Award as "the year's best new nonprofit publication."

Peter lives in Springfield, Illinois, with his wife and three children.

Contents

Preface

This book is about management. It is also about faith, as the two are inextricably intertwined for staff and volunteers of faith-based organizations. I have tried to examine traditional management issues in the unique light of the manager's faith and to put the issues that so often vex staff and volunteers in that same perspective.

I do not know your faith. I don't know which teachings you follow or how you label yourself spiritually. For the purposes of this book, that doesn't matter. And, in researching the book, I found many teachings in many sacred texts that appear to me to give good, solid guidance to all faith-based managers. As a result, I've included them in the pages that follow.

I know from my interviews that some readers may be upset by seeing a variety of different holy books quoted here. I also know that many, many people encouraged that same ecumenical perspective on management. Personally, I think it makes for a stronger book, one that can speak to many people from many backgrounds and many faiths.

The various citations from the Bible, Talmud, Qur'an, and I Ching that I have included are, of course, subject to interpretation by the reader. You may agree or disagree with my use or my interpretation of these passages, and that is fine. All I can tell you is that they spoke to me. If they can help you to be a better manager and ultimately, to achieve the good wishes I send your way on the very last page of the last chapter, then I have achieved my goal.

Acknowledgments

For me, this book was different. The ideas, stories, suggestions, and hints in my first three books came almost entirely from my experiences with not-for-profit organizations as a staff member, board member, and consultant. I relied on my notes from those interactions and from the articles, training materials, and lectures that grew out of my consultations. There was minimal research and I conducted no interviews.

This time, all that changed. While I have worked with many local, statewide, and national faith-based organizations as a consultant and trainer, a book that is this focused on one particular sector deserved a lot of research. That meant much reading and many conversations with people who are staff and volunteers in faith-based organizations of all sizes and types. Thus, I am indebted to many, many individuals who selflessly shared their time to give me their perspective on what makes a faith-based organization special. Their insights into their work, their roles in our communities, and their faith were more than informative, they were truly inspiring.

Additionally, for this book I had two editors instead of one. Bob Follett, my good and true friend and the editor of my first three books, didn't abandon me just because this book was published by John Wiley & Sons. He again saw much more in my early drafts than was really there and showed me the way to find it and put it into words. Martha Cooley, of John Wiley & Sons, provided much needed counsel on the strategy for the book, the most appropriate target audience, and the ways to appeal to and give value to you, the reader. Both these editors deserve my thanks, and I give it wholeheartedly. After you read the book, if you like what you see, remember that most of the good stuff here is in large portion due to Bob and Martha. Blame the bad stuff on me.

1
Introduction

If any of you lacks wisdom, let him ask God, who gives to all men generously and without reproaching, and it will be given him. James 1.5

They are all straight to him who understands and right to those who find knowledge. Take my instruction instead of silver, and knowledge rather than choice gold; for wisdom is better than jewels, and all that you may desire cannot compare with her. Proverbs 8.1–11

PRELUDE

In this chapter you will learn about:

> ➤ The special challenge of the faith-based organization
> ➤ The benefits of reading this book
> ➤ A chapter-by-chapter overview
> ➤ How to get the most from this book

Welcome. I am gratified that you have chosen this book to help you improve your faith-based organization. I am very aware of the fact that my readers have invested some of their precious time with me, so I assure you that I will do everything I can to make your investment one that pays off handsomely for you, your staff and, most importantly, the people your organization serves. I know that you want to have a quick turnaround from reading to application because you are in a hurry. Your organization's mission cannot wait, your personal calling cannot be deferred, the people you serve deserve no further delay. This book is full of proven concepts and ideas that are demonstrated through examples from many not-for-profit organizations, many faith-based, some not. Each chapter also contains many hands-on suggestions for you to apply immediately in your work.

1

This book is written to help the paid and volunteer leadership of faith-based not-for-profit organizations. Whether you are the pastor of a small church, the deacon of a large one, or the executive director of a soup kitchen or foster parent organization, this book will have many benefits for you, your organization, and the people that you serve.

WHY THIS BOOK, AND WHY NOW?

I have been volunteering and working in, around, and for not-for-profits my entire life. My parents were lifelong volunteers and on the boards of many organizations in our home community of Hartford. The summer that I was fifteen, my mother informed me that I was not going to sit around all summer, but was going to do something useful! That something useful turned out to be a summer-long stint as a volunteer in the emergency room at Mt. Sinai Hospital in the north end of Hartford. My eyes were opened, not only to a side of life that I had never even imagined, but more importantly, to the dedication that the staff throughout the facility brought to their work. About halfway through the summer, we had a particularly difficult shift that saw auto accidents, beatings, and gunshot victims come in faster than the staff could handle them. By the end of the shift I was exhausted, both physically and emotionally, and the fatigue fueled a foul and frustrated mood. Life was unfair (not an unusual revelation for a fifteen-year-old). There was just too much pain, too much poverty, too many people to help. I was in the middle of my first true altruistic funk, and I'm sure I looked it. I was greeted by the administrator of the hospital on my way out. He took me aside and asked me how I liked my job, how the hospital staff were treating me, and in general, how I was doing. I informed him that, to put it mildly, I was not doing well. I remember voicing my frustrations and concerns, as well as my feeling that I could not possibly keep up and do my share to help. I told him, "It gets very depressing. I don't know how the ER staff keep up their energy, their spirits, and their hope. How do they do this work?" The administrator's answer was one that has stayed with me to this day. "They don't do the work. God does it through them. That's where they get the strength, the hope, the compassion and the commitment to their calling." That evening I went home and looked up the word *calling* in the dictionary. And somewhere inside I knew I had to work in or around organizations with that kind of passion, that kind of dedication, that kind of energy.

Such passion, dedication, and energy show up in many, if not most, of our not-for-profit organizations. Whether they serve in hospitals, museums, animal shelters, schools, symphonies, the YMCA, Special

Olympics, Boy or Girl Scouts, or any one of a myriad of other entities the staffs and volunteers of not-for-profit organizations bring a very special set of qualities to bear on their mission. They are uniformly underfunded, underappreciated, overworked, and some days, just plain overwhelmed. Despite all this, they keep coming back for more, and that is why I have chosen to work with and for them, really for all of you, for all of my career.

So what happens when you take that level of commitment, that level of energy, that level of passion and then you amplify it with a huge dose of faith? How are faith-based organizations different? How does "having God on your side" change things? As one Baptist pastor told me, "Your secular not-for-profit has its mission, and that's great. But we add to that the great *commission*, and that's what makes it amazing!"

In writing this book, I talked to literally hundreds of people who are involved in serving faith-based organizations as staff and volunteers. Their faith, their energy, their commitment, and their dedication should ring clearly throughout this text. They certainly inspired me to keep going in the task of trying to put into words ideas and suggestions that I know will make your organization more mission-capable.

But we should start at the beginning. In the remainder of this chapter, we'll review why it is that faith-based organizations present such a special challenge. I'll give you some reasons—some mine, some from organizations I worked with, some from scripture. I hope that these reasons will help you see why good management is good mission, even if it isn't as much fun or as satisfying as preaching, healing, teaching, or other kinds of direct service. Next, we'll review the benefits that you will get by reading the entire book. There are many, and as I said earlier, I want you to get a very high return on your investment of time and money. Third, we'll preview the remainder of the book, chapter by chapter. I'll give you thumbnail overviews of what's in each chapter and hopefully whet your appetite for what's to come. Finally, I'll give you some suggestions on how to get the most from your reading and some tips on how to implement the ideas that you like quickly and successfully.

A. THE SPECIAL CHALLENGE OF FAITH-BASED ORGANIZATIONS

I suspect that we should start by defining what *"faith-based"* means in the context of the remainder of this book. To me the faith-based organization is one that is closely aligned with a religious faith or a denomination of a faith. The most obvious examples would be a church, a synagogue, or a temple. But to limit our discussion to these kinds of organizations would not do the subject justice. Why? Because so many other organizations also strive to meet a mission that is inspired by their faith. Organizations such as Catholic Charities, the Salvation Army, The Fellowship of Christian Athletes, Lutheran Social Services, and B'nai Brith, to list just a few nationally known "name-brands," fit into my definition. So do local church-run schools, hospitals (including Mt. Sinai in my earlier story), homeless shelters, nursing homes, and overseas missions. Organizations as large as colleges and universities and as small as a local soup kitchen or homeless shelter qualify. It doesn't matter if the faith behind the mission is obvious from the name or not. What matters is that the faith was there at the beginning of the organization, has been there throughout its growth and development, and most importantly, is evident in the actions and policies of the organization today.

As we go through this book together, I will provide you with ideas and examples and in some cases will distinguish between the two large subcategories of faith-based organizations, which quite often, have widely different interpretations of a particular issue or problem. One of these subcategories, which will be called *places of worship,* includes churches, temples, synagogues, meeting houses, and any other places where people gather to display fellowship and to learn more about and praise their God. Places of worship, of course, come in all shape and sizes. Some have budgets in the thousands, some have budgets in the hundreds of millions. Some congregations number in single digits, some in the tens of thousands. However, while many places of worship have ancillary or affiliated schools, nursing homes, retirement centers, or missions, the primary focus of the place of worship is spiritual teaching, spiritual growth, and the creation of a faith-based community of believers.

The other major organizational subgroup consists of *community service organizations.* These groups focus on providing one or more community services to both believers and nonbelievers. They often have to deal with more secular issues, such as legislation, licensing, funding streams, government regulations, and the like. They are often, but not always, larger than places of worship, and quite often they employ a large paid staff, whose members may or may not be members of the faith that sponsors the employer.

But what all these organizations share is a mandate to pursue a mission that results in both worldly good for their service recipients *and* spiritual growth for those individuals, as well as for the staff and volunteers who serve and manage the organization. It is this mix and, in successful organizations, synergy of purpose that makes faith-based organizations special and especially challenging to manage.

What kind of challenge?

❏ **FOR EXAMPLE:** You are the head of a soup kitchen sponsored by an evangelical Christian church group. You provide food to all who present themselves and help find shelter for those who need it. Your organization has a reputation as a safe place, staffed with good people, both paid and volunteer, serving reasonably tasty food. Your volunteers come almost exclusively from the churches that sponsor your organization, and they are numerous, hard-working, enthusiastic and, most importantly, essential to your continued operation. Thus, you are smart to keep them happy.

As you have many years on the job, you have learned that there is a place and a time for bringing the Word of God to the people you serve. Too soon, and you may chase them off; too late, and you lose the opportunity to help them find Jesus. You and your staff are comfortable that you have balanced your mission of worldly works with your calling to save the unsaved. Lately though, you see some of your newer volunteers greeting people at the door and sitting with them while they eat, and something doesn't seem quite right. You have fewer "returns"—people who come back for a second or third meal—and many people who do come to eat leave right away, even though they previously often stayed for a second cup of coffee and some conversation. You investigate and find that your new, enthusiastic volunteers are also recently converted Christians, who are full of both enthusiasm and evangelism—they are almost literally not letting people get both feet in the door before they start to talk to them about Jesus.

You meet with the volunteers in question and talk to them about your view that you need to feed people first with food and then with fellowship. You explain your experience with the hungry and how you have found that leading by example works better than leading with a hard sell, no matter how well intentioned. To put it mildly, they disagree and argue that the highest priority is to proclaim the word of God at every opportunity. They contend that you may have only one chance with hungry or homeless persons, and so you must talk to them now and not let them leave without hearing about how they can have a personal relationship with God. This debate is long, impassioned, and unresolved.

The following Sunday, you are scheduled to talk about your organization in a number of the Sunday school classes that provide your organization with both a significant amount of funding and a large number of volunteers. Predictably, the issue of evangelism comes up again, and as you leave, you are concerned about the continuation of both a needed stream of income and an even more important source of workers. Do you change your philosophy to meet those of your benefactors? Or, do you continue to face this issue in the same way as in the past?

This kind of conflict is not unusual in a faith-based organization. It can center on evangelism, on abortion, on homosexuality, on women in the ministry, on things inside the organization, or on things outside the organization, such as the 1997 Southern Baptist boycott of Disney. When you layer worldly concerns on top of a foundation of faith, interesting, challenging, frustrating, and often wonderful things happen. How better to manage the outcomes is the reason for this book.

B. THE BENEFITS OF READING THIS BOOK

This book is particularly written for staff members, policy setters, and volunteers of faith-based organizations. Additionally, it is intended for the many people who oversee more than one organization of the same type, such as a geographically defined group of churches. No matter which of these important roles you fill, you will find information and ideas that you can put to immediate and mission-beneficial use in the following pages. But what will you learn, and how will you benefit from your investment of time? At least in the following ways:

1. You will learn the seven characteristics of the successful faith-based organization, how they are formulated, and how you can achieve and retain them in your own organization.
2. You will learn how being involved in helping a faith-based organization presents special challenges—and special rewards.
3. You will learn the appropriate roles of staff, board, and volunteers in your faith-based organization and how to make sure that each of these parties knows whose role is whose.
4. You will learn the spiritual approach to staff management, one that includes an emphasis on trust, guidance, and goal setting for both the supervisor and the supervised.
5. You will learn about financial stewardship and how to get the most mission for the resources that you have been given.
6. You will find out about the connection between your mission and marketing, and how to use some well-established techniques to further both your spiritual and worldly goals.
7. You will find out how to identify and use your special gifts as a leader in your organization and how to plan your organization's future course.

8. You will learn the key techniques necessary to recruit, motivate, and retain volunteers in your faith-based organization.

9. Finally, you will examine how to keep close to your faith and your faith-based mission in a very secular, demanding, and rapidly changing world.

There is much more, of course: examples, hands-on ideas, and scriptural context. But I promise you that you will come away from this book with these nine areas of management in much clearer view than when you started.

C. CHAPTER-BY-CHAPTER OVERVIEW

This book is divided into eleven chapters, each focusing on a particular issue such as governance, staff management, finance, or marketing. Each chapter is set up to help you receive the most benefit from your reading. Let's go over the features that you will find in every chapter.

Immediately following the chapter title, you will find one or more quotations from Scripture that provide a spiritual basis for the philosophies, ideas and suggestions that follow. You may well want to use these scriptural excerpts as a basis for further study on your own or discussion with your pastor, priest, or rabbi. People of faith have their world view strongly affected by their spiritual perspective. Thus, there should be a very real link between your faith and your management style. I strongly encourage this mix of management and spiritual growth; I think that they both fall under your job description if you are a staff member or volunteer in a faith-based organization. There are other scriptural references throughout the text, but the noted excerpts are the key ones for the chapter. (Please note that the scriptural citations are mine, and that if you disagree with me on their application to the various points I made throughout the book, that's fine. But they spoke to me, so I included them.)

Second, you will find a **PRELUDE,** which is a brief summary of the major subjects that I will cover. In the body of the chapter you will find two features. ❑ **FOR EXAMPLE** will indicate a story or short example from the faith-based, not-for-profit, or business world. These examples are designed to illustrate a point or an idea in the text. The ☞ **HANDS ON** symbol is good news for readers who want ideas that they can immediately use; it means that just such a suggestion will be provided for you. The intent is to help you apply what you have just learned and give you a hint, idea, or gentle nudge to get you started.

At the end of each chapter are three additional features. The first is a **POSTLUDE,** in which I review the key ideas that I have presented, as a reminder and summary. Then, in the working chapters (four through ten) you will find a ✓**Checklist,** which will provide you with specific items to examine in your organization. The final section of each chapter, entitled **Questions for Discussion,** provides you with a number of questions that you can use with your fellow staff members and volunteers to analyze the uses and impacts of the ideas that are contained in the chapter.

Now that you know the design of the chapters, let's look at their sequence and content.

Chapter One: Introduction

This is the chapter you are reading now. It provides a short discussion of why faith-based organizations are special, what comprises a faith-based organization, a listing of the benefits I promise to deliver as you read the book, a short description of the contents of each chapter, and some ways that I recommend to ensure that you get the most out of the book.

Chapter Two: The Special Calling of the Faith-Based Organization

In this important, context-setting chapter, we will examine some key questions: What sets the faith-based organization apart? Why are you special? What special challenges do you face? Do you have just a mission or a greater commission? And most importantly, why is good management worth the effort and how is it tied to your faith, your mission, and the people you serve?

Chapter Three: The Characteristics of a Successful Faith-Based Organization

There are seven characteristics of a successful faith-based organization. This chapter will list them one by one, go into detail about what they mean, and outline how your organization can achieve and maintain them. The chapter also contains an organizational self-assessment chart, so that you can examine your organization and determine how it measures up to my list of standards.

Chapter Four: The Duties of Staff and Board

Governing volunteers and employees have different roles and responsibilities. Whether your governing body is called a board of directors, elders, a governing council, or trustees, there are some overall responsibilities that the leaders must fulfill. Whether the staff consists of one part-time, bivocational pastor or 5,000 medical personnel, there are clearly defined staff roles and responsibilities that also need to be performed. This chapter will list these for both the staff and the board. It will also discuss how to recruit and retain a strong governing body.

Chapter Five: Staff Management

If you supervise staff or volunteers you have a special role and responsibility. This chapter will discuss management in a spiritual model and include practical models for delegation, evaluation, discipline, communications, and motivation.

Chapter Six: Financial Stewardship

This chapter will cover the most important parts of financial stewardship, including budgeting and reporting, financial controls, and how to (and how not to) use volunteers in financial oversight, and will list the information that you really need in order to manage your organization well. I'll also take some of the mystery out of finance by including a list of key financial terms and their meanings.

Chapter Seven: Leadership in the Faith-Based Organization

All successful organizations need leaders, and this is true for yours. But what are the essential characteristics of good leaders? Do your gifts match this list? How can you move to improve your skills? This chapter will show you how to go beyond mere supervision into the realm of leadership.

Chapter Eight: Faith-Based Marketing

Good marketing is good mission. To perform your mission well, you must be effective at marketing. The rules of marketing apply to every church, synagogue, hospital, and soup kitchen. In this chapter, we'll examine why that is, what the marketing cycle is, and how you can apply it to your faith-based organization. We'll examine your markets, how to get more out of marketing materials, and how to obtain the feedback you need from your constituencies.

Chapter Nine: Vision and Planning

One of the key facets of good stewardship is planning your organization's path into the future. In this chapter we'll discuss the reasons to plan, look at a time-tested planning process, and provide you with an outline of a strategic plan, a marketing plan, and a business plan.

Chapter Ten: Getting the Most from Your Volunteers

Nearly all faith-based organizations use volunteers beyond their governing bodies. Whether they take the collection during worship services, staff the gift shop in a hospital, or help send out mailings from the thrift shop, volunteers are an essential part of your organization. This chapter will show you how to find, train, motivate, and retain excellent volunteers.

Chapter Eleven: Final Thoughts
There is still more to cover, and we'll do it in this final chapter. It is essential that in a rapidly changing world, both you and your organization hold on to your core values. I'll show you why and how. We'll also look at the issue of flexibility and how to achieve and maintain it while still valuing and honoring your organization's traditions. Finally, we'll examine ways to stay motivated to the mission, year-in and year-out.

Resources for Further Study
This section includes a listing of other resources, including print, training, and Internet locations that may be of help to you. Some readers always want to follow up with more study. I admire the life-long learner and have provided a starting point for further study.

Does this sound like a lot to cover, a bunch of stuff to learn and retain? It is, but the results of implementing the ideas in this book can be to make your organization much more mission-capable, much more focused, and much more of what it can and should be for your community and your faith.

D. HOW TO GET THE MOST FROM THIS BOOK

Now that you know what's in this book for you, let's take a moment to think through how to use the book most efficiently and effectively by looking at the ways that you and your staff and volunteers can get the most from reading this book. Again, I want you to get the highest level of return from your investment of time and money.

First, read the book through in the order in which it is written. I know that if you are like most readers, there are certain areas such as planning, volunteers, or finance that you are most interested in, but I urge you to read the book in order. I wrote the chapters in this order for a reason: they build on each other, each subject leading to the next. Try to avoid jumping around, and read it through once from cover to cover. Then if you need to go back, you can reread the parts that you need to focus on the most. If you don't you will run the risk of focusing only on the issues that you believe are in need of improvements and not taking a look at areas where you may have an organizational blind spot.

Second, this is your book. Just as I am sure your pastor, priest, or rabbi tells you about your holy text, mark up the book with notes, underlining, and sticky notes to help you get more and remember key things. By making notations you can retain more content and refer more quickly to important ideas later.

Third, read the book as a team if you can. Read a chapter, pass it around to your key staff and volunteers, and then use the questions at the end of each chapter to talk through ways to implement the ideas in each section. If you can afford to, buy multiple copies so that you can expedite the process. If you can't, fine. It will take a little more time, but going through the book as a group ensures that you will give all of my ideas a more complete examination, and it can build consensus for any changes that you may find are needed.

Finally, remember that this is, at the end of it, just a book. I am just a human being. There is no divine wisdom here, no mandate from God. I am not Moses, and this is not a new set of commandments. You, your staff, and your volunteers need to carefully consider my ideas and my suggestions and use the ones that you feel are right and appropriate for your faith, your organization, and your constituencies. There should be no blind acceptance, no action taken based on these writings that is not well thought through.

Not every one who says to me, "Lord, Lord," shall enter the kingdom of Heaven, but he who does the will of my Father who is in heaven. Matthew 7.21

The one who would have the worst position in God's sight on the Day of Resurrection would be a learned man who did not profit from his learning. Hadith of Darimi

POSTLUDE

In this chapter, you learned why faith-based organizations have a special management challenge and reap special rewards. You learned about the dual outcomes of worldly good and spiritual growth that drive the faith-based organization and how this presents certain challenges in management, planning, and resource allocation.

Then, you learned more about this book and how to get the most out of it. I outlined the nine major benefits of reading the book, gave you a summary of each chapter, and provided some suggestions on how to get the most out of our time together.

In the following chapters, you will put this information to good use. Our first task will be to examine why your faith-based organization is special and why exceptional management skills are needed in your day-to-day, weekly, monthly, and long-range activities. That is the subject of the next chapter.

QUESTIONS FOR DISCUSSION: CHAPTER ONE

1. What makes our organization special? Does our basis in faith strengthen us? How? Does it ever hold us back? How?

2. Can we fairly assess ourselves based on how well we manage our resources, on how good we are at being stewards?

3. Is there any information we need to gather as we continue through this book to judge ourselves fairly?

4. Should we read the remainder of the book as a group? If so, whom should we include?

2

The Special Calling of the Faith-Based Organization

If you will obey my voice and keep my covenant, you shall be my own possession among all peoples; for all the earth is mine, and you shall be to me a kingdom of priests and a holy nation. Exodus 19:5–6

You are the best community that has been raised up for mankind. You enjoin right conduct and forbid indecency; and you believe in God. Qur'an 3.110

PRELUDE

In this chapter you will learn about:

- ➤ What sets your organization apart
- ➤ Is it just a mission or a great commission?
- ➤ The need for good management in a faith-based organization

What makes your organization special? There must be *some* difference between your organization and others that are secular, or I would not have defined yours as a *faith-based* organization. Is it just faith that sets you apart? What baggage and benefits come along with your faith? (Do you work for the mission, or are you literally on a mission from God?) I think that you *are* different, that you *are* special, that you *do* have both baggage and benefit from your ties to a certain religion or denomination. I also believe deeply in the concept of stewardship and that good stewards use each and every resource at their command to pursue their missions. Good management, including marketing, personnel, finance, leadership, and planning, thus becomes part of good stewardship.

Why is this so important? Because more and more places of worship are becoming community service organizations, and more and more faith-based community service organizations are expanding because our social safety net is not supporting the increasing numbers of our neighbors who are in need. We're in an era in which the federal government's role is diminishing and federal mandates are being transferred to the states, which are delegating functions directly to already overburdened counties and municipalities.

We've also learned that simply throwing money at problems doesn't solve them and in some cases makes them worse. You can't buy your way out of disintegrating families, increasing violence in schools, drug abuse, or any others of the myriad of social and political ills that beset us. You need to lead, to coach, to parent, to counsel, and to preach your way out. Money is part of the answer, certainly. No money, no mission. But so are a set of core values and beliefs that faith-based organizations bring to the table and that they are supposed to exemplify and practice.

So who will step into the breach? Who will take on these problems? Who will fill the voids as they appear? Who can serve better at the local level than our places of worship and our faith-based community service organizations? If not we, then who? And if we don't do it well, how long will we be able to continue helping?

❏ **FOR EXAMPLE:** In the mid-1980s, one of the most rapidly growing churches in our community realized that it had reached a moral impasse. As fundamentalist Christians, the leadership and the congregation took a strong stand against abortion, demonstrating, lobbying and letter writing. But as this action went from being something new to something predictable, they began to ask themselves: What *effect* are we really having? If we *say* we believe in something, are we really *showing* it or just giving it lip service? They decided to take a huge step, and instead of just counseling women to let their babies come to term, they would offer to adopt them, especially the ones with severe disabilities. Soon families in the church were adopting infants with disabilities; youngsters who were considered medically fragile, sometimes two or three in a family.

Medical equipment had to be acquired, parents and siblings had to be trained in its use, support networks for respite care had to be established, and an entire infrastructure in the church had to be developed to support these families and their new children. At last count, well over 100 of these disabled children had been adopted.

This church put its money, its families, and its faith to the test to serve the community. Whenever I drive by this church, I think of the term *service.* These families epitomize the idea that I saw embodied in the words that appeared at the end of the Order of Worship at still another local church that my family recently attended: *The worship is ended. Now the service begins.* I like that idea. A lot.

❏ **FOR EXAMPLE:** Across the nation, faith-based organizations are rapidly trying to patch together a system of assistance to respond to the new needs arising from welfare reform. Whether it is job training, family counseling, or antiaddiction services, these organizations are responding to a very real need and a very real opportunity in their local communities. Let's look at a very short partial list. In Mississippi, an organization called Faith and Families tries to bring the benefits and beneficence of church congregations into play by matching recipients with a local church. The congregation provides the services and spiritual support to help the recipient to get off and stay off welfare. In Lansing, Michigan, the Church of the Nazarene has started a Quality Living Program which is a twelve-week course, run by members of the congregation, that combines Bible study with techniques of developing and staying on a family budget. In Florida, local churches have started a hunger hotline, which matches people in need of food with food pantries run by the congregations.

What these organizations epitomize is the need to put their faith into action. I can clearly envision the discussion among the staff and volunteers as they considered the needs in their community, the workload of available service providers, and the benefits of bringing service and faith together in synergy. After much consideration, meditation, and prayer, the ringing question had to be: If not the people of God, then who?

But there is concern outside the faith-based community regarding whether these well-intentioned people can get it right. Will there be adequate training for volunteers who interact with welfare recipients and sufficient financial controls to accommodate the often large welfare-to-work contracts that some organizations are receiving? Would such concerns be justified if it were your organization described above? Are you well managed enough to expand the ways that you help your community if you were called upon to do so?

A. WHAT SETS YOUR ORGANIZATION APART?

What sets the faith-based organization apart from other community service organizations, the ones we normally call not-for-profit? After all, your faith-based organization is a not-for-profit entity, subject to the same rules as secular not-for-profits. You need a governing body and a

charitable purpose. If you apply for and receive tax-exempt status under
section 501(c) of the Internal Revenue Service code, you need to fit into
the same categories of religious, social, research, educational or fraternal
activities as any other not-for-profit operation. You need a budget (which
is never big enough to meet all your needs), a special identity (which not
enough people in your community recognize), and volunteers and/or staff
(whom you can't compensate for their full value).

Does this situation sound familiar? I'm sure it does, and it would also
ring true for just about any of the thousands of secular not-for-profits I've
worked with since 1982. You see, at the surface, your organization has
many of the same issues, many of the same rules constraining it, many of
the same motivations guiding it as the secular not-for-profit. But the
moment you dig a little deeper, you realize that the faith-based organization is in many ways playing on a different field, with serious effects on
the way it can and does operate. I think that it's time to talk about what
these differences are and how they affect your organization.

1. Mission

As I was writing this, I looked through our local newspaper's Directory of
Worship, which includes a listing of all of the places of worship in town
and the times at which they have services. There is also a part of the directory for paid advertisements. Here I saw churches proclaiming themselves
"The Church Where Faith Meets Life," "The Church with a Sense of
Humor", and "The Church That Brings You Home." Every place of worship identifies itself slightly differently, sometimes through a slogan,
sometimes through its interests in the community. I don't mean to equate
a slogan with the higher calling of a mission, but the concept is important:
What does your organization stand for? What does it do?

❏ **FOR EXAMPLE:** Some places of worship decide that they will provide
a religiously inspired school. Some become involved in overseas mission work, through either financial aid, volunteer work, or both. Some
churches, temples, and synagogues sponsor Boy or Girl Scout troops.
Some dedicate a large part of their volunteer capital to helping the
homeless, to Habitat for Humanity, or to dealing with gangs, broken
homes, or the results of divorce. In most cases, these specializations
occur naturally as a result of a crisis in the community, an interest in
the congregation, or a request from the recipients of the service.

Then we have our community service organizations, some of which
specialize in a particular issue and some of which are general human service or educational organizations.

❑ **FOR EXAMPLE:** The Fellowship of Christian Athletes and the Promise Keepers are two organizations that are relatively focused on one population (athletes and men, respectively). Catholic Charities and the Salvation Army are examples of organizations that offer everything from, in the words of one Catholic Charities staff person I talked to, "soup to nuts" (free food to mental health counseling). These are the generalist variety of community service providers. Their mix of services has evolved, again from a unique history of original focus, community need, community request, staff and volunteer interest, and funding source mandate.

In both the latter two examples, the organization has chosen to specialize in a mix of services to identify itself, its staff, and its volunteers on the basis of its mission statement. That mission statement may evolve over time, or it may stay the same decade after decade. In fact, faith-based organizations are less likely to change their mission statement than secular ones, in major part because most faith-based organizations have some larger organization overseeing them. We'll talk more about that below.

However, mission statements for faith-based organizations hardly ever point simply to what the organization does in terms of worldly good. The statement is almost always placed in a context of religion, which takes the faith-based entity beyond mere mission while at the same time placing a set of implicit and explicit constraints or limits on the organization.

Let's look at a few examples of mission or purpose statements for some faith-based organizations.

❑ **FOR EXAMPLE:** *"Associated Catholic Charities of the Diocese of Galveston-Houston* is a sign of God's love and compassion in the community. The mission of Associated Catholic Charities is to extend to all persons the healing ministry of Jesus Christ. Associated Catholic Charities provides culturally-sensitive social services to those in need without regard to race, religion or socio-economic status. As an advocate for social justice, Associated Catholic Charities empowers the community through action and education asserting the principle of human dignity. Proactive response to the needs of the community guides the growth and development of Associated Catholic Charities."

❑ **FOR EXAMPLE:** The mission of the *Fellowship of Christian Athletes* is "to present to athletes and coaches, and all whom they influence, the challenge and adventure of receiving Jesus Christ as Savior and Lord, serving Him in their relationships and in the fellowship of the church."

❑ **FOR EXAMPLE:** *"Promise Keepers* is a Christ-centered ministry dedicated to uniting men through vital relationships to become godly influences in their world."

❑ **FOR EXAMPLE:** *Mission of B'nai Brith:* "To promote the security and continuity of the Jewish people through the enhancement of Jewish identity, the strengthening of the Jewish family, advocacy on behalf of Jews around the world and service to the community on the broadest principles of humanity."

❑ **FOR EXAMPLE:** *YMCA of Greater New Orleans:* "The YMCA, reflecting our Judeo-Christian heritage, is a family of volunteers, members and staff helping the people of this community achieve their God-given potential through development of body, mind and spirit."

❑ **FOR EXAMPLE:** *Hope Lutheran Church, Selden, New York:* "To make Christ known to all people we proclaim a message of healing and hope through Jesus Christ and invite them to share with us in worship, fellowship, and service."

❑ **FOR EXAMPLE:** From the Salvation Army Act of 1980: *"The Salvation Army's* objects are the advancement of the Christian religion ... of education, the relief of poverty, and other charitable objects beneficial to society or the community of mankind as a whole."

In all these mission statements there is an element of faith that both enables and restricts certain activities and actions, as well as providing an immediate set of values for the organization to use.

Thus it's not just about mission, it's about both mission *and* faith. The added foundation of faith provides your organization with a supplementary dimension that empowers and focuses your efforts in ways that you need to channel to the benefit of the people you serve. And, your faith base adds a set of limitations that you need to live with, incorporate into your operations, and manage your way through.

2. Governance
Who sets policy? All secular not-for-profits have a group of governing volunteers that set policy, adopt budgets, develop strategic plans, hire the head staff person, and are the fiduciaries of the organization, that is, the people who are personally responsible for the actions of the entity they supervise. Most faith-based organizations have this structure as well, but in the faith-based organization there is often a mix of governing models.

The local governing volunteers may not have authority to hire and fire over their staff and, as we will see in the next section, sometimes do not even have the authority to select their chief staff person. The local governing board may really be only an advisory group, with the real decisions on budget, policy, and other key issues made at a different level or even in a different community.

The governing volunteers in a faith-based organization almost certainly have to fit into a larger regional, state, and national framework. Whether this is a diocese, a synod, a presbytery, or a parish, this framework comes with the territory—in business terms, it is part of the franchise.

The result of this is that the governing volunteers have to work within a framework of policies and values, which they may have little say in setting and which may be controversial or even counterproductive in their local communities.

❏ **FOR EXAMPLE:** Recently, my family attended church with the family of our eldest son's best friend. It is a small congregation, and we know the minister and his wife. To our initial disappointment (but to the benefit of this example), the minister was on vacation, and the sermon was taken up by a report from a representative of the presbytery that included this church regarding the decisions taken at a recent national meeting of the church hierarchy. He reported actions and presented the language of new policies on church outreach, missions, and other relatively mundane topics. Then he spoke about the issues of homosexuality and adultery, both in the ministry and in the volunteer leadership of the church. There was rapt attention in the audience, accompanied both by nods of support and gasps and murmurs of dismay with the decisions of the national body. As I listened to the ensuing questions and discussions, it was easy to see a moral fault line running through the congregation. Like the San Andreas and other geologic faults, the dissent was building up pressure and storing energy for an eventual release. Would the release be a minor temblor or a major earthquake? Would people settle down and accept the decisions or literally split with the church? I wondered, how do you manage, administer, motivate, in short, lead such a group of people when your core values are provided to you from outside the group?

This is a challenge that, as I said earlier, comes with the territory, but is often unpredictable. Just because I know and accept that my overseeing denomination sets policy doesn't make it easier to implement when the overseers make choices that aren't easily digested by my congregation. Of course, many of our faiths have their roots in just such decisions and the resulting dissent. But that doesn't make managing your place of worship any easier when such issues present themselves.

❏ **FOR EXAMPLE:** The Daughters of Charity National Health Systems Inc. is a six billion dollar health care system, which includes 49 hospitals in 12 states. In 1997 it was ranked among the five largest health care systems in the United States. It is owned by the 1,100 U.S. members of the Daughters of Charity order of Catholic nuns. It is a big business in a tough and competitive marketplace, one where mergers and alliances are carved out weekly. In 1996, the Daughters attempted to merge the Carney Hospital in Boston, which it had run for over 130 years, with the Partners HealthCare System, a secular health care system. However, after long negotiations, the transaction was rejected by the cardinal who was the head of the Boston Archdiocese. The reason? Some parts of the Partners system perform abortions. Thus, the management of the hospital system had to refuse an advantageous business proposition that would have enhanced its mission capability. It understood that faith outweighed mission in this instance.

A governance linkage. Another governance difference that is unique to the faith-based community is the linkage between a place of worship and the community service organization. For some community service organizations that are sponsored by places of worship, there is a *quid pro quo* to the effect that some of the governance positions are filled by members of the sponsoring congregation. This has its benefits and its drawbacks. The benefits are that there is a close linkage between the community service organization and its supporters, which improves communication and can maintain a steady supply of both financial and volunteer support. The downside is that, just as in the soup kitchen example in the last chapter, the congregation members who are also governing volunteers can sometimes take a very narrow view of the world, seeing it only through the sometimes inflexible lens of strong faith, and restrict the community service organization's effectiveness.

A loose governance structure. On the other end of the scale, smaller faith-based organizations, particularly places of worship, often have a very loose governance structure, with few or no lines of authority in the traditional business sense. This is sometimes an outgrowth of size, sometimes an outgrowth of belief.

❏ **FOR EXAMPLE:** One fundamentalist Christian church intentionally has no bylaws, the standard operating rules of a not-for-profit organization, publicly declaring that the Bible is the only set of operating rules needed. This is probably not unique, but I have to admit that I was both surprised and appalled when I found out about this choice. Shortly thereafter, I asked a good friend of mine, who one of the church's elders, how this had occurred, and how the volunteers worked their way around procedural issues such as selection of elders and deacons, removal of same, selection of the pastor, or conflict of interest, all things that are usually found in the bylaws. My friend, who in his work life is a corporate executive with both a CPA and MBA (and thus familiar with procedure and business-like activities) smiled and said "It's been that way since the church was founded in 1901" And the procedural conflicts? "It just always seems to work out." I shook my head in wonder and he added, "If you think that's unusual, you ought to see our budget process! When I was first on the finance committee, I worried night and day about the finances of the church. The elders told me to relax, that God would show us what He wanted us to do. And, of course, He did. Now the younger guys on the board do all the worrying and I'm the one telling *them* to relax. You've got to have faith."

And, of course, you do. In this church, the culture had developed around having very loose organizational structure, and this has worked well. But, having too loose a governance structure can prove disastrous, and we all too often see the results in a headline reading something like *"Church Official Embezzles $200,000 over Five Years."* Whenever I see such a headline I am first saddened and then incredulous at the attitude of the staff and/or supervising volunteers who were supposed to have a set of checks and balances in place to prevent such an occurrence. "Five *years*?," I would say, "Where were the auditors? Where was the board? Who was watching the cookie jar?" And, unfortunately, the structure was too loose, too trusting, to have anybody watching adequately.

3. Finance

What about money? Isn't it the same for any not-for-profit? A budget is a budget, after all. Hardly. The faith-based organization looks at its finances differently from the secular organization, and the sources and resources it counts on are often completely different, Faith-based community service entities are most like their secular cousins: they often receive funds from federal, state, and local governments, apply for and receive foundation support, and are recipients of United Way funds.

On the other hand, places of worship derive nearly all of their income from tithes and offerings, with a smattering from bequests and, for organizations that run a religious school, from tuition. This means that the organization can look at past trends, but that from week to week, from worship service to worship service, they really don't know how much income they will have.

4. Staffing

Unlike nearly all secular not-for-profit organizations, you may have severe restrictions on staff selection. Staff may have to be of the sponsoring faith or of a certain sex and in Catholic organizations, a certain number of (or even specific) positions may have to be filled by nuns or members of a priestly order. For the head staff person, limitations on who can be hired can also be troublesome, but most faith-based executives whom I have talked to consider that this infrequent difficulty is more than compensated for by having staff who at least theoretically share their faith, their perspective, and their values.

The most notable staffing difference comes in the way that some faith-based organizations pick their leader—they don't. In nearly all secular not-for-profits, the board selects the head staff person, usually called the executive director. In many faith-based organizations, someone other than the governing board (usually in the hierarchy of the sponsoring faith) picks that person and assigns him or her to the organization. This person may be called an executive director or a rabbi, pastor, or director. Whatever the title, the issue is that the governing volunteers don't get to work with a person whom they chose. In some cases, they aren't even asked for their opinion. The organization may not even get someone from the community, the state, or even the region of the country, someone who knows the local customs, politics, and issues.

This crucial difference is most common in places of worship but is also prevalent in community service organizations, such as the Salvation Army. And, it can affect the relationships, levels of trust, and morale of the staff. The power to hire and fire the top staff person is a key function of most governing volunteers, and organizations that don't allow this activity are, in my opinion, at a distinct disadvantage.

5. Volunteers

More than any other part of the not-for-profit sector, faith-based organizations rely on their ability to motivate, recruit, and retain volunteers to keep things running. This goes way beyond the governing volunteers. Whether they are making copies, stuffing envelopes, teaching Sunday school, delivering meals, pushing the hospital book cart, serving a meal, passing the offering tray, or performing any of the literally thousands of other tasks that need to be done, volunteers are the true backbone of many community service organizations and nearly all places of worship.

This is not to say that other not-for-profit organizations don't use volunteers. They do, both in governing and in provision of service, but the level and depth of dependence on volunteers is much greater in faith-based organizations.

Each of these differences puts into stronger relief how special, unique, and blessed your organization is. How you manage those differences is the key. Will your dependence on volunteers be your downfall? Or will it be an inconsistent funding stream or a governance system that you don't completely control? Or, will you find ways to turn these differences into strengths, letting them define your unique gifts, special perspective, and higher calling?

B. IS IT JUST A MISSION, OR A GREAT COMMISSION?

> *All authority in heaven and on earth has been given to me. Go therefore and make disciples of all nations, baptizing them in the name of the Father and of the Son and of the Holy Spirit, teaching them to observe all that I have commanded you; and lo, I am with you always, even to the close of the age.*
> Matthew 28:18–20

For Christians, this is the paramount teaching of Jesus. For Jews, the Ten Commandments are a cornerstone of guidance in life. For Muslims, it is the Five Pillars of Islam found in the Qur'an. God tells all people of faith what He wants them to do. Different faiths hear different voices and have different rules to live by, but for the faithful, the Word of God is the ultimate inspiration and guide.

We've all heard the phrase "He's a man on a mission!" referring to a friend or co-worker who is particularly focused on his purpose or goals in life. Such focus and purpose are laudable, and successful not-for-profits of all stripes share this characteristic. Being mission-driven is the point of being a not-for-profit and, unfortunately, too many organizations forget their mission, or underutilize it, forsaking the tremendous motivating and focusing tool that a mission can be.

To put it another way, all not-for-profit staff and board members need to believe in their mission. If they don't, they can't put in the extra effort, the extra time, the extra energy that their mission and their organization so often need and nearly always receive. Why do people put so much into organizations that pay them so poorly? Because they care and because they believe in their mission and that their mission makes a difference in their community.

Of course, you and your staff and volunteers have an even higher calling. You don't just do a job, meet a need, or provide a worldly good. You and your organization need to understand the reality of the situation: as a faith-based organization, you are on a mission from God. If you believe that, and if you can pass that belief on to your fellow staff and volunteers, you can empower your organization in ways you can only imagine. The motivation, the energy, the willingness to take risks that come from this belief can (not to put too much of a point on it) part the Red Sea. *Then Moses stretched out his hand over the sea; and the Lord swept the sea back by a strong east wind all night and turned the sea into dry land, so the waters were divided.* Exodus 14:21.

You see, secular not-for-profit staff members or volunteers believe in their mission. You don't stop just at *believing* in your mission, you have *faith* in it!

C. THE NEED FOR GOOD MANAGEMENT IN THE FAITH-BASED ORGANIZATION

If you are so well armed with your faith (*The Lord is my strength and my shield.* Psalm 28:7), if it motivates you so much, why do you need to manage yourself well? Won't God simply provide? Yes, He will, but I firmly believe that we also need to do some of the work. As stewards, we need to make the best use of all our gifts and all our resources to pursue our mission, our faith, and the directives of God.

Among those resources are management techniques that can help us get the most good out of our necessarily limited financial, material, and human resources. Stewardship, in my view, requires us to look around and use every tool, every resource at our command to get the job done. And, as long as we are faithful in our implementation, the end result of our activities will be favored by God. Thus, marketing, public relations, cash flow management, personnel policies, building management, budgeting, and strategic planning all become tied to making our organizations more mission-capable, more able to do good in the world. The more of these tools we use, the better our organization will run, and the more people we can help in God's name.

1. You Are Held to a Higher Standard

Oh, yes. One more thing to consider, and to remember well. As a staff member or volunteer of a not-for-profit organization, you are held to a higher standard of conduct and an increasingly high standard of performance as compared with your peers in business or government. As a staff member or volunteer of a faith-based organization, you are held to an *extremely* high standard of conduct and an increasingly high standard of performance. Let me explain both things.

First, the standard of conduct. We know that we are all imperfect and that we strive to follow our God's laws and teachings. But as people of professed faith, we have gone on record as saying that we agree with our faith's standards of conduct. Whether that standard is the Ten Commandments (e.g., Thou shalt not steal, Thou shalt not commit adultery) or any other teaching from Scripture, we are expected to abide by it. And here is the issue: those both inside *and outside* the faith expect us to behave *according* to our faith. When we fail to uphold those standards, we are liable to be targets of intense scrutiny, merciless criticism, and extensive commentary.

❑ **FOR EXAMPLE:** A business executive is accused of sexual impropriety, perhaps of harassment. Unless the person is extremely well known, the story probably will not receive mention in the paper or on the local television. But if the accused is a priest or a pastor will you hear about it on the six o'clock news? You bet. Why? Because the same offense perpetrated by a trusted figure is more offensive—and more newsworthy.

❑ **FOR EXAMPLE:** In our community we have had at least three cases of embezzlement at least that I know of in the past year. The widely reported case occurred at one of our local churches, where one of the staff had stolen well over $100,000 over a number of years. There were perhaps seven prominent stories in the paper at various points as the case unfolded after the theft was discovered, after the thief was charged, during the trial, and after sentencing. Shortly after the initial report, I ran into one of the deacons, and I asked him about the case. He told me the details, and I commented that unfortunately they were getting a lot of unwanted press. His response was, "Yeah, we had two cases of embezzlement at my company in the past five years, the latest just last month, and both for a lot more than here at church, but no one outside the company cared. The paper covered it in less than 50 words on page 15."

Why did no one care? Because internal business affairs are considered of low interest unless they affect a consumer directly. But church affairs or the affairs of an organization (faith-based or secular) that receives United Way or governmental funding? That's public and subject to scrutiny and to a great deal of media coverage, which, as we all know, is not always fair. So our internal management and control systems need to be up to speed. We need to manage our funds well, define conflict of interest, be specific in our personnel policies about acceptable and unacceptable behavior, and, in general, use well developed management skills to prevent scandals.

2. You Can No Longer Hide Poor Management Behind a Veil of Being a Charity

On a second front, all not-for-profits used to be "cut a break" because of their charitable status. If the location of service was a little shabby, if the service itself was a little inefficient, if the staff was not 100 percent competent, people often smiled and were tolerant, as they would be of a small child or a pet. "After all," they would say, "it's just a charity, what do you expect?"

Those days are long gone. People now want outcomes, efficiency, and effectiveness from their community's not-for-profit operations, whether they are secular or faith-based. I have been telling people for years that when the public interacts with your organization, they hold you to the same service and competence standards that they received *from their most recent excellent retail transaction.* They don't care if the service was provided by a paid staff member or a volunteer, they want what they want, they want it now, and they want it well provided. If, before they call you or visit your offices, they have just gotten off the phone with Land's End, or come from Nordstrom's, you have some pretty tough standards to meet. How would you hold up?

☞ **HANDS-ON:** Let's see how you measure up in the medium by which many people first interact with your organization, the telephone. We're going to run a little test. Think up five or six moderately obscure questions to ask the person who answers the phone at your organization.

   For Community Service Organizations: The questions will depend on your service array and constituency, but they could be about insurance, or a facet of a particular program (time, date, location), or a qualification for financial aid, or anything just a little out of the ordinary.

   For Places of Worship: The questions will depend on the size of your church, temple, or synagogue or the kinds of ministries, choirs, scriptural classes, and so on. But you could ask about a certain kind of ministry, who is in charge of it, and whom you could talk to to learn more about it; about day care during worship; about youth group overnights; or about anything just a little out of the norm.

Now that you have your list, *don't call anyone!* The receptionist will probably know your voice. Have friends or neighbors call while you are sitting next to them. After they are done with the call, ask them how courteous, knowledgeable, helpful, and pleasant the staff was. Did they get their questions answered? If follow-up action was promised, did it occur? This simple test will tell you a lot about how people are first treated when they interact with your organization. And, as you will learn in our chapter on marketing, everything everyone does every day in your organization is marketing; thus every interaction is crucial.

The management point? If your staff members are not well trained, if they don't have the knowledge they need about your services or don't know how to find it quickly, if they are not concerned with customer satisfaction, people will go elsewhere, because they won't tolerate poor service, even from a charity.

There is no excuse for not going about the task of becoming and remaining well managed. The excuse that you are just a poor charity doesn't hold. Your responsibility as a steward mandates it. The fact that you have more on your plate than two people can reasonably do in 24 hours is not an adequate excuse. The fact that it is much more fun to minister, to teach, to heal, to counsel, or to care for people than to manage, budget, discipline, maintain, plan, or set policies is flat-out no excuse. This is and will remain part of your job. If you really don't have the time (one of my favorite lame excuses and one that we will deal with a bit later in the book), then you need to delegate. If your board has not allowed you to hire someone to whom to delegate, sit down with the board members and talk to them about the management needs of the organization. If they won't allow you to hire someone and won't help you come up with the resources to pay an assistant, then it is the board's job to do the management tasks, whether it is accounting, personnel policy development, or building maintenance.

There really is no place to hide here. If you don't invest the time, staff, and money in good management, you are just plain delinquent in your job. Why? Because your organization suffers, and ultimately so do the people you serve, whether they are a congregation, a set of patients, a school full of children, or a group of the homeless. And those people are depending on you to manage the organization well enough that your services are not merely provided, but that they are provided with consistency, with excellence, with caring, and with a clear evidence of your faith. On those benchmarks, how do you think you measure up?

If management hasn't been a priority for you, I completely understand. I know why it hasn't, I know how you got here. But just because you haven't made a major effort in this area, it doesn't mean that you can't or shouldn't start now. You have to.

If the management of your organization has been one of your major areas of work, I assure you that you still have places to improve. How do I know? Because your organization is run by humans, and we all have our flaws, our blind spots, our strengths, and our weaknesses. We bring these flaws to our jobs, and they show up in our areas of responsibility. So look again and see where you can improve. Even your strengths can get stronger, even your core competencies can be expanded. I know the old adage: If it ain't broke, don't fix it. My father was an engineer, and he loved that line. But he always added to it, "But just because it isn't broken doesn't mean you can't *polish* it."

So whether your organization is a lean, efficient, management machine, or a novice in the discipline of management, the remainder of this book provides you with all the core tools you will need to make the transition from where you are to where you need to be. The longest journey starts with the first step. Let's get started. The next chapter will lay out for you the characteristics of a successful faith-based organization and provide you with a self-assessment tool that will help you gauge where you are, at least according to my set of standards.

POSTLUDE

In this chapter we have covered the all-important issue of what sets your faith-based organization apart from other not-for-profits. We looked at five specific things that set you apart, making for both special benefits and unique challenges. These were *your mission, your governance, your finances, your staff, and your volunteers*. We delineated these for worship centers and community service organizations. We then examined what kind of mission you are on and noted that it really goes beyond just a traditional mission. It is much more than that when faith is there with you. You are, literally, on a mission from God. Finally, we looked at the need to become better managed and at how good management turns into good mission, more people helped, and more people brought to your faith. And that, of course is the whole point, isn't it?

You are on a mission from God, and all the work involved in developing and maintaining good management is worth the effort. You need to know what standards to set for yourself and for your organization. Just how far do faith-based organizations go in managing themselves? What are the characteristics of a successful, well-managed faith-based organization? That's what we will examine in Chapter Three.

QUESTIONS FOR DISCUSSION: CHAPTER TWO

1. Do we feel that our organization is on a mission? On a mission from God? Are we enhanced by our faith?

2. How often do we discuss spiritual issues as we consider management decisions? Is this enough, too much, too little?

3. Do people outside our organization see us as spiritually driven? How do we know? Is that perception good or bad in terms of pursuing our mission?

4. What are our community's standards for places of worship and faith-based community service organizations? Are we just a charity, or are we held to higher standards?

3

The Characteristics of a Successful Faith-Based Organization

Now there are varieties of gifts, but the same Spirit. And there are varieties of ministries, but the same Lord. And there are varieties of effects, but the same God who works all things in all persons. Corinthians I.12:4–6

PRELUDE

In this chapter you will learn about the seven characteristics of successful faith-based organizations. These organizations all do the following:

- ➤ Have a foundation of faith and a focus on mission
- ➤ Have volunteers who fill key roles, knowledgeably and competently
- ➤ Have staff members who use their gifts and let others use theirs
- ➤ Pay close attention to markets
- ➤ Value excellent stewardship in finance, strategic planning, and resource management
- ➤ Value flexibility within the value structure of the faith
- ➤ Are focused on achievable growth

These characteristics are found in faith-based organizations that are consistently successful in their mission, in service provision, and in keeping close to their faith.

You will also find a self-assessment tool that can help you take an objective look at your organization and help jump-start the process of moving you forward. By the end of this chapter, you will know a lot more about where you are now and will have a good compass to help you get where you need to be.

All successful organizations have characteristics in common. But why are they successful? Are there common traits that inevitably lead to their success? Is there a special mix, a unique potpourri, that becomes a slam dunk of certain success?

No there isn't. There are no guarantees, no assurances of ultimate triumph, of final victory, at least in worldly terms! But it is more than just luck. There are things that excellent, consistently successful organizations have in common, and these are not, as you might have suspected, generic. More often they are very special, and very targeted, to an individual industry or ministry.

❑ **FOR EXAMPLE:** Let's look at a pizza parlor. What are the characteristics of success in such an establishment? A partial list would include:

Good pizza ("good" being a very subjective term)
Fast service

Delivery

Clean restaurant

Polite service

Consistent taste of the pizza

Competitive price

Central location

Enticing menu

Now these characteristics might not be the key characteristics at another kind of organization, even if it is in the same industry. Look at Exhibit 3-1. Here we can consider the fanciest, most elegant restaurant in your community. What would the characteristics of success be there? Would they be basically the same as for the pizza parlor? Let's look.

Exhibit 3-1   Pizza Parlor Versus La Ristorante Elegante

Pizza Parlor	La Ristorante Elegante
Good pizza	Superb food
Fast service	Diners want to linger
Delivery	Diners want to eat in a luxurious environment, not in front of the television
Clean restaurant	Immaculate restaurant
Polite service	Doting and attentive service

Exhibit 3-1   Continued

Pizza Parlor	La Ristorante Elegante
Consistent taste of pizza	Consistently superb
Competitive price	Price relatively unimportant
Central location	Can be central or out of the way
Enticing menu	Enticing menu

See the differences? They are important, and yet the two organizations are both considered non-fast food restaurants. In vastly different industries or economic sectors, there would be even more differences. For example, one of the key things at the pizza restaurant was product *consistency,* so that customers could come back repeatedly and find the same excellent pizza. In the software industry, the key is consistent product *innovation.* You wouldn't pay again for the same software, the way you would cherish paying for the same good pizza. In software, if it doesn't have new features, new bells and whistles, it's not competitive.

Okay, I hope I have made my point: There are specific traits that when used together can describe a successful organization in any given industry. Now, what about you and your faith-based organization? Are there central, core characteristics of success that you can attempt to emulate? You bet. And I've gathered them here for you to review, to consider, and, hopefully, to adopt.

A. THE CHARACTERISTICS OF SUCCESSFUL FAITH-BASED ORGANIZATIONS

The following are the seven characteristics that I think are essential if your place of worship or community service organization is to become and remain a successful faith-based organization. As you review these, understand that they cannot be taken selectively. They work together, each supporting the others and in turn receiving support. You can't just focus on characteristics one, two, five, and six, for example, and believe that achieving those will get you most of the way there. That's like saying that if I have an engine, wheels, tires, and seats, I have a car that will go somewhere. What about the transmission, the battery, the fuel? So read through my list and consider each characteristic in the light of your own organization. Are you comfortable with your status? Is there room for improvement? Is the issue a low-priority, a moderate problem, or a crisis? How do these characteristics fit together in the larger strategy for the success of your organization?

Now, before you rush off to fix the first problem that you see, read through the remainder of the characteristics to get the entire picture. If you are confused about where your organization is in relationship to my benchmarks, following the listing of the characteristics I provide will help you scale and score your organization in relation to the important indexes below.

1. Successful Faith-Based Organizations Have a Foundation of Faith and a Focus on Mission

Yours is, after all, a *faith-based* organization. The adjective brings all kinds of special benefits and unique challenges as we discussed in Chapter 2. Your faith needs to be the basis, the foundation, the rock upon which your organization stands. And yet, your organization not just about your faith. Within your faith and as a result of it, your organization has chosen a set of services on which it is focused hopefully with an emphasis on compassion and quality. It may be a place of worship or a community service organization, but you still need to define a mission and focus your energies and your resources toward accomplishing that mission. Successful faith-based organizations are very focused. They never forget that their faith is the reason that they *exist* but their mission is the reason for *being.* Put another way, a lot of very religious friends of mine talk about their faith as the identity, the core of who they *are.* If that is true for organizations, then the faith is what they are, and the mission is what they *do.* Both faith and mission are essential; one cannot survive without the other. If your organization identifies itself as a Christian, Jewish, Muslim, or Buddhist organization, the faith needs to be visible and apparent to people both inside and outside the organization.

Then, there's the mission statement, and that's a bit trickier. The question is: What is it that we do? This can lead to some interesting and problematic discussions.

❑ **FOR EXAMPLE:** A good friend of mine described budget meetings at his Congregational church near Chicago, where he is head of the board. There is always a concern from some on the board about "how little of the budget goes to mission, as opposed to staff salaries and church operating expenses." These people want more of the church's money to go to missionary work, to feeding the hungry, and to the other community good works that the church supports. But, of course, others on the board counter that with "What the staff does, what the buildings provide us, those *are* our core mission. Pastoral guidance, worship, fellowship, counseling, and support of each other are really what we are here for. The outside stuff is good, and it's important, but it isn't our *mission!*"

Sound familiar? I can predict that most readers who are involved in the financial decisions at their place of worship have heard this discussion in one form or another. And, sometimes it winds up being just the opposite.

❏ **FOR EXAMPLE:** Another church (this one in Virginia) in which I have friends on the budget committee argues this same issue from another side: It is an evangelistic Christian congregation, and many of the leadership feel strongly that the mission of the church is to pour all of their efforts, particularly those of the staff and volunteers, into evangelizing people who have not already "found Jesus Christ as their personal Lord and Savior." These people contend that this is the only mission of the church and in fact, is the Great Commission we talked about in Chapter 2: *Go therefore and make disciples of all nations, baptizing them in the name of the Father and of the Son and of the Holy Spirit, teaching them to observe all that I have commanded you; and lo, I am with you always, even to the close of the age.* Matthew 28:18–20. The other side of this discussion comes from those in the leadership group who believe that attention needs to be paid to those who are already members of the church and that these people need pastoral care, counseling, fellowship, and the like.

Two sides of the same coin? Yes, in part. And neither of them is patently correct or seriously wrong. This kind of discussion has to be worked out by the people involved—it's their church, their stewardship, their responsibility. But in both cases the discussions were healthy, because the groups were defining who they were and what they were about.

Now, you might think that these kinds of discussion are most prevalent in places of worship, where the line between faith and mission is thin and often blurred. But it also pops up in community service organizations, particularly when they try to grow too fast, or don't stay focused on their core mission.

❏ **FOR EXAMPLE:** A perfect example of this is Promise Keepers, the men's ministry that rocketed from near anonymity to national prominence in 1996, culminating in its sponsored March on Washington in 1997. Formed to promote spiritual growth and its attendant family and community involvement among men, this ministry was by 1997 a multimillion dollar operation, with much staff, many plans, and apparently not enough focus. By early 1998, the Promise Keepers were laying off most of their staff, cutting back on their core stadium assemblies, and, from all reports, in serious trouble financially. They may, by the time you read this, refocus their energies, stabilize their efforts, and get back on their feet. They may not. But at the height of their success, they had a nearly unlimited number of plans to expand and promote their faith, which is laudable. The problem, apparently, was that they forgot their *core mission* and ignored the fact that whatever they did, they had to do *well*.

The first rule of secular not-for-profits is mission, mission, mission. Not for faith-based not-for-profits. For you, it is faith first, mission a *close* second. So, whether you are a place of worship or community service organization, use your faith as a foundation and then, like all successful organizations, focus your resources, skills, energies, and efforts on a mission that you believe in, can perform with excellence, and believe makes a difference in your community.

2. Successful Faith-Based Organizations Have Volunteers Who Fill Key Roles Knowledgeably and Competently

As I noted in Chapter Two, many faith-based organizations are heavily, even critically, dependent on their volunteer core. Your organization almost certainly uses volunteers in many roles as well. A crucial mistake that leaders often make is to confuse enthusiasm for a job with competence. In other words, just because your volunteers are eager, willing, and excited about a job doesn't mean that they can do it in a high-quality manner or even marginally well.

Excellent faith-based organization have to ensure that enthusiastic volunteers are recruited, trained, and then retained, just as with staff. Just because you are not paying people doesn't mean you can't have high expectations of them nor does it mean that you can't turn their enthusiasm and willingness to help in another, more appropriate direction if they are not suited to the first, second, or even third task that they attempt.

❏ **FOR EXAMPLE:** Judy volunteered for a teen center sponsored by her local Jewish community life center. She had been involved with helping adolescents nearly all of her adult life. At the center, she ran a support group for teens from families in some sort of turmoil, often working 20 to 30 hours per week in the evenings and on weekends. Over the years, she had related well to the teenagers and had enjoyed success in keeping her charges out of trouble.

Judy looked around her community and saw many more children in need than she had time to help. She envisioned an expansion of the program, adding two more volunteers who could, in her words "triple our effectiveness." She sold the program expansion to the director of the center with the promise that "This will be a totally volunteer-based expansion. There won't be staff time or costs involved. We have the space, and I'll recruit the people." The director agreed, on those conditions.

The problem was that Judy, while a talented counselor and enthusiastic mentor for kids, was a lousy administrator of adults. She was a poor planner, had unrealistic expectations of her fellow volunteers, which she was unable to communicate and unwilling to enforce, and didn't have a clue about time management. All of these problems didn't matter when she was working alone, but when she was a manager, the issues showed up front and center. And, of course, the program grew, but not in size, just in the amount of time, effort, and energy that it took for the staff to clean up Judy's constant messes.

Here, the director mistook enthusiasm for competence and made the all too common mistake of assuming that someone who is talented in one area will be equally expert in another. Excellent organizations carefully recruit, guide, train, and manage their volunteers. For many faith-based organizations, this is such a crucial component of their organizational capacity that we will spend all of Chapter 10 on this issue.

3. Successful Faith-Based Organizations Have Staff Who Use Their Gifts and Let Others Use Theirs

Once your organization grows beyond the capabilities of its volunteers, it needs paid employees, commonly known as the staff. We are taught that we all have gifts that *God wants us to use. But to each one is given the manifestation of the Spirit for the common good.* Corinthians I, 12:7 In excellent faith-based organizations, staff are allowed to use their efforts where their strengths are, and volunteers perform the rest of the tasks. Where there are not enough staff and volunteers, the board approves hiring more staff—staff with specific training or experience in the areas of need. The idea is to keep the set of the skills that the organization needs available through a combination of paid and volunteer resources.

Of course, staffing and staff management have a very wide range in faith-based organization, running from a small-town church's bivocational pastor to a statewide Lutheran social services organization with thousands of employees. Even within places of worship, there is vast disparity in the size of staff. The rise of the megachurch has brought about a concomitant development of megastaff, sometimes numbering in the hundreds. The issues in such an organization are vastly different from those in a church with three or four hired staff members. But no more challenging.

❏ **FOR EXAMPLE:** Immediately after I graduated from college, I did a tour in VISTA (Volunteers in Service to America), which was then the domestic equivalent of the Peace Corps. Volunteers were matched with communities in need who had applied for people with particular skills. We were paid $200 per month ($194.48 after taxes—I remember it *clearly*), from which we were expected to pay our living expenses. The idea was that if we were to help the poor, we should live among them, a philosophy that I completely agreed with.

I was a paramedic and was placed in a small rural community of 500 people in northwest Louisiana, helping to establish and maintain a community health clinic. I arrived in town with no idea of where I was to live and was immediately introduced to the pastor of the local church, who had a room available in the parsonage for $50 per month. I said yes immediately and moved my two bags of personal belongings in right away. As it was Friday afternoon and I didn't start work until Monday, Pastor Bob invited me to go with him to work on Saturday and see the local country a bit. This sounded good to me. He told me we would leave at 6 AM sharp.

I was ready at 5:45 AM and was greeted by Pastor Bob dressed not as a preacher but in greasy overalls and carrying a toolbox. "Where are we going?" I asked. "To work," said the pastor. "I'm a plumber most days; I only preach on Sundays and Wednesday evenings. And, of course, the occasional funeral wedding and counseling. But we're on the road today to a customer with a stopped-up septic tank!" We got back to the house around 8 PM, smelling like that tank. I was exhausted, having, of course, been enlisted to help. Pastor Bob stayed up until midnight working on his sermon for the next day. I was asleep before my head hit the pillow.

Pastor Bob preached at two churches 15 miles apart. During the week he lived 70 miles away. He worked 60 hours per week plumbing and 20 to 30 hours per week as a pastor. He was one of the happiest, hardest-working people I have ever known. Oh, yes, I almost forgot. On Sunday, when I went to church, I increased the size of the congregation by 10 percent—and that was his big church. Later that first month I asked him the undiplomatic question, "Isn't this an awful lot of work for 20 people?" His answer was "Yes, it is a lot of work, but it's God's work. I'd love to have more people come to church. If we did, I could afford to get some help in the church offices, and we could get the pianos tuned and perhaps fix the roof. But God isn't sending the people just now. I'm content to wait until He's ready."

Within the past year I met the Senior Pastor at a church with a congregation of 4,000. He has a staff of 25 working for him. I talked to him for a while about his responsibilities and all the people who depended on him in his congregation. His response was very interesting. "You know I started out as a country preacher? I had fifteen people each week in the pews, and three of us in the choir. I worked harder then, a lot harder, because I also was a teacher and coach at the local high school. But in a small church you know all the people, you get to really help people with real problems. At this level, I only have time to go to staff meetings and board meetings, preach three times on Sunday, and deal with personnel and budget issues. The problems are different, and somebody has to solve them. I guess that's me. I still get to preach, but I don't seem to pastor much anymore."

The two preachers were at the opposite ends of the size spectrum. They both had lots of work, important work to do. Both liked their jobs. One wanted more parishioners, which would get him more staff. One wanted to be closer to people again. Both wants are common in faith-based organizations. And it isn't just true for the head staff person, it's true for staff throughout the organization.

And that's the issue in all faith-based organizations. How do you meet the challenge of recruiting and retaining excellent staff, people who do their jobs well, with enthusiasm and high energy, and yet are willing to give up the higher salaries they could earn in the private sector to work in your community service organization or place of worship? If they are willing to make such sacrifices, can and should you hold them to high expectations? Should you discipline and even discharge them if they don't meet those expectations? How do you use the faith to motivate them, or do you need to?

The answers to those questions are what we'll cover in Chapter 5 on staff management.

4. Successful Faith-Based Organizations Pay Close Attention to Their Markets

Let me put it simply: Good marketing is good mission. I know what you are thinking. Our organization wouldn't stoop to something as crass and commercial as marketing. Here's the surprise, you already do. But the question is: Do you do it well?

All organizations, faith-based or secular, for-profit or not-for-profit, have to pay attention to their markets if they are to be successful. That means knowing who comprises your markets, asking them regularly what they want, and giving it to them to the extent you can. When you think about it, you probably do that already. You have many, many markets, perhaps more than you realize.

❏ **FOR EXAMPLE:** Many churches across the country have instituted so-called family nights, which both parishioners and the public can attend and at which they can have a meal, play a game, use the gym, do a craft activity, and in general have some of that much vaunted but too rare quality family time. It is an incredibly popular evening in most communities, precisely because it does what I talked about before: It identifies a market (families) and gives them what they want (a mechanism to help them connect with each other in a safe location with good values). That is pure marketing, And not crass at all. And I am almost certain that your organization has programs, ministries, and outreach that focus on particular markets, such as teens, broken families, singles, or seniors, and works to appeal to their particular wants.

❏ **FOR EXAMPLE:** The buses that run to and from many retirement communities, toting people around to their doctors' offices, the supermarket, the mall, and church, are a very popular feature for the residents of these communities. Why? Because it allows the target market (residents) freedom from worry about what will happen as they drive less and less or even lose their driving privileges. Furthermore, from a business point of view, this makes excellent sense as a selling point in trying to induce people to live in the community. Why? Because the service removes an impediment to deciding to join the community. Potential residents know *before* they decide to live in the community that they will be able to get around, no matter what their physical situation and no matter what the weather.

Think about this for your organization. Are there impediments to people coming to your organization? Guess what? You don't know unless you ask your markets! So, good marketing is an integral part of a successful faith-based organization. Furthermore, becoming a good marketer takes a lot of work. Marketing has many component parts, and we'll spend all of Chapter 8 on this crucial issue.

5. Successful Faith-Based Organizations Value Excellent Stewardship—in Finance, Strategic Planning, and Resource Management

A primary rule of all not-for-profits, whether faith-based or secular, is mission, mission, mission. Right behind that rule is a second one: "No money, no mission." I know, I know: God will provide! And He does, but not always monetarily the day before payroll needs to be paid! As stewards it is your job to use your resources wisely. This includes good financial management and controls, realistic budgeting, which allows for adequate checks and balances between staff and board, and conflict-of-interest policies for volunteers and paid staff. It also means that the organization has an up-to-date strategic plan and that the annual component of the plan is used as the basis for budgeting; that there is a five-year capital expenditure plan which is updated every year; and that the capital assets of the organization, whether vehicles, computers, kitchen equipment,or buildings, are well maintained.

This discipline is difficult for many faith-based organizations. They are so focused on doing good that they feel there is no value in doing good *well.* But you need to stop and think about it. If your organization only has so many resources with which to accomplish its mission in any given month or year, doesn't it make sense to use those resources as efficiently and effectively as possible? By doing so, you get *more* mission for the money! In contrast, if you don't maintain machinery, buildings, and equipment, they wear out faster, break more often, and in the end, cost more. And money spent for repairs that could have been avoided and for replacements that could have waited a few more years is money poorly, irresponsibly spent. Other things need to be maintained as well: personnel policies, financial controls, quality standards, bylaws, and insurance coverage. Without regular attention, these key management controls will fail sooner, also costing the organization money, energy, and morale.

❑ **FOR EXAMPLE:** I know of a couple of faith-based organizations that don't carry liability insurance on their building. Why? "Because we don't have much net worth. And anyway, the only people who are around our property and who would get hurt are our parishioners, and they would never sue us." Think again. What about the visitors to the church (in one case) or temple (the other), what about delivery people, the postal carrier, the meter reader? Would they not sue? And, if the organization is sued, the board members are *personally* liable for any damages resulting from the lawsuit. Why? Because having liability insurance is considered a standard business practice, and board members are liable for something called mismanagement. Not carrying insurance certainly meets that criterion. I can understand neglecting an issue like this, or forgetting about it, and I can certainly be sympathetic to an organization that is temporarily unable to afford an insurance premium. But making a conscious decision not to insure? It makes me even more sure that when God gave out gifts, He didn't ration the amount of stupid He handed out.

❑ **FOR EXAMPLE:** I also know of many, many organizations that do not have personnel policies or haven't updated them for five, seven, or even ten years. Personnel issues are incredibly complex and technical, and if you have even one employee, you need them. I know it seems as if this is a lot of work for very little reward and there are better things to do with your time. I assure you, there aren't many. One staff begets two, and then four and then six and then ten, and then a lawsuit or a discipline issue, or a dress code problem, or a "misunderstanding" about work hours, reimbursement policies, or evaluation or promotion criteria. How would you like to play in a softball or basketball league in which all members assumed that they knew the rules, but no one bothered to write them down? How long would it be before an argument stopped the game? Not long. The same holds true for your organization.

In both of these examples, the staff and volunteers avoided the hard and sometimes dull work of management for the more enjoyable activities of helping people. But just, as we saw good marketing is good mission, so is good management. Excellent faith-based organizations are well managed from one end to the other. They train their staffs, maintain their property, attend to their finances, and look to the future in a planned strategic manner. You can too. In Chapters Six, Seven, and Nine, I'll show you what you need to know in finance, leadership, and planning.

6. Successful Faith-Based Organizations Value Flexibility— Within the Value Structure of the Faith

If you pay attention to your markets (and you need to), what will you do when the markets' wants change? Will you ignore the changes or will you become market-driven? If you are a for-profit business, the answer is clear: adapt or die. If you can provide what the market wants, do it. In the faith-based organization, the answer is much less clear. Whether you change depends on a number of things, but the most important of these is the value structure of your faith.

❏ **FOR EXAMPLE:** Remember the story about the Daughters of Charity hospital merger, which was discussed in Chapter 2? The merger, which was intended to adapt to a changing reimbursement market, was rejected because of a faith-based value.

☞ **HANDS-ON:** Imagine yourself the director of a nursing home run by your faith. Managed care, Medicare, and Medicaid have all cut into your income streams, and among the key elements of your value structure are the facts that your nursing staff spend extra time with patients and that you have counselors and spiritual advisors in house 24 hours per day to minister to both residents and families immediately when they are in need. Now that service array is being threatened by budget cuts. You can no longer afford to keep the spiritual advisory staff on duty for 24 hours. You need to be flexible and to accommodate to the financial realities of the market, but at the same time, this service is a core one in your viewpoint. What do you do?

❑ **FOR EXAMPLE:** A government funding unit that supports your organization's 200 foster homes has a new program add-on. It has decided that to reduce future child welfare demand, it is necessary to limit teen pregnancy, a goal that you agree with and applaud. To implement this goal, however, the funder is requiring your organization to provide information not only on pregnancy avoidance but also on birth control methods and even to distribute condoms on request. Your organization has, in the past, counseled teenagers on the ethics and morals of the situation and on God's teachings on the issue. But now you are required to do something that may, in your mind, encourage promiscuity while at the same time reducing out-of-wedlock births. How flexible are you on this issue?

You can see the problems here. Your faith-based values have to be your limits, but they do not mean that you *never* change. For example, many faith-based organizations provide much needed services for HIV-positive people, and AIDS did not even become an issue until the early 1980s. Just because these organizations had not dealt with someone who was HIV-positive before, did not mean that they couldn't or shouldn't when the need became evident.

In fact, much of the basis of my premise in Chapter One, that more and more faith-based organizations are becoming involved in community service issues, is evidence that these organizations *are* flexible, and are meeting community needs. But how far should you go? How flexible should you be? We'll talk a lot more about this in Chapter Eleven.

7. Successful Faith-Based Organizations Are Focused on Achievable, Maintainable Growth

Successful organizations grow. Why? Because part of success in a faith-based organization comes from reaching more people. Also, from a management point of view, larger organizations have more economies of scale, allowing for a higher percentage of expenses to be in direct service, and a smaller one in administration.

But how much growth is good? Can there be too much growth? Yes, absolutely. Unchecked growth exhausts cash reserves, stresses out management systems, overflows buildings, and affects quality. Thus my adjectives, *achievable* and *maintainable*. Growth should be *achievable* within a value system that is focused on excellence, that is concerned about staff burnout, and that pays attention to the wants of its many markets. It should be maintainable within the constraints of cash flow, consistent quality, and administrative supports.

❏ **FOR EXAMPLE:** A faith-based community service organization on the East Coast was told that it would receive a $150,000 increase from its major funder for one of its main core services, family counseling. The previous fiscal year, it had negotiated a fee per counseling session with the funder and was very pleased that it had stood firm on its commitment not to lose any money on the service. Thus the service was a break-even proposition for the agency for the first time in years. Now the funder wanted to increase the number of reimbursed counseling visits but not change the rate per session. The agency agreed. It was sure that its existing counselors could handle the load, and in fact that the counselors and the administrative support *could* handle the extra sessions. What could not support the growth was the organization's working capital, the money that it had on hand to pay its bills between the time it provided a service and the time it received payment. This organization, like so many faith-based organizations, had steered away from trying to make a profit, had spent every dime it got every year on what it considered to be urgent needs, and had very little cash on hand at any time—*as a policy of the board.*

The result in this case? Since the funder reimbursed bills in 45 days and since the agency billed the funder at the end of every month, this meant that the agency had to find 75 days (45 days plus one month) worth of the additional $150,000 in cash to be able to afford the increased counseling load. That came to $30,822, of which the organization was about $30,000 short. And no one would lend it any money, as it had a policy just to break even.

The result was a good one, actually. The organization decided not to take on the extra counseling sessions for a year and set a goal of having the extra cash the following year so that they could expand at that time. It did *not* do what far too many organizations do, which is to go ahead and take the money and figure out the consequences later. The administrators thought about it first and not only considered the mission load on their counseling staff and administrative structure but also looked at cash and discovered, to their great chagrin, that they needed net revenue (commonly called profit) to be able to grow.

Growth is good; it is a characteristic of successful organizations and a goal that your organization should have. But within reason, within limits. Don't let your reach exceed your organizational grasp. We'll talk about this issue more when we discuss stewardship and planning.

So there they are, the seven characteristics of success that your faith-based organization wants to emulate as it moves ahead. Remember, you don't want to be satisfied with achieving just two, three, or even four of these. You want to attain and then maintain them all. In the following chapters, we'll talk a lot more about the specifics of these characteristics and provide you with more examples and a lot of hands-on ideas. There will be things to apply to your organization and checklists to review. But for now, let's get away from general characteristics to much more specific analysis of your current status.

B. AN ORGANIZATIONAL SELF-ASSESSMENT

So now you know the seven characteristics of faith-based organizations that are consistently successful. But how does your organization measure up? I'm sure you were gauging your organization and yourself as you read my list above. And, it was hard to really tell how you fared as there weren't discrete items included about which you could say "been there, done that" for some and "oops" for others. Well, here's that list.

Exhibit 3-2 is a short organizational self-assessment chart for you and your fellow volunteers and staff to apply to your organization. It is designed to get you started, not to be the end-all and be-all of organizational standard setting. The assessment is broken into a number of critical sections, and several important questions are asked. By no means are these all the questions. They are simply the most important ones that for the most part can be answered easily by yes or no, and are designed to make you think about other things that are included under the section.

Go through the assessment as a group, and then score yourselves in each area. Don't panic if you are in the low range. Don't celebrate *too* much if you are in the high range. The low range allows you the opportunity to get much better! The high range is good news, but there is always an opportunity to improve.

Exhibit 3-2 Organizational Self-Assessment		
Criteria	**Scoring**	**Your Score**
Mission		
Has your board reviewed your mission in the past 5 years?	If yes, 5 points	____
Is your mission statement prominently displayed in your organization?	If yes, 5 points	____

(continued)

Governance

Does your governing board have a quorum at 90% of its meetings?	If yes, 3 points	_____
Do you have an active committee structure?	If yes, 2 points	_____
Are 90% of your board slots filled throughout the year?	If yes, 2 points	_____

Staffing

Is your staff turnover at an acceptable level?	If yes, 2 points	_____
Do you invest in at least 40 hours of training for every staff member every year?	If yes, 4 points	_____
Do you encourage staff from all levels of the organization to serve on staff committees?	If yes, 3 points	_____
Do you have personnel policies that have been updated in the past 24 months?	If yes, 2 points	_____

Volunteers

Do you have policies for recruiting, training and if necessary, dismissing volunteers?	If yes, 4 points	_____
Are at least 90% of your volunteer position needs filled within 30 days?	If yes, 2 points	_____

Finance

Does your staff and board both participate in budget development?	If yes, 2 points	_____
Have your financial policies been updated in the past 24 months?	If yes, 3 points	_____
Do you have an annual audit?	If yes, 3 points	_____
Has your organization had net revenue in four of the past 5 years?	If yes, 4 points	_____
Do you have conflict of interest policies?	If yes, 4 points	_____

Planning

Do you have a current strategic plan?	If yes, 4 points	_____

(continued)

Do you have a current marketing plan?	If yes, 4 points	_____
Do you let outsiders and all staff review your draft plans?	If yes, 3 points	_____
Do you have a 5-year capital spending plan?	If yes, 3 points	_____

Growth

Is your growth planned?	If yes, 2 points	_____
In each of the past 5 years, has your organizational revenue grown?	If no growth, 0 points	
	Up to 3% per year, 3 points	
	3.1–8% per year, 4 points	
	8.1%–12.0% per year, 2 points	
	>12.00% per year, 1 point	_____

Marketing

Have you identified your three to five key target markets?	If yes, 3 points If no, minus 3 points	_____
Have you asked those markets what they wanted in the past 24 months?	If yes, 4 points	_____
Is customer satisfaction an organizational priority for every staff person?	If yes, 3 points	_____

SCORING SUMMARY

Mission	
Governance	
Volunteers	
Finance	
Planning	
Growth	
Marketing	
TOTAL SCORE:	

At the least, *you should score at least 5 points in every category except finance, where 10 is the minimum target score. Overall, your total score should be above 48.* If you didn't score that well, help is on the way in the following chapters!

POSTLUDE

In this chapter, you learned the seven characteristics of successful faith-based organizations. You learned about why such traits are important in any industry and why faith-based organizations are no exception. The characteristics are as follows:

Successful faith-based organizations:

Have a foundation of faith and a focus on mission

Have volunteers who fill key roles knowledgeably and competently

Have staff who use their gifts and let others use theirs

Pay close attention to markets

Value excellent stewardship in finance, strategic planning, and resource management

Value flexibility within the value structure of the faith

Are focused on achievable growth

Then, we went through a brief organizational self-assessment, and I hope that you did well. But now that you have a little idea of where you are, and where you want to go, let's get on to the specifics. The place to start is with the differing roles of staff and volunteers, and that is the subject of Chapter Four.

QUESTIONS FOR DISCUSSION: CHAPTER THREE

1. Which of the seven characteristics of successful organizations are we strong in? Where are we weak?

2. What steps can we take immediately to strengthen our weak areas? What should we plan for in the next fiscal year?

3. What items in the organizational self-assessment chart did we not score well on? How can we correct them?

4. Are there any other characteristics of success that are specific and special to our kind of organization? Do we emulate them? How can we do better?

4

The Duties of Staff and Board

If the whole body were an eye, where would the hearing be? If the whole were hearing, where would the sense of smell be? But now God has placed the members, each one of them, in the body, just as He desired. Corinthians I. 15–19

PRELUDE

In this chapter you will learn about:

➤ The differing roles of staff and board
➤ Board roles and responsibilities
➤ Staff roles and responsibilities
➤ Building and retaining a strong board

In every grouping of people, there is a need for role differentiation. In the home, husbands and wives may fill traditional roles, with the wife doing the cooking, for example, and the husband in charge of the yard work. Or, as in our household, those roles may be reversed or may be flexible depending on who has the time. In school, there is a great difference between the roles of teacher and principal and yet another difference between the roles of teacher and teacher's aide. Organizations that succeed in getting their tasks accomplished consistently have their people focused on the desired outcome and at the same time, are very aware of the individual role that each person plays in accomplishing the desired outcomes. Each agree to fill their role to the best of their abilities, and if they do, the whole group is more likely to achieve success.

All religions have their teachings about what they consider appropriate roles, as well. The relative roles of employers and employees, family members, and teachers and students are thoroughly documented in the

Old and New Testaments, as well as in the Koran. The purpose of these teachings is to help us understand how we can best work and live with our fellow inhabitants of the planet.

When people don't know their roles (because either they haven't been told, they haven't been trained, or they want to do something else), you can see the results very quickly. Not knowing an appropriate role is not uncommon for a governing volunteer. Often there is no board job description, no orientation, and no guidance, and thus the volunteers make up the job duties as they go along or learn by example from their peers (who probably never were trained, either).

More often, though, problems arise when governing volunteers or staff members know their roles and refuse to limit themselves to their assigned duties. Board members try to manage the day-to-day activities of the organization. Staff members try to set policy without board approval. Neither of these things leads to a good result. An executive and an assistant, a chief operating officer (CEO) and his or her board, an athlete and a coach, a musician and a conductor—all of these are examples of people who work together but who bring different talents to the task and who accept different roles to get the task accomplished. What if one of these people decides to try a different role? Imagine an athlete who, in the middle of a contest, decides he or she wants to play a different position. A catcher, for example, who suddenly starts to pitch. What about an orchestra's tuba player, who leaps across to the piccolo section and asks to play that instrument instead? Or a hospital administrator who decides that administration is just too boring and tries a little open heart surgery one afternoon. In each case, things would not go well for the team, for the orchestra, or for the patient.

It is no different in your organization. You, your staff, and your governing volunteers need to each know your roles, play them well, and leave the tasks that are to be completed to those who are most suited to do so. *For to one is given the word of wisdom through the Spirit, and to another the word of knowledge, and to another faith, and to another the gift of healing by the same Spirit.* Corinthians I. 12:8–9

But where do you draw the line? In this chapter, we'll look at the differing roles of paid staff and governing volunteers whom, for simplicity's sake, I will call "the board." I'll show you why and how the two jobs are different and give you some examples of what happens when the lines of demarcation are crossed too often. Then, we'll focus in on specifics for boards and staffs. What should they do? When should they do it? To whom are they responsible? How can you tell where you are now? We'll hone in on all of these.

Finally we'll look at ways in which you can recruit and retain a superior governing body. You'll find out that these volunteers are just like any other group of people to whom you want to appeal. I'll show you how to recruit, orient, excite, and then keep your board.

A. THE DIFFERING ROLES OF STAFF AND BOARD

As noted earlier in this chapter, the staff and board in your organization should have different roles. But to be effective, both groups need to define and know their roles and to stick to them.

Let's start with the board. Whatever you call them—elders, deacons, boards of governors, or boards of directors—this group of people are (1) volunteers and (2) in charge of your organization's policy and direction. Board members are what the legal system calls *fiduciaries*. This means that they are *personally* responsible for the actions of the organization, even when state statutes hold boards not accountable for some actions taken by board members.

The key for boards is that they are in charge of policy, not management. Management is the purview of the hired staff, not of volunteers whose involvement is not, and should not be, full-time. This is not necessarily an easy distinction to draw or to keep, particularly in crises. Additionally, at different stages of an organization's growth and development, it is more important for volunteers to be closely involved in the operations. And, some board members need to be more involved than others, for example the board president and treasurer.

We'll deal with all of these issues a bit later, but I want first to go over the issue of what are and what are not appropriate policy issues for board consideration. The items listed below are all things that your organization may or may not consider at the board level. Note that this is not a complete list, just a set of examples. See how many sound familiar and how many are discussed at your board meetings.

Strategic plan goals and objectives

Annual budgets and monitoring their implementation

Adding a new program or ministry or ending an existing one

Adding a new building

Obligating debt

Adopting personnel, finance, and other policies

Hiring, disciplining, or firing the head staff person

Approving the start of a capital fund drive

Establishing an additional corporation (for a foundation, for example)

Reviewing and approving an annual audit report

Now the flip side of the coin. There is much too much that goes on in most board meetings that is the purview of management but that the board, for a variety of reasons, refuses to let management take care of. Over the years, this has caused me a mix of frustration, amusement, and downright amazement, depending on the situation, my role in the meeting, and how badly I wanted the meeting to adjourn! The list below is a *much* abbreviated version of examples that I have gathered from board meetings that I have attended as either a participant, a staff person, or a consultant. As the humorist Dave Barry is wont to say, "I am not making this up." The numbers in parentheses that follow the item are the number of minutes that the discussion consumed.

The color of the paint in the staff lunch room. (26)

Whether or not a budgeted expense of $19.50 should be spent this month or next—in an organization with an annual budget of over $4,000,000 and no cash flow problems. (37)

Which candidates should fill a certain (very) low level staff position. (24)

Whether the invitations for the annual meeting should be issued on blue or white stationery. (42)

Whether or not to fire a staff person other than the senior minister (92).

Advising staff members on how to do the technical portion of their jobs (counseling, nursing, education, daycare), which the board members knew absolutely nothing about (10 zillion).

In all these examples and dozens of others that I could detail for you, the board members forgot, accidentally or intentionally, that their role was policy, not operations. It's not difficult to have this happen, and some of the reasons are understandable, if not defensible. Many of the things that boards should deal with are long-term, and they are sometimes esoteric and rarely hands-on. Thus, it is understandable that such issues as the paint color or the firing of an employee are a welcome change to a board member who really wants to "get something tangible done," an expression I have heard used a thousand times. Deciding whether to fire a staff person *is* tangible. It's something that a board member can get his or her hands around. So is deciding on the color of the lunchroom, or the expenditure of the $19.50. But the problem is that those activities, while tangible, are not appropriate, and in fact, are a waste of board time and capital. These are management decisions, ones that should be left to the staff to make.

The other reason for discussing this kind of minutiae is less common, but more crucial, a lack of trust in the staff members. This crisis in confidence may be about the staff members' competence, their credibility, their vision for the future, or even their honesty, but the overall issue boils down to this: The staff can't (or won't) do this right, so we (the board) have to do it for them. Again, an understandable opinion, and one which many would argue is the epitome of good stewardship. The board members are acting in the capacity of checks and balances. Isn't that what they are there for?

Certainly one key job of board members is to act as a check and balance on management. But it is not to perform management's job, even if the managers are incapable or have lost the trust of the board. In such situations, the board's job is to hire new management personnel and to let *them* do the job of managing the organization.

☞ **HANDS-ON:** Let's take a minute to look at your board's level of policy setting. Take out the minutes of the board's meetings for the past year. Read them through and ask yourself how much of the discussion was policy and how much was minutiae? If you find too much small stuff and not enough big stuff, ask why. For most organizations the reason is simple—the small stuff is more fun and more immediate and gives the board members a feeling of accomplishment. To fix this, focus on ways to make the board see that policy is valuable, that big picture decisions will affect more people in more ways for a longer time than their discussions and decisions on smaller issues. Remind them that they only have so much time to invest in the organization. How is the organization going to get the most from that investment? From *everyone* doing his or her job well.

Now let's examine another common clue that a board is too involved in the day-to-day operations of the organization: board members call or come in all the time. If your board is constantly in the building or on the phone with you, asking for details of the operation or even more general questions such as "What's new today?," you may well resent the interruption and the time it takes to attend to their questions. To stop this bad habit, the question to ask yourself is: Why are they doing this? It could be that they don't trust you. It could be that they are not getting enough information to feel comfortable in making policy decisions. It could be that they have not been trained in their appropriate role as board members. Or, it could be a combination of these reasons. But the bottom line is that you need to have the board back off and let the staff run the organization.

☞ **HANDS-ON:** If this is a familiar situation, try this method of dealing with it. Approach your most trusted and most sympathetic board member and relate the situation from your perspective. Ask for this member's ideas on why it is occurring, including the trust issue. Be straightforward and firm, noting that minutiae managing is not a board job. Ask for suggestions on how to solve the problem. These may include more board education, more board information, or a frank discussion with the entire board at the next meeting. What you want to do is to let board members know that the staff needs to be trusted to do its work. What you don't want to do is to alienate sincerely interested board members, cut off communications, or engender a feeling that the staff is trying to insulate itself from board oversight. It's a tricky balancing act, but it's one that needs to be attended to sooner rather than later.

☞ **HANDS-ON:** Another approach is to use today's technology to speed up your work, while at the same time appealing to your board's desire for more information. The solution? Once a week, twice a month, or just monthly draft an e-mail (or have your staff do it) that incorporates the key activities of the past few days or week. Then send it with one click of your mouse to all of your board who have e-mail. This is quick, slick, and easy but has a couple of downsides. First, nearly every organization has one or more board members who are not wired, and if they don't have fax machines at work or at home (your backup for people who don't have e-mail), you can't give them the same sense of *immediate* information that you are providing to members who are more technically equipped. Second, information like this, once it starts, becomes an instant tradition and an interminable task. So, consider adopting such a technique carefully. If you are doing it to get information to a board that really needs it, fine; if you are merely avoiding dealing with a board that is too detail-oriented, you are just delaying a problem and making more work for yourself or your staff.

Let me also note here that every organization has its own culture, and part of that culture is its tradition of the level of board oversight. If your culture (or the tradition at a state, regional, or national level) calls for a hands-off board, you may well have trouble getting board members involved enough to truly fill their fiduciary roles. On the other hand, if your history is rich with board involvement at the detail level, think hard about trying to change that in just one or two board generations. You may only be tilting at windmills. You may need to consider other ways to put all of that interest and energy to good use; this may mean more involved committees or larger projects that are more volunteer-driven, such as special-event fund raisers, building projects, or community service. Don't get wedded to the idea of an ideal balance between board and staff. There isn't such a balance that makes the most sense across the entire not-for-profit sector. But there is one for your organization. Try to find it with the least expenditure of time, energy, and emotion. Then, if you want to change it, recognize that such a change will take time and effort, and a lot of it.

B. BOARD ROLES AND RESPONSIBILITIES

Given the strategic (for the board) versus day-to-day (for the staff) role breakdown, for what specifically is the board responsible? Within most not-for-profits this list is long but nearly standardized; that is to say, that it is pretty much the same for the board of the animal shelter, the symphony, a private school, or a trade association.

But in the faith-based sector, things are a little more complicated. Many readers are affiliated with organizations whose board is really an advisory board and not a policy one. How can you tell? If your organization chooses its chief staff person, if it develops and adopts its own budgets without outside oversight, if it can write its own strategic plan, buy a building, or add or cancel a program without approval, then your board is a *policy* board. If you have outside oversight on any of the items listed, your board is an *advisory* board.

☞ **HANDS-ON:** If you have an advisory board, that's fine, but you need to find out what responsibilities your board has. Talk to the state or national body of of your denomination and ask for written responsibilities of the advisory board. Even if you have these, ask for the latest set. Then make sure you distribute these to your board and talk them through. Are you complying with all of them now? If not, how can you get up to speed?

Below is my list of responsibilities for *policy* boards. Understand that while the board is responsible for the things on this list, some of the tasks are delegated to staff, auditors, or organizational counsel. However, the board is ultimately responsible for everything on this list. They are, as I have said before, fiduciaries, *personally* responsible for the actions and outcomes of your organization. Use this list to make sure that your board members understand their roles and their responsibilities.

1. Fulfill the Beliefs of the Sponsoring Faith

Mission, mission, mission, underpinned by your faith. That's what we've been talking about all through the book so far, so here is the core role of the board: making sure that your organization stays true to the tenets of the sponsoring faith. Whatever your dogma, you need to make sure that your actions, marketing material, and staff and volunteer activities all reflect that faith. This is, of course, easiest in places of worship, where teaching that very belief structure is the core activity. There are day-to-day reminders of the faith in the activities of the organization, from worship to counseling to ceremonies such as weddings, funerals, and baptisms. In community service organizations, it is more likely that staff and board will get caught up in chasing dollars, providing needed service, and forgetting the core beliefs that are their foundation.

❑ **FOR EXAMPLE:** One group that has, in my opinion, fallen victim to this inattention to its founding faith is the YMCA. In the past ten years I have done a great deal of training and consulting to Ys across the country and thus have seen their organizations up close. They are, for the most part, well-run, mission-focused, and dynamic organizations. Their communities benefit from their existence. But, as I tell them all the time, they need to refocus on one leg of their three-part mission to improve the mind, body, and spirit of the community". It's the spirit part that I think is lacking in many Y's. Remember, their name is the Young Men's *Christian* Association, and yet many are not associated with churches in their communities, which would seem to me to be a natural mix, especially for youth programs. It is my belief that YMCAs would not only find great benefit from paying attention to the spiritual side of their service triangle but would find that the community welcomed such a benefit with open arms. Who is ultimately responsible for such a policy change? The board. (*Note:* There are some YMCAs that are really focused on the spiritual side, and I applaud them.)

Your board, in monitoring the job that staff and other volunteers are doing, needs to review these outcomes in light of the tenets of your faith. If they feel that the faith is not being lived up to, they need to take remedial action immediately.

Now in saying this, I acknowledge that such discussions are nearly always based on deep-seated feelings and as such, may be emotionally charged. But they need to happen if your organization is to stay on course with its beliefs.

☞ **HANDS-ON:** To ensure that your organization is on track in the faith area, I suggest a one-day retreat comprised of your board and key management staff. If your organization is part of a larger state or national organization, you may want to consider inviting a representative of your larger organization or your sponsoring faith, if that is appropriate. Review the tenets of your sponsoring faith, and then ask this question: What does our organization do, *specifically,* to promote and support these tenets? Now, ask the reverse question: Do we do *anything* that conflicts with our faith or its major components?

Encourage participation and urge your board members to voice even small concerns about your consistency with the faith that sponsors you. Use this time to identify and hopefully, to put to rest confusion or misconceptions about your mission, services, and interpretation of your role in your community. What you do not want to do is leave anyone with the feeling that they should not ask a "dumb question" or should not rock the boat. You want people to voice their concerns. The idea of this retreat is to allay those concerns and to build confidence in the board that you are about God's business as your faith interprets that business.

I will almost guarantee that this discussion will be spirited and at times difficult. But if you air all the issues fully, you will come away with a new sense of shared values and mission, a new zest for the challenges that confront you, and a new or renewed peace of mind from knowing that you are on the right path spiritually.

2. Fulfill All IRS, State, and Local Reporting Requirements

Put simply, this means keeping your collective nose clean. You have a tax-exempt status from the state in which your organization is incorporated. Most readers' organizations also have applied for and received an organizational federal income tax exemption from the Internal Revenue Service (IRS). In some states organizations must register to be allowed to solicit donations.

In all cases, these situations call for regular and often quite specific reporting. Nearly all states require an annual corporate report submitted to the attorney general, the secretary of state, or both. Nearly all states and the IRS want to see your mission statement whenever you modify it. If your organization has unrelated business income, it is required to report that income annually on a form called the 990T. You may even have to file certain forms with your county or city.

Why do I put this boring, tedious, and extremely important requirement here? Isn't this what staff is supposed to do? Of course it is. But it is crucial to remember that it is the board who is ultimately *responsible for seeing that it was done.* If it has not been done, it's the board that federal, state, county, or city officials come after, not the staff.

So, get an audit. One of the things your auditor is supposed to do is to make sure that you comply with all the ever-changing rules. Make sure that your auditing firm clearly understands that you want it to monitor this issue, and make sure that your board members read the auditor's report.

I know that many faith-based organizations, particularly places of worship, eschew audits as too expensive and as evidence that the governing volunteers don't trust the staff. The volunteers don't want to spend their limited revenues on something that implies, at least in their minds, that the staff is suspect. Besides, said one elder of a church I worked with, "You hardly ever hear of churches who really have a major problem in this area. After all, these are people of God. You have to have faith."

Pardon me while I pick myself up off the floor from a fit of laughter. No, not because of the part about faith. You do have to have faith. But you also need to use the brains and the experiences that God has provided you. I asked this elder if his church had insurance for fire, flood, earthquakes, or tornados. His answer was: "Of course! That's only prudent." What I barely managed to keep myself from saying was "Gee, you hardly ever hear of churches burning down. You need to have faith!"

If you want to do your job as a board member, get an audit. Your staff members will thank you, not criticize you, and if they do object, start worrying.

3. Fulfill the Responsibilities and Contractual Obligations of the Funders

Here's another place where an audit is crucial. The people who fund you (if you get outside funding from a foundation, United Way, or a government body) have certain things that they want done as a result of giving you money. These are called *contractual responsibilities and obligations,* and guess who, inside the organization, is ultimately responsible to see that they get fulfilled? That's right, the board. The kinds of obligations I'm referring to are varied and will be specific to your organization's funding mix. But they are all things that your governing board needs to ensure that your organization can and will do during the time span of the funding.

❑ FOR EXAMPLE: A homeless shelter staffed primarily by a group of volunteers from a local synagogue got part of their funds from the local county and some from their local United Jewish Appeal. The county wanted fifty overnight beds available throughout the first six months of the grant period and a five bed (10 percent) increase in the second six months. The county wanted assurances (in the form of licenses and inspections) that food service was clean and safe and that any counseling provided to shelter recipients was aimed at getting them jobs. The county also wanted its funds audited at the end of the grant, and to have "professional staff on site 24 hours a day." And, as a government agency, the county administration required that the shelter's personnel policies be nondiscriminatory in all ways.

The United Jewish Appeal's expectations were less detailed, but it also wanted an audit report, which was to be done differently from the one required by the county. All of these expectations had to be reviewed by the board before agreeing to take the funds. As a primarily volunteer-driven organization, could it afford professional staff on site all day every day? Was there enough capacity in the shelter to add five beds? Could the organization afford the audits? Was its counseling currently aimed at employment of clients or merely getting them housing? If the board members believed that the organization could not comply with the funders' requirements, what should they do?

Do any of these kinds of requirements sound familiar? I suspect that they do. Does your governing board know the obligations that it is contracting for when it approves the receipt of grant or contract dollars? It should, and if not, the time to start is right now, with a review of outstanding obligations to any and all funders.

☞ **HANDS-ON:** Not only should you initiate an internal review of all your funder-driven obligations, but you should also institute a policy of reviewing such obligations before you sign on the bottom line. Additionally, don't always automatically agree to every requirement of a funder. In many cases, funders, who often provide monies to dozens or even hundreds of organizations, mail out boilerplate contracts, often not differentiating between the size and administrative capabilities of their grantees. Thus, after you review the expectations of your funder, a conversation may be in order to establish what is negotiable and what is not. Talk about outcomes rather than focusing on process, and then suggest to the funder what alternative might suit their needs. For example, some funders say they need an audit, but that may mean an audit just of their funds, not of the entire organization, the former being much less expensive and time-consuming than the latter. Get clarification on expectations before you sign for the money. And if concessions and adjustments are made, get them in writing. The worst thing that can happen is to get an oral okay on, for example, a program audit rather than a full organizational one from a certain employee of a funder and then have that employee leave during the funding cycle and be replaced by a new employee who is much less flexible.

4. Set Policy and Establish Organizational Goals

Let's talk for a moment about the word *policy*. A policy is defined as a plan of action adopted by an individual or group. Note the use of the term *plan of action*. In other words, policies are guidelines for action, plans of actions, statements of belief; they are *not* actions themselves. Thus, board members need to stay on track by setting policies and then stepping back and letting the staff and volunteers implement them.

Earlier in this chapter, I provided a list of examples of policy work and a list of minutiae. Go back and review them now to see if you still feel that your governing board sticks to policy or find that it gets involved in the murky and dangerous area of implementation and day-to-day management.

All of this caution regarding policy versus minutiae management does, of course, have its exceptions. In my opinion, there are three situations in which a board should be involved in the day-to-day management of a faith-based organization. These are:

1. *At start-up.* When an organization first forms, it will almost always do so under the auspices of a group of committed volunteers, some of whom form the initial board. At this stage, there are no employees to do the management work, and thus the board members need to do it themselves. This stage should end when employees are hired, but it is often, and understandably, very difficult for the board members to back off from caring daily for their "baby."

2. *In cases of imminent financial organizational demise.* What I mean by this is not that the organization is merely having a bad fiscal year. What I do mean is that the organization may not survive for the next 60 to 90 days unless stringent action is taken. Here, not only is close board involvement important, but it may be essential to survival. Of course, if the organization has reached such a pass, it may be that the board was not minding the store closely enough in the preceding months.

3. *In cases of moral or legal improprieties in the office of the head staff person.* The crucial term here is "head staff person." If your executive director, headmaster, or head pastor (by any name) gets into trouble with the law or is accused of some moral impropriety, the board needs to get involved immediately and stay on top of the situation until it is resolved. However, if a similar problem crops up with any other staff person, then the issue should be resolved by the executive director, *not* the board.

With these three crucial exceptions, you need to have your governing board focus on policy, not day-to-day management.

5. Hire and Evaluate the Head Staff Person

As I said earlier, some boards of faith-based organizations don't actually hire a head staff person; that position is filled at a higher level of authority. This is most often true in places of worship but can also occur in some community service organizations. However, most faith-based organizations' boards have as one of their most important decisions that of filling the top staff job. If your top staff person's tenure is long, there may well have been many board people who have come and gone and never had to worry about filling the top spot. And they are probably glad of it: recruitment, interviewing, and making the final decision are tough, thankless, and critically important jobs. But whether or not they helped to hire a head staff person, all board members should have taken part in at least an annual evaluation of the top staff person.

This is an important board job, but one that many board members fear and try to avoid. Their lamentations go something like this: "I'm not a rabbi (preacher, educator, administrator, etc.); I don't know how to run this organization. That's why we hire staff! So how can I possibly evaluate someone who has the staff's job skills? I don't know enough."

The secret is that you do! You *can* evaluate how the organization is doing in relation to the goals in its strategic plan; how the organization is perceived in the community; how effective the communication and information flow is from the staff to the board; how close the staff comes to making its budget every month, quarter, and year; and whether your chief staff person has the ability to lead, to think the big, strategic think, and to be a model of your faith. All these are crucial issues that you have the information to review and provide an objective evaluation, not necessarily as individuals but almost certainly as a group.

Good people want to know how they are doing. They want to know when they are doing well, and they want to be told where they can improve. Sit down with your head staff person and develop a set of criteria against which you will measure his or her actions. Then, at least annually, go through the process of developing an evaluation and giving it to the CEO in writing and orally. I suggest using a small committee to draft the evaluation, getting board approval and then meeting with the CEO as a group of two or three board members. Don't make it a reenactment of the Spanish Inquisition. Report the good things and the not-so-good things that you feel have occurred. As always, if you criticize something, have an alternative solution or a suggestion for remedy.

6. Help Develop, Adopt, and Monitor Budgets

As I've already said at length, board members are fiduciaries and thus are ultimately responsible for all actions of the organization. Nowhere is this responsibility more visible and more vulnerable than in the development of your organization's budget. On the surface, your organization's budget details how you anticipate obtaining income and how you plan to spend it, usually for a one-year period. But look beneath the surface. The budget is your strongest statement on your priorities, on how you will actually implement your strategic plan. It is policy put into action; it is literally putting your money where your mouth is.

And, since policy is the governing board's responsibility, your board needs to be very involved in the development, adoption, and monitoring of the budget. Not every board member needs to be steeped in the minute details of the budget, but it is important to have a finance committee which does go through the numbers line by line. The finance committee then brings a suggested budget to the board for its review and approval. This keeps the job a board function without requiring every board member to spend huge numbers of hours on it.

After adoption of the budget, the board will need to monitor its implementation. I have always believed that a budget is a contract between the staff and the board. The board has in effect said "If you can bring in this much money, you can spend that much on those things." Thus, instead of questioning every dime that the staff spends, the board should make sure that the staff is within the budget, or complying with the contract if you will, and if the staff is on budget, the board should leave the staff alone.

We'll look at financial management in depth in Chapter Six, which will include lessons for both staff and board members. I'll show you a budget monitoring template that is thorough and excellent for oversight and allows your board to have the time to work on things other than just finances at their meetings.

7. Establish Personnel and Financial Policies and Ensure Their Implementation

Here is an area in which many, many boards get into trouble. I have already told you at least ten times that the board's job is to set policy. And I suspect that, like most readers, you agree. But do you limit your definition of "policy" to just program decisions, budgets, and planning? Don't. Policy setting also includes deciding on the limits within which staff, volunteers, and board can operate on a day-to-day basis. Your organization needs personnel and financial policies, even if you only have one employee or a budget of $25,000. These policies need to comply with local, state, and federal law and with the rules of any funders you may have. They need to be regularly reviewed by the board with the assistance of an expert in the field. For the financial policies, this can be your banker and your auditor. For the personnel policies, consult a human resources expert.

This is very technical stuff, which to most people is just boring, bureaucratic paper wasting. But just because you may think it is, don't put it off. Policies not only set defined limits for acceptable behavior, they are the tools the organization can use to prevent certain misbehaviors and botched results.

I am aware that some professionals say that you shouldn't have any personnel policies, as they become a contract and make you open lawsuits. At least as of this writing, I don't see a compelling enough case for such drastic action. Having no personnel policies leaves you with no rules, no limits, and it has not been my experience that the benefits of having no contract outweigh the dangers inherent in such a vacuum. So get a professional's advice, but don't shirk this important board responsibility.

8. Nominate and Elect Officers

Boards need to elect their own officers. Many faith-based organizations have a membership or congregation that elects the organizations's leaders (deacons, elders, lay advisors), and this is good. But to have the general membership also elect the officers is somewhat akin to having a university student body elect the captain of the basketball team. Your organization's bylaws should allow for your board to elect its own internal leaders every year or two.

9. Represent the Organization in Public

Anyone on the board is part of the organization in a tangible way, both inside the walls and out. What this means is that a board member represents the organization in a *de facto* manner all the time and may be asked to speak for or about the organization in a formal setting on occasion. This can produce both excellent and disastrous results.

❏ **FOR EXAMPLE:** A church-sponsored nursing home had started 20 years earlier with simple levels of care (in some states called *sheltered care*) and over the years had expanded into higher and more intense levels of care, called *skilled nursing* care. All the services had been delivered at the organization's nursing facility, and that building had naturally been the focus of much board attention and fund raising over the years as the property was expanded and improved.

Recently, the organization had decided to develop a hospice program. The reader should know that there are two kinds of hospices, facility-centered and home-centered. This organization chose the home-centered model, in which the caregivers go into the home of the dying person and provide care there. The staff and board had discussed this choice briefly, focusing more on the budget and community service implications of starting the program than on the more technical issue of giving care in or out of patients' homes.

The local chamber of commerce invited one of the board members, a prominent businesswoman, to report at its quarterly meeting on the status of the nursing home, which was a large employer in the relatively small community. She gave a compelling presentation on the organization's growth, excellent service levels, and strong commitment to the community. Then she was asked to discuss the new hospice service and gave a lengthy answer supporting the need for such care, describing its excellent results for patients and their families, and stating that if the needs assessments were correct, *even more expansion of the building might be necessary.* "Why is that?" asked a listener. *"Because we'll need more rooms to hold these patients."* "So these patients will be cared for at the facility?" *"Absolutely. That's where we provide all of our care."*

What happened? From then on, everyone in town "knew" that the hospice was an inpatient facility. The hospice opened, and for five solid years, as patients and families found out that services were provided in their homes, they felt that they were getting second-rate care, since their perception of quality service was based on their misconception regarding the location of that service.

The board member had certainly not wanted to damage the organization but had answered a crucial question about an issue that she was not familiar with. She assumed that care would be given in the location that had been the focus of so much attention for so many years.

☞ **HANDS-ON:** Make sure when board members speak publicly, that two things occur. First, that staff provide a written and oral briefing on the key issues that the board member will cover. Second, have a staff person accompany the board member to provide answers to any technical questions that may arise. I suspect that, had there been a staff person present at the chamber of commerce, there would not have been the long-term damage that there was.

10. Raise Money

Last, but certainly not least, board members need to be involved in raising funds to keep the organization pursuing its mission and exemplifying its faith. Ten years ago this was not, at least in my view, a mandatory part of the board's job description. But it is now, as fund raising of all kinds is so much more competitive. If your community service organization is trolling for dollars with a foundation, a corporation, or your local United

Way, the involvement of a volunteer is critical and may even be a prerequisite to any serious consideration. If your organization is a place of worship, your board needs to lead in terms of their own tithes, offerings, and donations.

For many boards, this is a major and crucial cultural change, one which may not occur in one or two years, but rather over the span of time needed for a majority of the board to go out of office and be replaced by new members who have never experienced a board without fund raising as part of its job.

There is, of course, a danger in a board spending too much of its time on fund raising, just as there is a problem with board meetings being consumed by budget monitoring, staff problems, or any other issue. The board has, as you can see from the foregoing list, many and varied responsibilities. Thus, fund raising is an important part of your board's job but not the only one. On the other hand, if you ignore your organization's ability to attract and receive donations of money, service, or goods, you are ignoring a crucial resource, one that may make the difference in your being able to pursue your mission. Fund raising is a good thing and one that needs both staff expertise and board involvement.

These ten responsibilities are the core of board service in your faith-based organization. Your board needs to attend to all of them, and your staff needs to make sure that the board members have the skills, information, and mix of expertise that they need to get the job done.

☞ **HANDS-ON:** I strongly suggest that you develop a board job description, one that lays out all the varied responsibilities of your governing body. Such a document, which does not have to be long, will put everyone on notice as they come on the board what the expectations are and will provide a benchmark for board self-evaluation. Starting with the list above, have a discussion with your board and senior staff. Look at the list, add to it, and modify it in any way that you see fit for your organization, your faith, and your local culture. Then print it up and provide it to all board members, including it in your board manual (to be described a bit later in this chapter).

☞ **HANDS-ON:** The next step is to go beyond a mere board job description to discuss the roles and responsibilities of your officers. A listing of roles of the board chairperson, vice chairperson, secretary, treasurer, and any other formal office holder again puts the organization on record as to who is charged with what tasks and makes it easier for new board members to understand the relative roles, areas of responsibility, and chains of authority. As in the case of the board job description, talk this through with staff and board, look at what other organizations like yours use, and then include the listing in the board manual.

☞ **HANDS-ON:** I have one more suggestion for your board to use to enhance its understanding of the impact of its policy decisions—volunteer at the line of service. This mostly pertains to boards of community service organizations, and what I mean is that policy setters need to see the situation at the point of service, which they can't do on a board tour. For example, I tell school board members that they need to spend an hour twice a year reading to first graders, eating lunch in the cafeteria while talking with students, or volunteering to help at an athletic event, book fair, or open house. For your organization it might be serving a meal, cleaning a bunk room in a homeless shelter, reading to a group of schoolchildren, or attending a group counseling session (if confidentiality allows). But whatever the service array your organization provides, there is almost certainly a place and time at which board members can help and see the results of their policies. It's the corollary of "managing by wandering around" that works so well in the private sector. And I'm not talking about a major time commitment for people who I know are already putting in a lot of hours in your organization. An hour or two per quarter is fine.

C. STAFF ROLES AND RESPONSIBILITIES

Within the context that I set above, staff also have distinct responsibilities, but in the case of staff there are two sets of these, one in relation to the board and one that pertains directly to the organization. Obviously, both sets of staff responsibilities move the organization toward its greater good, but you need to be aware that there are two distinct sets of duties to consider, remember, and be accountable for. Let's look at both sets in some detail.

1. Staff Responsibilities to the Board

Staff and board are in a two-way symbiotic relationship: they can't exist without each other. Board members need staff to do certain things for them in order for the board members to be able to perform their duties. Here is my list of the things that staff members need to do, do regularly, and do well for the board.

Provide accurate, timely, and focused information. I hope that, in a faith-based organization, the term "accurate" applies without question. But accurate, in my view, goes beyond just telling the truth. It also means presenting both sides of an issue, discussing both the positive *and* the negative results of a certain action or policy. Without complete knowledge there can be no true understanding of an issue, and without that understanding, board members can and will make poor and potentially harmful decisions.

Timely does not mean as the board members arrive for their meeting. What it does mean is that board and committee members should receive their meeting packets at least *three working days* before the meeting at which they will consider the materials. Board members need time to read, absorb, reflect, and prayerfully consider their actions and the often conflicting priorities of their organization's many needs. To ask them to do this while the material is being discussed is tantamount to sabotaging the process and the board's ability to set policy. Of course, no one can ensure that a board or committee member will actually read his or her material prior to arriving at the meeting site, but staff at least need to get the information in board members hands to give them a chance to read, make notes, and come prepared with questions.

Focused information does not mean just one side of an issue. I intend this term to convey the need for staff to let board members know about the most important issues that they should attend to. Board members are involved with their policy-setting activities only four to six hours *per month* on average. Compare that with a senior staff member averaging 50 to 60 hours *per week,* and you can see why it is critical that staff members, who have been hired as specialists and experts, channel the limited time of the board to considering only the most important issues. Please note, though, that this responsibility does not give staff license to limit what a board member can see. If a board member raises an issue or wants to see information on a particular trend or topic, the staff should comply with that request as long as the information requests are not frivolous and don't threaten an issue of confidentiality.

Inform the board of new developments. You don't want your board members to find out about crucial developments, good or bad, in the paper or on the local news broadcast. Whether the development is a happy one, such as a grant award or local press coverage of a new program, or bad news such as suspected criminal activity that includes an employee or volunteer, board members should know about the situation as early as possible.

☞ **HANDS-ON:** Here is where e-mail is such a great tool. Start now to develop a board e-mail list, and when there is an important issue, send all of your online board members the same information at the same time. For those who aren't yet wired, send a fax. Remember, though, not to exclude board members who do not have the benefits of the latest technological wizardry. Make sure that they are called by phone or sent the materials by messenger. Finally, don't use e-mail as a "set and forget" part of your communications effort. I know of many critical messages that went undelivered simply because the recipients didn't check their e-mail for a day or two. If you really, absolutely have to get the information to people, you need to fall back on the phone or on hand delivery.

Orient and continually train the board. Staff are on the job full-time, and I know that sometimes it feels as though you have two or even three full-time jobs. You often feel as if you live your job. You know everything you can about your organization, your community, and the challenges your organization faces. But volunteer boards simply do not have the time to amass that kind of expertise—that's why they have staff.

Thus, it falls to the staff not only to educate themselves but also to keep the board continually up to date. Since board members are involved in their policy work only 6 hours per month at the maximum, staff members need to regularly orient them with regard to the basic functions of the organization as well as the more technical and timely issues facing them. It boils down to this: you can't just do a one-evening orientation and hope that it will hold in the memory of any of your board members. It won't. Think back to your first day on the job. How much of what you were told do you remember? Not much, I'm sure. Neither do your board members, and through no fault of their own. So it's up to the staff to keep reminding the board about all the many things that your organization does, as well as to inform it of current events and future issues. We'll look at how you do this a little later in this chapter.

Support the recruitment of new board members. Board recruitment is a staff/board partnership. In the next section on building and retaining a strong board, we'll look at the recruitment process and how staff and board members need to work together to develop the policy body that the organization needs. But suffice it to say here that you don't want the board recruitment process left to the board alone. It isn't fair to them, to you, or most importantly, to the organization.

Support board committees. Staff members need to provide the same support for the committees of the board as they do for the board itself. This often can and should mean that different staff members support different committees. For example, the director of finance might be the lead staff person for the finance committee, the director of human resources could staff the personnel committee, and so on. Spreading around staffing responsibility has three advantages: it allows the work to be divided among many staff, it allows the board to see how many good staff the organization has, and it is a great staff development process. But the bottom line is that the staff needs to help committees get their jobs done.

Attend board meetings. I'm a great believer in having staff attend board meetings. Not only do I think that the head staff person should encourage subordinates to report on issues for which they have responsibility, but I go further than that: I think that all staff should be allowed to attend any board meeting they want to. Before you fall over with disbelief, read on a bit. First, the largest and most divisive issue in many organizations is the resentment staff have over the "secret" nature of board meetings. Believe me, they talk about what goes on and share rumors, which we all know are dangerous things. They assume that something untoward must be going on since they aren't "good enough to attend," a phase I've heard dozens of times. The solution: Let them come, but on your terms.

☞ **HANDS-ON:** I encourage you to encourage your staff to come to board meetings, but *with the clear understanding that they are observers, not participants.* (The only exception to this would be for staff members who are actually reporting to the board.) If your organization is like most, a fair number will attend the first meeting after they are allowed in and then never come again, since they will find the meetings boring. And, of course, you can ask people to leave when you are discussing personnel issues or other issues that merit confidentiality. However, opening your doors will end the concern about board meetings being off limits. Try this, it works!

Follow policy decisions of the board. Unless your board is just an advisory board (and thus the staff actually works for a higher echelon of authority within your faith's structure), the staff should follow the policy decisions of the board promptly, thoroughly, and with enthusiasm. If the board has made a decision that the staff, particularly the senior staff person, disagrees with, that staff person should let the board know, and I would hope that this would have been done prior to the decision being made. I strongly encourage the head staff person to make recommendations, provide cautionary advice, or urge the organization's policy makers to stretch and take risks, depending on the situation. I also urge board members to encourage frank and complete input and ideas from their paid staff. Thus, in cases where there is disagreement, the discussion should be lively and include all sides of the issues.

But, once the governing body makes its decision, that's it. The staff and any dissenting board members need to be on the team, loyal to the decision, and to carry it out with both excellence and enthusiasm. If your staff members fundamentally disagree with the policy on a moral or spiritual basis, their choice should be to resign from the organization. I recognize that such a drastic action is much easier said than done, but staff members who choose to stay in such a situation should do so with the understanding that they must be loyal to the organization and its policies.

2. Staff Responsibilities to the Organization

Now we need to look at another set of staff responsibilities, those that the staff has to the organization. In Chapter Five, we'll look at the way that I think you need to manage your staff, but here I want to quickly walk through the things that staff are responsible for, as a counterpoint to the board responsibilities that we've already reviewed.

Focus on faith and mission. You read earlier that the board has a responsibility to focus on faith; so does the staff. As a faith-based organization, your staff must ensure that your policies and your programs support the core tenets of your faith and on a day-to-day basis, that those policies are implemented in a faithful manner. Of course, as a not-for-profit you need to focus on your mission as well, regardless of whether you are a place of worship or a community service organization. How do you do this? Should you just place your mission statement on the wall? Should you just make sure that members of your staff behave themselves? While both of these are good ideas, I suggest a little more rigorous approach. My list of things for you to attend to is as follows:

- Be a faithful role model. First and foremost you need to evidence your faith in your own words and deeds. You also need to believe passionately in your mission and work to promote it every day. I strongly urge you to start each staff meeting and board meeting with prayer and a brief devotion or meditation. You may want to do this yourself or to circulate the responsibility among the staff or board.

- Have the tenets of your faith and your mission statement visible, available, and often discussed. I advise secular not-for-profits to have copies of their mission statement on the table at every staff and board meeting, so that people can constantly be confronted with the reason for the organization's existence. For faith-based organizations I suggest the same thing, but to add to that a list of the tenets of your faith. You want this list visible, available, and often discussed.

- Talk about your faith and your mission when you recruit staff. Make it clear that your expectations of behavior are high and be specific about what you will and will not allow.

Report fiscal information regularly. It is a staff responsibility to let the board and the volunteers know what is going on financially, regularly, which means at every meeting. If your board only meets quarterly, you should let your executive committee or management council see financial reports every month. The budget that you and your board set up is a contract for fulfillment by the staff and for monitoring by the board. The staff needs to do its part and to let the board know what is going on—regularly.

Act as a check and balance on the board. Just as the board is a check and balance on the staff, the staff provide the same function for the board. If the governing volunteers begin to act in ways not consistent with good management principles or in ways that don't support the mission or your faith, staff need to speak up and to use their persuasive and political skills to stop the slide into mismanagement or toward a wrong direction.

Make the most of all resources, including the board. Earlier I noted that all staff and board members are stewards of their organizations. Stewards make the most of all the resources at their command to perform more mission. One of those resources that staff have is the board. Thus, it is appropriate for staff members to ask their board for help, expertise, connections, information, or ideas if they think that the board can provide help. It's also fine for board members to refuse if they can't or if they have other obligations.

There is also an inherent idea hidden here. To get the most out of your board as a resource, its members need to be trained and kept up to date. More on that in the next section.

Ensure that the board's skill set matches the needs of the organization. As I said above, board recruitment is a joint board-staff effort and responsibility. We'll cover the recruitment process in some detail below, but let it suffice here to say that the staff role is to ensure that the long-term needs of the organization for certain board skills are met by the skill set that is present on the board in any given year.

D. BUILDING AND RETAINING A STRONG BOARD

Now that you know the key responsibilities of staff and board in your organization, let's examine the crucial issue of building and retaining a strong board. I am a true advocate for a strong board model of governance, with a strong staff to balance the organization. But the first part of the equation is a strong board, one that meets the need of the organization now and in the next few years. I think of your board as a market, just like any other. That may sound crass on first reading, but let me explain.

When I was the young executive director of a regional not-for-profit, my organization's service area was over 150,000 square miles and I had 45 board members, many of whom had to drive two hours each way to attend meetings. As a result, there were often times when we didn't have a quorum and sometimes months that would go by in which I couldn't fill an empty board slot; people weren't willing to make the kind of commitment it took to be on our board. I complained loudly about my board's lack of commitment to a friend, who was the CEO of our largest hospital. He smiled benevolently and told me it was obvious that I didn't know about the "rule of 24." As I didn't, I asked him to explain.

"When we are born," he began, "God gives us all gifts. Some of us are artistic, some musical. Some of us are great organizers, some great thinkers. Some are athletic, some altruistic. Each of us gets his own mix of God's gifts. But there is just one gift that we all get exactly equally, and that is 24 hours in a day. What we do with our lives is based on what we choose to do with this gift each day. Your board members have choices. They can choose to watch TV, eat dinner, meet with family or friends, engage in a hobby, sleep, garden, listen to music. Or, they can choose to come to your board meeting. Are you making it *worth their while* to take a part of their 24 hours to attend your meeting? By the behavior that they are demonstrating (not coming to the meetings), I would say that it is your fault, not theirs, that they are not there. It is your job to make it so appealing that they will invest part of their 24 hours with your organization."

After that conversation, I have never thought the same way about board-staff relations. I realized that, just like any other marketing situation, the staff has to make it valuable enough to the board members to get them away from their families, their jobs, or their recreation. With my board, I started by asking them, for the first time, what *they* wanted from their board service. I found out that they wanted to feel more a part of the organization, that they wanted us to have more concrete outcomes and that they wanted to be given important tasks so that they did not just feel that they were rubber-stamping staff work. All these items, when I reflected, were valid wants, and wants that I was not meeting as their senior staff person. You can do this too, and we'll look at how as we go through the sequence of recruitment and retention listed below.

Some faith-based organizations have their board appointed by a higher echelon of their faith. The church hierarchy may simply select lay persons to serve on a particular board. If this is the case for you, there is still information here that you can use; simply skip the section on board recruitment, but don't if your organization has *any* input into the board selection process.

1. Recruit the Board You Need

I doubt that any of you would hire a staff person without requiring some experience prior to hiring. For example, if you needed a nurse, you wouldn't take someone who didn't have education as a registered nurse or a licensed practical nurse. Nor would you ever think of hiring staff persons and not assigning them to a particular role, providing them with a job description, or evaluating their performance. But we do all these things with our boards. We essentially take anyone willing to serve and tell them to go do good works. Earlier I showed you a list of board responsibilities, which I hope you have used to develop a job description for your board. But how do you get the right people in the right board slots at the right time?

First, you need to have a rotating board. What this means is that you have board terms, and that board members have some limit on the number of terms that they may serve. My suggestion is two three-year terms as a maximum, with some required time off (a year or two) before a person can stand for election again. While this is tough to implement if you have a board that had been in place for 15 or 20 years (as is the case with some organizational boards), it really is worth the effort. New people on a board bring new ideas, new perspectives, and new enthusiasm, which is not to say that your current board doesn't have ideas or energy. It's just that turnover is a good thing. The Dead Sea is the only body of water on the planet that doesn't support life. Why? Because the River Jordan empties into it as its inflow, and there is no outflow—no turnover.

Second, you need to look to your strategic plan to see what skills you will need on your board over the next five years and then compare that skillset with the skills of your current board. From this exercise, you can construct a list of skills that you will need to recruit to lead your organization over the coming years.

❏ **FOR EXAMPLE:** When I joined the board of our local Association for Retarded Citizens many years ago, the board consisted of family members, a few politicians, and the occasional businessperson. Over the next ten years, we built or acquired over 25 group homes, added hundreds of staff, and became the largest provider of services to people with disabilities in central Illinois. To accomplish that, we recruited architects, builders, bankers, lawyers, realtors, and human resources professionals on to the board. And when that expansion was done, those people rotated off the board to make room for people who had the skills to lead the organization into its next major initiative, community-based employment.

What skills does your organization need? People who passionately believe in your mission? Yes. Businesspeople? Yes. Legal advice, accounting, engineering, educational, marketing and other expertise? Perhaps. Only you, your staff, and your board can really decide. But decide you must, and then go about the process of recruitment.

The third step is recruitment, and that, as I have already noted twice, is a joint endeavor of the board and staff. Recruitment is not a task that should wait until the week before the nominating committee meets; it is an ongoing effort. Keep a list close at hand of the skills you need and of potential board candidates. Network in the community to look for people who might be good additions to your governing body, and when you meet with them to discuss their possible service, remember not only to talk about what your organization does, but also to let them know what the organization will expect of them as leaders. Then ask them why they are interested in serving. Listen carefully. This will be your first chance to figure out what they want from their service so that you can give it to them and keep them motivated to serve.

And don't forget your faith in the recruitment process. If your organization is a place of worship, you will almost certainly recruit exclusively from your congregation. Many but not all community service organizations encourage board members from outside their denomination or faith, often as a way of broadening their community network and sometimes as a way of accessing a specific expertise. I'm not going to make a recommendation here: I've seen it work well both ways. Just remember to think the issue through and discuss it thoroughly *before* you start to recruit.

Don't take just any warm body for your board. Figure out what skills you need, and then go out and get them. Your organization will really benefit from the effort.

2. Mentor, Train, and Retain

Now that you have the board members you need, how do you keep them? By mentoring, training, and working to retain them for their full terms of service. Let's start with mentoring. This is a great way to increase the likelihood that a new member will stay on your board and will reach the point of actively contributing as soon as possible.

☞ **HANDS-ON:** When a new board member is elected, the board chairperson should appoint a mentor for that member. Let's say that the new board member's name is Ed and the board chair asks Len to be Ed's mentor. As this is quite an honor—the board chairperson obviously trusts and admires Len—Len agrees. What does Len have to do? Before the first board meeting that Ed will attend, Len calls him and suggests that they get together before the board meeting, perhaps for dinner. Len walks in with Ed and introduces him to each board member in turn. Then, for the next six meetings or so, Ed and Len sit next to each other, so that Ed can turn to Len and safely ask the "stupid" question (which is rarely stupid at all). Len can quickly explain jargon, background information, and so on. Between meetings, Ed calls Len to make sure that he got his monthly board mailing and to find out if he has any questions. As soon as Ed is ready, usually in about six months, Len backs off and lets Ed be on his own.

Such mentoring will really increase your new board members' understanding of their role and of your organization's culture and language and will also speed their ability to make significant contributions.

The second job to is to train, train, train the board. This means not only having an orientation session when they are new, but also regularly educating, informing, and reminding them of what is going on inside the organization, as well as what is going on outside that will affect the organization.

☞ **HANDS-ON:** Don't just settle for a one-time orientation. Make board training a regular part of every meeting. I suggest that you incorporate board training as a fifteen-minute item on *every* board agenda. Review your main programs, one at a time. Go over public policy or events in the higher echelons of your faith. Discuss state of the art (best practices) in your area of service. In short, remind board members of your core issues and give them context for their policies. Here's a hint. Members who have been on your policy body for a while may think that they already know it all; if you have this orientation session at the beginning of the meeting, they will drift in late. If you have it at the end, they will either actually leave, or just tune it out. My suggestion is to have your 15 minutes of orientation *just before the finance committee report.* That way you are assured that everyone will be in their seats and at their most alert.

☞ **HANDS-ON:** Your organization needs a board manual. Some organizations use their manuals as a place to store their board materials. I think that this is a mistake. Your board manual should be an educational text, the place your board members turn for information between meetings. It should have in it the key things that your board needs to understand its job. The manual should be a reference too, which your board members can use to find important information, clear up confusion, or answer basic questions about the organization and their role in it. Included, at a minimum, should be:

- A copy of your Mission Statement
- A copy of the Tenets of your Faith

- A copy of your Bylaws
- A list of all board members, their addresses, phone and fax numbers, and e-mail addresses (both work and home)
- A list of Committees, their members, meeting time and place and the responsibilities of each committee
- A table of organization with staff names, titles, and phone numbers
- A list of current goals from the strategic plan
- A list of jargon, with definitions in plain language
- A copy of your current budget
- A copy of your board and officer job descriptions
- Names, addresses, phone numbers, and e-mail addresses of your organizational attorney, accountant, and any other regularly retained consultants
- A brief (one paragraph) description of each of your programs or ministries

3. Motivate Your Board

The third leg of the board stool is to motivate board members to participate to the maximum of their abilities and to weave their volunteer efforts for your organization into the fabric of the conflicting demands of family, work, and faith. This is not an easy task, and the two best tools you have are your mission and your organization's sponsoring faith. You need to regularly celebrate the value that your organization has in your community and personalize that value by letting your board members know about the person-by-person successes, the lives altered and improved, the families reunited, the people fed, the homeless housed.

We do much too little celebrating in our organizations. We seem to spend all of our time trying to fight the latest fire, plan how to overcome the next obstacle, and see into the future to foretell the next critical need. We all need to step back and look at the good works. *And God saw all that He had made, and behold, it was very good.* Genesis 1:31. I'm not advising you to have huge celebrations or throw a big party, which simply beats your collective chest. What I do want you to do is to remind each other through individual examples of how much your organization helps. Don't let the people part get lost in the shuffle of budgets, plans, and policies.

And then there is your faith. We've already talked about what sets your organization off from secular ones. You know it, I know it, but does your board know it? You need to tell them early and tell them often. People of faith are motivated by their faith to do wonderful things. We've all seen that in our own lives. Don't neglect reminding people that their work on the board can be an evidence of their faith. Again here, I need to caution you about misinterpreting my intentions: Don't try to give people a guilt trip if they miss a board meeting now and then. Don't threaten them with God's wrath or accuse them of faithlessness if they don't volunteer for every opportunity to serve.

❑ **FOR EXAMPLE:** A minister friend recently told me a story about his early years as head pastor of a small church. He was a self-described firebrand, pushing himself and his flock to grow the church to minister to the community, and providing literally dozens of opportunities to meet, serve, volunteer, and be together. As he told me, "We had activities, meetings, services, or service opportunities seven days a week, and we thought we were being accessible and available and giving people choice. But we weren't." As my friend described the sequence, he mounted the pulpit to urge people to participate, to serve, to share fellowship, and to worship together. He quoted Scripture, wrote columns in the church newsletter, and even called parishioners to urge them to join a new group when it started. His intention was to get each member of his congregation to participate in *something* other than Sunday worship. What the congregation thought they heard him say was that God wanted them to participate in *everything* the church offered. And many did. And marriages suffered, children were ignored, work was deferred, careers put on hold. My friend still grieves about this, fifteen years later. It was never his intention to use his faith as a club for motivation. But that's what happened.

So motivating your board by examples of success and by faith is fine. They will give you more service and give it more often if you do. Just don't overdo it.

Finally, I want to offer you one final perspective on your board. Later in the book, we'll cover how using traditional and time-tested marketing techniques can help you promote your faith and provide your mission. At its core, marketing is figuring out who your customers are, asking them what they want, and trying your best to give it to them. Why is this important here? Because I want you to think of your board as a market, and a very important one. You have to have a committed and talented group of governing volunteers. Just remember that these volunteers also have wants, and that you have to ask them what those wants are to meet them. You can never just assume you know. Talk to your board members about what they like and what they dislike regarding their service. Listen carefully and try to give them more of the former and less of the latter, if at all possible.

POSTLUDE

In this chapter you learned a number of crucial things about the key players in your organization: the governing volunteers and the paid staff. You were shown how the board members are fiduciaries, who are responsible for strategic policy decisions, while staff members are responsible for carrying out those policies on a day-to-day, week-to-week, and month-to-month basis. Both groups are supposed to act as checks and balances on the other and in doing so, to build a better organization.

Then you learned about the responsibilities of boards, which are as follows:

1. Fulfill the beliefs of the sponsoring faith
2. Fulfill all of the IRS, state, and local not-for-profit reporting requirements
3. Fulfill the responsibilities and contractual obligations of the funders
4. Set policy and establish organizational goals
5. Hire (if allowed) and evaluate the head staff person
6. Help develop, adopt, and monitor budgets
7. Establish personnel and financial policies and ensure their implementation
8. Nominate and elect officers
9. Represent the organization in public
10. Raise money

Next we turned to the staff. As you saw, there are two sets of staff responsibilities, one to the board and one to the organization, both of which are important and which should work in a coordinated manner to move the organization forward. The staff responsibilities lists we reviewed were as follows.

Staff responsibilities to the board:

1. Provide accurate, timely, and focused information
2. Inform the board of new developments
3. Orient and continually train the board
4. Support the recruitment of new board members
5. Support board committees
6. Attend board meetings

Staff responsibilities to the organization:

1. Focus on faith and mission
2. Report fiscal information regularly
3. Checks and balances on the board
4. Make the most of all resources, including the board
5. Ensure that the board's skill set matches the needs of the organization

Finally, we turned to ways in which you can recruit, motivate, and retain an excellent board. The key point here was that you need to think of your board as a market, just like any other, and to find out what board members want and provide it to them, whether what they want is a challenge, meaningful things to do, fellowship, personal recognition, or a feeling that they are making a difference.

You should now have a good handle on this important set of relationships and responsibilities. And, while the interactions between your staff and board are crucial, so are staff members' interactions with each other. We commonly call this staff management. That is the subject of our next chapter.

CHAPTER FOUR CHECKLIST

In this, the initial "working" chapter in this book, I have for the first time, included a *Checklist*. The idea of the *Checklist* is to give you a set of specific things to examine in your organization right away. For example, in the *Checklist* for this chapter, you will see the items Board job description and Board manual. This should remind you to check whether your organization has such items, whether they are up-to-date, and whether you are satisfied with the contents. All remaining chapters will include *Checklists*.

Chapter Four Checklist

✓ Board job description

✓ Officer job descriptions

✓ Staff job descriptions

✓ Board manual

✓ Board orientation process

✓ List of committees and their duties

✓ Bylaws review

QUESTIONS FOR DISCUSSION: CHAPTER FOUR

1. Do we use our board to maximum advantage? How can we get more out of this critical resource?

2. Do we get enough information to our board early enough in a format that they can use to the best mission effect?

3. Do we focus enough on mission and faith at our board and committee meetings? How can we do better in this area?

4. Do we have the skill set we need on our board? Will it continue to meet our needs for the next three to five years? How can we meet any unfilled needs?

5. Do we allow for appropriate interaction between staff and board? Do both groups know the limits of such interaction?

5

Staff Management

Masters, grant to your slaves justice and fairness, knowing that you too have a Master in heaven. Colossians 4:1

The world stands upon three things: upon the Law, upon worship, and upon showing kindness. Mishnah, Abot 1.2

PRELUDE

In this chapter you will learn about:

➤ A Spiritual model of supervision
➤ Delegating to others: A need to trust and empower
➤ Evaluation: Holding people accountable
➤ Discipline: Setting limits and enforcing them

If your organization is like most faith-based entities, you have some number of employees. Paid staff are a crucial resource for any not-for-profit organization, as they do the day-to-day work of implementing the board's policies. As we've seen in Chapter Four, staff are also responsible for activities as varied as providing a check and balance on the board of directors and ensuring that the underlying tenets of the organization's faith are followed. This is no mean feat, and your faith-based organization needs the best staff it can find, afford, and retain to ensure that your mission is carried out with competence, enthusiasm, and compassion.

Your staff need to believe in the organization's mission. If they don't, they will not be full participants in the implementation of that mission. The staff also need to have the skills to do the job well. As I said in Chapter One, people expect excellence, not just a caring and kind heart, from the employees of faith-based organizations. And such expectations are almost always dynamic; that is, they change, over time. That means that the staff needs to be constantly educated to improve services to meet the change of expectations. Developing a culture that reveres life-long learning is key, as are managers who model that behavior.

So, your staff need to do a lot of things, and you as a manager are responsible for leading, motivating, communicating, delegating, evaluating, and in some cases, disciplining the employees for whom you are responsible. That's a big task in an organization that often can't pay its employees even close to what they are worth, in which the management team may not have much formal management training, and in which the culture, while claiming to be people-based, may actually be fairly hierarchical, unsupportive, and cold.

If you supervise employees and if any of the organizational description sounds familiar, this chapter will help move you into being a better manager and a better supervisor.

In the following pages, we'll first look at what I consider a faith-based method of supervision. It is founded on some Old Testament wisdom, wisdom that is as meaningful and effective for today's organization as it was when it was written over two millennia ago. Then, we'll examine the main ways in which you interact with your staff members: delegation, evaluation, and discipline. In Chapter Seven, we will take a separate look at what I consider crucial leadership skills: motivation, innovation, communication, flexibility, and lifelong learning. Of course, all of these skills also affect the way in which you interact with your staff. However, too many leadership texts focus on the big picture part of management. While such large-order thinking is important, you also have to run the organization, or your part of it, on a day-to-day basis. That requires supervision skills, which is the focus of our discussion in this chapter.

A. A SPIRITUAL MODEL OF SUPERVISION

We are taught many positive behaviors through the texts of our religions. Whether it is from God's Ten Commandments, the wisdom of Proverbs, the parables of Jesus, or the Pillars of Islam, each of our major religions provides us with a guidebook for life and our actions and interactions with each other.

If supervision of staff is anything, it is interaction with others. So what does your faith teach you about those interactions? Does it invoke honesty, fairness, respect, and nurturing? Certainly. Does it call for leaders to lead? Absolutely. Does it require sacrifice? Unquestionably. Does it put you up on a pedestal? Or allow you to treat employees like galley slaves? Or encourage you to work employees to death (or to divorce)? I suspect not.

Managers in faith-based organizations must manage, *based on their faith.* You need to lead by example, evincing your faith in all that you do.

That includes your interactions not only with people *outside* the organization, but also those inside. If you are a rabbi, steeped in a tradition of life-long learning, how can you not budget for more continuing education for your staff? If you are a minister of a Christian congregation, preaching a gospel of love and forgiveness, what message does it send if you hold a public grudge against an employee or ignore a certain staff person? Again, because of your profession of faith, you are held to a higher standard.

But our faiths do provide us with guidance to be excellent managers. All the important issues are covered in our holy texts. The question for us is how we will implement them in a secular, competitive, and often less than forgiving world.

Let's examine a few parts of Scripture regarding employers. We are taught that employers must not oppress their employees (Deuteronomy 24:14, *You shall not oppress a hired servant who is poor and needy, whether he is one of your countrymen or one of your aliens who is in your land in your towns*), must be considerate (Job 31:31, *Have the men of my tent not said, "Who can find one who has not been satisfied with his portion?"*), and must be just and fair (Colossians 4:1, *Masters, grant to your slaves justice and fairness, knowing that you too have a Master in heaven"*). And, don't you want to be treated fairly, justly, considerately, and without oppression?

The following are my tenets of a faith-based manager. What I've done is take the characteristics that I have seen in successful organizations like yours (whether places of worship or community service organizations), and put them into a framework for you to consider. This framework is just that, a bare outline of the kind of staff supervisor I would like you to be. As there are huge differences between supervising 150 staff persons at a YMCA and 2 at a small temple, I will attempt to illustrate the ideas with examples from large and small organizations.

1. Treat Others, Including Those You Supervise, as You Would Want to Be Treated

Look familiar? It should. Every reader learned this as a child. It is one of God's great teachings to us, so simple and yet so profound. We all would like to be treated well, and in survey after survey, people want basically the same three things: to be treated with respect, to be told the truth, and to be treated fairly.

In your work as a supervisor, you need to constantly be asking yourself: Am I treating people the way I would like to be treated? Sounds simple, but it is not as easy as it seems. Many supervisors have thought that they were treating people well, when their employees were constantly comparing their behavior to that of Attila the Hun. Could this happen to you? Certainly.

Think of your early career. Nearly everyone has worked for someone whom he or she disliked or who was unfair, dishonest, or a general pain. I can almost guarantee that during that period, you said to yourself: When *I* get to be a supervisor, I'll *never* treat people like that. Perhaps you don't, from your perspective. But what do your employees think? Are they saying the same thing about you that you did about that long-ago supervisor?

Let's do some reality checking on each of these core values and, if you are honest with yourself, you can see how you stack up.

• *Respect:* Showing people respect means a lot of different things. It means respecting their individuality, their different gifts, their backgrounds, and the diversity of ideas that they bring to your organization. On a more day-to-day level, it means saying *please* and *thank you,* remembering that they have a life beyond work, listening to their problems and their ideas openly, and not being judgmental about non-work issues unless they affect your organization.

• *Honesty:* I hope that all my readers believe that they are honest. But in reality, do you always tell people the truth? When you say to a staff person, "I'll get back to you on that tomorrow," is it a covenant, or just a way of ending the meeting? If you have no intention of getting back to this person in the next 24 hours or even at all, don't say it. Your people are listening. And remembering. You don't have to tell everyone everything — some information is better not shared. But *everything* that comes out of your mouth *must be the truth as you know it.* Every time. Unfortunately, our society does not put a high premium on this.

❏ **FOR EXAMPLE:** We are, as a society, getting more and more casual about this issue. We don't value honesty, and in some areas such as paying our taxes, are even ridiculed for being honest. Our culture even has ignored the true meaning of a popular saying because *we don't listen to what we say.* How many times have you heard, or yourself used, the expression, "Well, to be honest with you…" What does saying this literally mean? It is a warning to the listener that you are about to *stop lying!* You are admitting that there are times when you are not honest! The term that should be used in these situations is "to be frank with you," which is a much more accurate way of describing the interaction.

Say what you mean, mean what you say, and think about what comes out of your mouth before it does.

• *Fairness:* While fairness is a subjective term, in a management context it means treating everyone the same, making everyone equally accountable, and enforcing the rules for everyone in the same manner. Unfortunately, we don't seem to be very good at this. We let a certain person break the rules now and then, allow one person to be consistently late for work, don't require some people to provide every receipt for cash reimbursement, have a different dress code for some people. Take it from me—this drives people nuts, both on the management side and on the staff side! How can you respect individuality if you make everyone fit the same mold? On the other hand, if you don't have standards, how can you hold people accountable? Shouldn't we all be able to act in a responsible manner?

Well, yes we should. Unfortunately, some of us are in adult bodies still trying to act out our adolescence. I firmly believe that you need a set of behavioral standards for your organization. You already have them for your faith. Why not for your workplace? The key question is: Do they apply to everyone? Of course, the answer is yes and no. There will always be an extenuating circumstance that requires managerial judgment to accommodate. What I want you to do is to reduce the challenges to the rules and thus to make it easier to be fair to everyone by following the steps discussed below.

☞ **HANDS-ON:** To increase the staff understanding of the rules and make it easier for you to enforce them, communicate better, and document your communications, distribute all policies and rules to staff in writing. Hold a meeting to review the rules and explain why they are in place and what they mean to the staff and to the organization. Ask for questions and insights into ways to implement them fairly. For every key policy, particularly personnel and financial policies, require that staff members sign a form saying that they have received the policy, had it explained to them, have been given the opportunity to ask questions, and agree to abide by the policy. The most common complaint among staff about discipline issues is, "No one ever told me." Now you *have* told them, and you can prove it if you need to. Then, hold annual reviews of all key policies. This is refresher training, which should be part of your normal staff training protocols. Regular review will remind people what the rules are and reinforce to them that you intend to hold people accountable to your organizational rules and values.

Treating people the way you want to be treated is not as easy as it seems. Try to be reflective on this issue, and make every attempt to see it from the perspective of the people you supervise.

2. Remember That You Are Here to Support Your Staff, Not the Other Way Around

As a supervisor, you have no job without having people to supervise. I view the best managers as those who recognize that the most important work of the organization is done at the line of service, not in the executive suite, and that the job of the executive is to get the necessary tools (training, equipment, space, etc.) in the hands of the line worker or volunteer who does the work at the right time. Thus management becomes a support function, not a fiefdom or dictatorship. You should be concerned with what you can do for your people, not the other way around. You should recognize that you succeed because of their hard work, not the reverse.

Again, this may take some stretching on your part, some rethinking of your role in your organization. Take a look at Robert Greenleaf's famous book, *On Becoming a Servant Leader,* if you want a great deal of insight into this perspective. Greenleaf's musings are excellent reminders that while we may have been chosen for positions of leadership, it is through that leadership that we serve our God, serve our communities, *and serve each other,* even the people that we work with.

I like to think of managers as coaches, or if you don't like sports analogies, conductors. People in both positions set the agenda, decide who plays, and are at the center of the action, but both realize that they succeed only through the actions of others; neither play themselves. The focus is on the players, but the organization couldn't function without the coach or conductor. This is as it should be, and as it should be in your organization. I don't think of the top staff person (executive, pastor, CEO) as on the *top* of the organizational chart, but rather at the *bottom,* supporting everyone else. It's a big load, a lot of weight on your shoulders, but one you can handle if you hire and retain good people and use them well.

3. Lead by Example

Leading by example is so important, and yet we seem to forget it all too often. To put it another way, you need to walk the talk. In Chapter Seven, we'll spend our entire time on leadership skills, but suffice it to say here that you need to evidence your faith, your values, and the actions, sense of responsibility, and work ethic that you want your staff to exhibit. If you want your organization to be innovative, don't resist every new idea. If you want your staff to go to constant refresher training, you go too. If you value lifelong learning, take some courses and let people know that you are doing so. If you want people to take responsibility for their actions, admit it when you mess up. All of our spiritual teachings tell us to put our beliefs into action.

On the other hand, if you whine about everything that is wrong, expect to have a group of whiners working for you. If you always have a reason why you are too busy to go to training, guess what—so will they. You reap what you sow, and you will have your staff follow your lead. So consider the direction in which you are leading them carefully.

❏ **FOR EXAMPLE:** As I was writing the first drafts of this book, my eldest son Ben was getting his driver's license. For three or four months he was taking driver's education learning all the rules of the road. As his "behind the-wheel" time approached, my wife and I starting being *much* more cautious in our driving, realizing that we sometimes did a rolling stop at stop signs, exceeded the speed limit, or sped up on a yellow light. We both knew that Ben had a newfound interest in our driving, and if we expected him to be a responsible driver, we needed to demonstrate that behavior.

Put another way, what parental statement was the lamest to you when you grew up? Probably what it was (and still is) for most kids: "Do as I say, not as I do." Don't subscribe to that theory of management. Walk the talk. *As you are so will you have rulers put over you.* Islamic Hadith of Baihaqi.

4. Set Limits, Give Assignments, and Hold People Accountable

Later in this chapter we'll discuss delegation, evaluation, and discipline, but the issue at this point is how you perceive your role. Even though you are there to support your staff, that does not mean that you give them free rein to make up their job description, set their own agenda, and come to work when they feel like it. Your job is to figure out the limits within which they can work (and make decisions), to give them assignments that match their personal skills, and to hold them accountable for their actions in the work environment.

This is no small task, and some days it seems as if it takes the wisdom of Solomon, the faith of Abraham, and the endurance of the Hebrews in the wilderness to get it all done. But get it done you must, because as a manager, whether in a place of worship or in a community service organization, it is your job to channel the work and the energy of the people you supervise into a cohesive outflow of service to your community. Just like the conductor of a symphony orchestra you harness the performances of many people to make a single outcome—in the conductor's case music, in your case service. No one else can do this. Someone must be in charge, but being in charge does not mean treating your people badly. Just treat them as you would like to be treated!

Now that we have listed the key parts of supervising, let's put them into action in delegating, evaluating, and disciplining.

B. DELEGATING TO OTHERS: A NEED TO TRUST AND EMPOWER

As you begin to apply my coaching model of supervision, our first task is to get you to really, truly buy into the need to delegate. I said earlier that coaches realize that they succeed through the actions of others. What that means is that you have to delegate some of the things for which you are ultimately responsible. You have to limit your job description to your job, and then keep yourself within that job description. You simply cannot be all things to all people all the time.

❑ **FOR EXAMPLE:** For most of his career, our pastor prided himself on knowing the name of every member in the church. When we had 400 families in the church, this was a daunting task. With more than 1,200 families currently, it is impossible. The pastor laments the change and, two or three times a year, apologizes from the pulpit for his inability to call everyone by name. I've talked to him once or twice about this and noted that he is showing good sense in realizing his limitations, and that the accomplishment of his other main goal, church growth, has brought him to this situation. He agrees and he understands, but he still doesn't like it much.

Remember that in Chapter Four I told you about the "Rule of 24"? To recap, this rule tells us that the only earthly gift God gives each of us equally is 24 hours in a day. In Chapter Four, I used the rule to illustrate why it is imperative to understand your board's motivation in order to make them choose to invest part of their 24 hours with your organization. Here I invoke the rule to hopefully make you realize that you, too, only get 24 hours in a day. Think about all the things that you are responsible for. How could one human being, even with God's help, get all that done every day? The truth? You can't. You need other people to help you and they are the people you supervise, the people to whom you delegate, Or, is it more accurate in your case to say *should* delegate? I hope not. You need to trust your staff, even if it hurts.

Here are my steps to better delegation:

1. Know Your Staff

You have to get to know the person behind the name if you are going to be a good delegator. You need to know that one of your staff's children (or parents) is very, very ill. You need to know that another person's wife just got a new job and is traveling a great deal. You need to know that a staff person just finished her MBA and is itching to try out her hard-won knowledge. Or that another spent three years in the Peace Corps and speaks fluent Portuguese. And which staff member is highly competitive and which is your best analyst, your best mediator, your best negotiator.

Why? Because if you know these things you can call on the right skill when you need it. You can back off when someone is under great stress, or offer counsel, help, or just a sympathetic ear. You can congratulate someone on his child's success, and console someone else about her loss. You have to take time to find out about your people, and it is an investment that will pay off.

It also helps to know where your staff are spiritually. I know, for example, that I can comfort some people who are having problems by telling them, "You will be in my thoughts and prayers." For others, that sentiment has no meaning at all. Your faith gives you a common language and a common perspective. You obviously have to treat the subject gently, but it is a good piece of information to have, as it can help you communicate and manage better.

☞ **HANDS-ON:** Don't just start by grilling people or by having them fill out a verbal questionnaire. This takes time, and people have to be ready to share. You can't force information out of them. And, here's another hint: People won't share with you unless you share with them. You have to be willing to open up a bit, be a little vulnerable, tell them about yourself. Otherwise, after a very short time people will understand that you are just taking and not giving.

2. Challenge Your Staff Supportively

The idea here is to give your staff new, interesting, and always somewhat challenging things to do. Push them. Make them stretch. If they appear hesitant, ask why? Perhaps they need some support, some more information, or just some assurance that you will be there to help if they get into trouble. And, of course, you will.

❏ **FOR EXAMPLE:** If you are a parent, and your kids are old enough, you remember teaching them to ride a bike. If you have more than one child, you remember that each child approaches this feat differently. Some can't wait, some are hesitant, and some are nearly paralyzed with fear. But all of them need a little advice and some demonstration, and then at the most critical moment, they need you to walk and then run alongside the bike with your hands near their waists, ready to catch them if they lose their balance. The child needs to know that you are there, and with that safety net, they can concentrate on learning how to balance. Then suddenly they are fine, off on their own, out of your reach, out of your protection, and, at least in the case of my three, brimming with pride.

Your staff need assurance that you will support them, that you are there for them, and that you will not be angry if they lose their balance.

Some things that you delegate will of course be routine, mundane, and easily accomplished. That's fine. But don't forget to throw in a few challenges now and then. It's how your staff grows, and how you keep them interested and motivated in their work. That having been said, there is also the other reality, that all of us have a limit to our skills. Most of us are never going to be able to run a four-minute mile, no matter how much we try, how well we are coached, or how supportive the coach is.

3. Be Available

Once you tell people what to do, you need to be available for follow-up questions, questions that may crop up in a minute, a few hours, or a few days. What you want to do is be not only physically available but also psychologically accessible to your staff. This means that you seek to make it easy and safe for them to approach you. I know dozens of executives who say that they have an "open door" policy, which they assume will solve all of their access problems. It doesn't, because what these managers don't realize is that their staff, for whatever reason, is inhibited or even afraid to come into the boss's office. So the staff members don't come, the questions don't get asked, and the job doesn't get done correctly. Don't be passive in this area. Go out and seek your people and find out what they need.

The idea of availability is to keep small problems, minor mistakes, or mundane miscommunications from becoming major messups. If your people know that they can safely ask a small question, if they know that you are a subscriber to the theory that "there are no dumb questions," then they will ask, you will be able to clear up the issue, and the job will get done better, sooner, and more efficiently.

☞ **HANDS-ON:** The key to availability is to *be available.* Here are three ways that you can improve your availability quotient.

First, as Tom Peters put it in *In Search of Excellence,* wander around. Every day, take a walk through the work areas of your organization, checking in with the staff you supervise directly and with other people to whom you may have given assignments. Do this at least once a day if you are on site, and don't race through the office giving off clues that you are too busy to talk.

Second, try to have an informal breakfast, coffee break, or lunch with the people you directly supervise once per week, or twice per month if weekly isn't possible. Have no formal agenda; just ask them what you can do for them, how their work is going, what else they need.

Third, if you have e-mail, use it. If you don't have it and you have more than five employees, get it. This is particularly true if you are out of the building a great deal (more than a total of a full day per week). Tell your staff that you will check your e-mail every night and then do it. Here's a hint—some staff will be more comfortable asking for help through the computer than in person. That's fine.

One final but very important note about availability. Many executives that I have met complain that being so available to staff takes up too much of their time, is too much like "wet-nursing" the staff, and they "have better things to do." I couldn't disagree more. You *don't* have better things to do with your time, since supervising *is* your job and being there for your staff is part of that job. Also, being available so that you can prevent a problem is not as difficult or time-consuming as picking up the pieces after something breaks.

4. Delegate Authority and Responsibility
Now, let's turn the table around and talk about making sure that you let go of *all* of any job that you delegate. If you give people just the work and none of the decision authority, you not only shackle them from moving ahead efficiently, you tell them clearly that you don't trust them. Also, you ensure that they will keep coming back to you over and over and over for input, diminishing the effectiveness of the time savings that delegation is supposed to bring you.

Give people the right to make decisions when you give them a task. If you tell them to design a new look for a newsletter, let them design it. If they are smart, they will ask for some limitations, such as number of pages or use of graphics, but then you should let them go and do their job, not bug them every 10 minutes about font, placement, "look," and so on. Remember I said earlier that one of the roles of the supervisor is to challenge people supportively? Here is where the rubber meets the road on that one. Give people the power to make decisions, and they will grow. Make all the decisions for them, and they won't. The corollary saying for this is: Give someone a fish. ... You get the idea.

☞ **HANDS-ON:** Some of your staff will love the idea of making decisions, but some will resist being on what they see as "the hot seat." This second group will need some coaching to begin to believe that they can succeed. Try this: A staff person who is given a job and comes back to you with a report often will have found two or three alternatives to solve a problem or finish a project. The employee will come to you, explain the situation, and then ask you, "Which way should we go?" or, "What do you want to do?" Try to be as neutral as you can and ask right back, "Which way do *you* think we should go?" Force them to choose, and unless that choice either violates your faith, is illegal, or would be a total disaster for the organization, say, "Sounds fine. It's your call, and I trust you to make it." I assure you, there will be staff who will *not* like this the first few times you use the technique, but they will grow in confidence both in their own decision-making capabilities and in the knowledge that you trust them.

☞ **HANDS-ON:** What to do when staff members don't come to you and they really mess up? What if they have used all this authority I have been describing and make a major league mistake? Should you punish them, read them the riot act, take away some responsibility? Get angry?

The answer to these questions is, *usually* not. Let me start to explain by invoking two sayings, one Japanese, one my own. The Japanese approach to this situation is: "Fix the problem, not the blame." Thus, if someone has made a mistake focus first on what you can do to stem or repair the damage. It doesn't do much good for people to take time yelling at each other about who left the stove burner on when the kitchen is on fire. First, put out the fire and save the house. So, start by assessing what happened and what went wrong, and work *with* the staff involved on fixing it. Don't *you* fix it alone; make them part of the solution.

Including staff in the solution is a demonstration of the second major issue here, your attitude in such a situation. Instead of saying, "Why are you such an idiot?" or, "Why did you do something so dumb?," you can practice restraint, review the current problem and its solution, and then ask "What did *we* learn from all of this?" (not what have *you* learned from this), and wait for an answer. The theory behind this comes from the second saying, mine, that had been invoked with everyone who has ever worked for me. It is the Primary Rule of Working for Peter, and it is this: *Make any noncriminal mistake you want, once.* What this means is that as long as your mistake is well-intentioned and not repeated, it's okay. Don't forget what you learned in high school: There are no failed experiments, just hypotheses that don't get proved true. The idea of experimentation is to learn whether or not something works, not just to have every idea proved true. So, as long as a person is not making a mistake repeatedly, figure out how to fix the problem and move on. You don't need to chastise them. Your good people are already doing that to themselves.

The bottom line here is that if you delegate a task and don't give people the authority to make the decisions necessary to do the job, you do four things you don't want to: inhibit their growth, take up an inordinate amount of your time supervising them, stunt their creativity, and tell them that you don't trust them.

5. Encourage Innovation and Problem Solving

Here are two of the greatest opportunities you have as a supervisor to improve your organization, grow your staff, and save yourself valuable time. Encourage people to solve problems on their own, but let them know that you will be there for them if they need you. This is a delicate balance and it requires being available and knowing your people well. When they come to you with a problem, ask them what they think is the answer, don't give it to them directly. When they list a bunch of choices and ask you which one you think is best, turn it around and ask them which choice *they* favor. And, as I said earlier, unless their choice is a disaster, let them make the choice.

On a much more important level, though, innovation challenges organizations because there is an inherent tendency to let ourselves be ruled by the inertia of tradition, as expressed in the statement: But we've always done it this way. One of my favorite buttons, sent to me by someone who came to one of my training sessions in New Mexico, looks like this:

I have nothing against tradition, but we can't let it blind us to good, positive change that makes us a better organization, helps us provide better services, or brings more people to our faith. Encourage your staff to suggest new ways of doing things, of being more mission-based, of demonstrating your faith, and of using your resources more efficiently and effectively. But make them rationalize why each change will result in those things. Make sure that you are changing for a valid reason, not just to change.

❑ **FOR EXAMPLE:** Many churches have gone through the pain of changing their worship service, most in the belief that it will make that worship more accessible and thus be more inviting to new members. The Catholic Church went through this with the changes brought about by Vatican II, when for the first time, Mass was presented in the local language, not in Latin. To understate the case, this was a controversial! But it doesn't have to be a momentous change to generate controversy. At my church, just a change in the music, from all traditional hymns to a mix of those songs and more contemporary music, had some people all riled up, but membership rose, which was, of course, the bottom line.

☞ **HANDS-ON:** One way to demonstrate your encouragement of innovation is to have a portion of employee evaluation dedicated to it. You need a question or criterion on the evaluation form that says something to the effect of: "What innovative idea, process, policy, service or product has (the employee) developed during the evaluation period?"

In the area of problem solving, remember this: You do not have all the answers. Other people can solve problems, too—let them. Give them the tools, the training, the authority, the support, and the coaching and then let them put that training into practice by allowing them to solve problems. Management is a team sport. Let everyone get some playing time.

Finally, in this area we need to deal with an item that is essential to any supervisor who encourages his or her staff to solve problems, and to innovate, namely, forgiveness. Remember the story in Genesis of Joseph, who was left for dead in the desert by his brothers and went on to become a prince in Egypt? During a famine that occurred 30 years after they had tried to kill him, his brothers appeared in his court asking for help. Joseph toyed with the idea of vengeance, but eventually forgave them, saying: *Do not be grieved or angry with yourselves, because you sold me here, for God sent me before you to preserve life.* Genesis 45:5. Although it may seem like it some days, your staff are not trying to kill you, or your organization! If Joseph could forgive, so can you. As one minister whom I heard said, "When someone wrongs you (or your organization), the real challenge is not to forgive and forget, but to forgive while remembering."

Again here, the issue is balance. Delegate as much as you can, and I know that for some readers this will involve learning to be comfortable with the idea of not doing everything themselves. For others, it will be a process of getting to believe that their staff can walk, talk, and chew gum at the same time. For many readers it will be a success. With some staff, though, it will not work, because certain employees just are not cut out for major responsibility or cannot handle the pressure of making decisions. Or, at some point, a particular staff person may have repeatedly made major mistakes and may no longer be considered a candidate for delegation. Then, what should you do? Read the next section on evaluation!

C. EVALUATION

The last two tools in our management quiver are ones that faith-based organizations too often eschew—evaluation and discipline. These two tasks are closely linked, and neglect of the first is often a sign of—and an excuse for—a desire to ignore the second.

Let's begin with evaluation, by which I mean the regular (at least annual) review of every staff person's performance against a backdrop of goals, values, and your faith. Again, just as with delegation, this is a basic, fundamental, and essential management tool. But too often I see organizations, particularly places of worship, which don't ever evaluate their people or only do it once a decade.

Look at it this way: your good people want to be told how they are doing, good or bad. The only way to help staff people grow, to help them move ahead with their careers, is to let them know their strengths as well as their weaknesses. The only way to ensure excellence in your organization is to measure yourself and everyone in your organization regularly. That means organizational and individual evaluation. (I assume that you want to be an excellent organization. Why would you settle for anything less?)

My rules for evaluation are pretty straightforward:

1. Evaluate Regularly, Both in Person and Writing

While I encourage people to perform evaluations every six months, the best many organizations can do is annually. That's fine, but make sure that the evaluation is structured and that it includes both in person and written components. This is a discipline, to be sure, and one that is easily put off by the crisis of the day, but failure to evaluate is just not good stewardship, not good management, and not good supervision.

2. Develop a Set Process and Form for Evaluation

By having a set process, everyone knows the ground rules. Will the evaluation affect an employee's salary? How? Will the evaluation be annual? At what time of year? Does the employee get a chance to respond? What input does the employee have in setting his or her goals? What responsibility does the supervisor have in the process? What criteria are included in the evaluation form?

Get all of this down in writing and have it reviewed both by a human resource professional and then by your personnel committee. Include it in your personnel policies, and let staff know why you are doing the evaluations, how you will do them, when they will occur, and what the outcomes are. If it is your first attempt at regular evaluation, go to a peer organization or your state or national trade group to get samples of evaluation processes or their evaluation forms.

The written form should include *at least* the following:

- The name of the employee and the supervisor
- The date of the evaluation and the evaluation period
- A review of the goals you set for the employee and the supervisor at the last evaluation
- A place for new goals
- A place for both the supervisor and employee to sign

Beyond that, it's up to you and your organization. As you develop criteria for evaluation, you may want to include things such as "evidences our faith" or "developed innovative practices" or other things that you value. Again, use suggestions from other organizations and then run them through your committee process.

3. There Should Be No Surprises in the Evaluation Process

The worst thing that you can do is to tell employees for the first time in a year that they are performing poorly or that they are great employees. If you do, you are not doing your job as a supervisor. The evaluation process should confirm and document what both the supervisor and the employee know and have regularly discussed—how the employee is doing. If an employee is stunned to see that he or she does not get a high rating in a particular area, it is evidence that communication has broken down during the year. One of the keys to good supervision is being available and giving regular feedback, both positive and negative. It is tempting to avoid the bad part, letting it slide until the formal evaluation. Don't succumb to that temptation.

4. Evaluate for the Entire Period, Not Just the Past Two Weeks

When you fill out employee evaluation forms, how do you fairly consider the employees' entire year? How do you remember all the good and not so good things that they have done over 12 months? If you are like me, you can't remember the good and bad things that *you* did a *week* ago, much less what a bunch of other people did 45 or 50 weeks ago. But to be fair you need to consider the entire evaluation period and to make sure that employees (who will definitely be aware that their evaluation is due in a few weeks) don't just go on a charm offensive to skew the results.

☞ **HANDS-ON:** Have a file folder for each employee you supervise and a pad of note paper on your desk. Each time an employee does something notable (good or bad) quickly jot down the date, what they did, and whether or not you talked to him or her about it (you should have). This should take less than a minute. Toss the note in the file. Then, at the end of the year, pull out the file, stack up the good notes and the bad notes, and review the entire file before you fill out the evaluation form. It will give you a much clearer view of the full year's performance.

5. Both the Employee and the Supervisor Should Be Evaluated

I know that this will be new to many readers, but I believe that the supervisor-supervised relationship is two-way, just like any other relationship; that is, it succeeds through the actions and contributions of both parties, not just one. Yet we traditionally only evaluate one person, the employee, and formally ignore the fact that employees cannot succeed without the help of their supervisor.

❑ **FOR EXAMPLE:** A faith-based community service organization with which I was involved had instituted a process by which the managers would be more involved in developing budgets for their areas. Each manager submitted his or her requests and associated rationales every year and then reviewed the requests and the resulting budgets with the executive director. The executive director then developed the entire agency budget for board review. During the ensuing fiscal year, the executive director monitored the progress of each manager's budget. To emphasize the importance of this process to the organization, the manager's evaluations included components for how well they did in the budget setting process and how close they came to making budget each year. All of this was well and good, but because of the actions of the executive director, unfair. Why? Because what I haven't told you is that after the board adopted the budgets, the managers didn't see their budget status again until the end of the year! When I asked one manager how much she had left in her supply and transportation budget, she replied, "Don't know. Don't have a clue. Don't ever see the numbers." In the next chapter, we'll talk about financial stewardship and why it is so important to share information, but the point of this story is this: How could the executive director hold the staff accountable for something that they had no control over and not even any knowledge of? The actions of the director negatively affected the staff's ability to do their jobs.

While having employees evaluate their supervisors may seem fraught with danger, it is actually a very helpful process to both parties if you ease into it. What you want to be sure of is that you develop the process in such a way that a supervisor who receives some negative evaluation comments from a staff person does not have the ability to then reduce or eliminate a raise for that person or revise an evaluation in order to get even.

☞ **HANDS-ON:** Develop a two-way evaluation process and format based on your values. I don't suggest that you implement this organization-wide right from the start. Begin with the people you supervise directly, and then spread it to the rest of the agency. Lead by example. You'll take some shots now and then, but don't overreact. Remember, criticism is an opportunity to improve, and I am assuming that because you are reading this book, you want to be the best supervisor possible. Having your staff evaluate your fairness, the quality of your communications to them, the directness of your assignments, the support you give (or don't give) them will all make you a better supervisor and will give you an essential insight into their perspective on your relationship.

The idea of the two-way evaluation is to formally acknowledge what we said earlier, that the people who work for you have great value and that you are their coach and supporter, not their dictator. It may be a stretch, a risk, but it is well worth it.

Evaluation is a crucial part of good stewardship. Telling people how they are doing (both good and bad) shows them that you are honest, frank, and have their interests in mind, as well as the interests of the organization. But sometimes even with good communication, even with regular reviews, even with you being available and approachable, people will step over the line. Then what? Then you need the next section.

D. DISCIPLINE

Now the unhappy stuff, the non-fun things, the part that most of us wish would just go away—discipline. There comes a time when, for certain staff, you have to drop the hammer. On them! If you have told them and reminded them of the rules and they have either broken the rules or made serious mistakes consistently, it is time for discipline. And, there is strong backup for you in your faith.

Let's look at some discipline rules to make this easier, more consistent, and less dangerous (in legal terms) for your organization to apply.

1. Have a Description of a Formal Discipline Process and a Listing of Unacceptable Behavior in Your Personnel Policies

The key here is to let people know early what is and is not acceptable behavior and further, to let them know what the process is for discipline. As with any and all items related to personnel, make sure that your policies are in line with both state and federal statutes and the most current thinking in the human resources field. This is *very* technical stuff—I call it *management neurosurgery*—so get an expert to help you set up the process, don't just use an off-the-shelf set of policies. Spend some money to prevent problems down the road.

2. Train All of Your Supervisors in How to Administer This Process Annually

I call this the management fire drill. Every one of your managers should be trained for at least two hours per year in how to apply your process and how to interpret your policies. Why? To keep their skills fresh. On the inevitable day when an employee acts up, do you want your supervisors to have not seen your discipline process for 36 months? No, you don't, because they have to administer the process in the right way and in the right order, or you may well be sued. Train, train, train, and hopefully you will *prevent* the fire from happening.

3. If You Aren't Going to Enforce a Rule for Everyone, Don't Have It in Your Policy

The worst thing you can do from a liability viewpoint is to be inconsistent in your application of your policies. Make sure that your supervisors enforce the rules for everyone every time. If you don't, you are just asking for a lawsuit from an employee who *does* get disciplined. And, even if it doesn't reach the stage of litigation, resentment will build in your staff.

4. Have a Feedback Loop for Your Governing Volunteers

I don't want your board or governing volunteers involved in day-to-day personnel issues, and I don't think that it is part of their job description to be involved in personnel problems. But it provides a healthy check and balance to let them know when grievances and severe disciplinary actions occur. Also, in most organizations the discipline and grievance process should reach a point at its very end at which there is an appeal to the personnel committee. But whatever you do, you don't want to totally exclude your board from this issue.

☞ **HANDS-ON:** Make a quarterly report to the board on the number (not the names or situation) of grievances and disciplinary actions taken in the past three months and compare that with the number in the previous quarter and year. Do this even if the number is zero. Thus, if the report looks like the first one in Exhibit 5-1, the board can relax. If it looks like the second, the board may want to ask its personnel committee to see if there is a problem. Again, board members do not need to know the names, issues, and so on until the process reaches them. But they do deserve to know if there are problems brewing.

Exhibit 5-1   Board Personnel Report

Full Time Staff 45	This Quarter	Last Quarter	Last Fiscal Year
Disciplinary actions	1	2	4
Grievances	0	1	1

Full Time Staff 45	This Quarter	Last Quarter	Last Fiscal Year
Disciplinary actions	5	2	4
Grievances	9	1	1

Discipline is not fun. It is not relaxing, nor is it something that most of us look forward to. But it is good stewardship, it does have a faith basis, and it is part of your job. Remember that most of us wait too long to discipline and we pay the price for letting things slide. Set your limits and enforce them fairly and consistently, and the people you want to keep as employees will respect you for it. Those that you don't want may very well go elsewhere, which will be yet another good result from doing the right thing.

A couple of final thoughts about employees. In our chapter entitled Faith-Based Marketing, we'll touch on the fact that, like your governing volunteers, employees are a crucial market. For most of you, the work of your organization would be impossible without paid staff. And, to get the most out of those staff people, you need both to follow the advice I have given you in this chapter and to *think of the staff as an important target market.* Like any other market, what do they want? How can you give it to them? How can you attract *and retain* the best people for the longest time? Keep this in mind as you ponder the ways you interact with your employees and as you think through ways to make your organization more market-oriented while remaining faith-based.

POSTLUDE

In this chapter, you learned about how to better manage your staff. First, we looked at my suggestions for a faith-based method of supervision, comparing it to a coach or a musical conductor, someone who succeeds through the actions of others. We examined the four tenets of my model of supervision which are:

1. Treat others in the way that you would like to be treated
2. Remember that you are here to support your staff, not the other way around
3. Lead by example
4. Set limits, give assignments, and hold people accountable

These four tenets form a framework from which you can lead your organization. Next, we turned to the issues of delegation, evaluation, and discipline, discussing each in some detail.

In delegation we listed the following tasks for you:

1. Know your staff
2. Challenge your staff supportively
3. Be available
4. Delegate authority and responsibility
5. Encourage innovation and problem solving

In evaluation, you had the following responsibilities:

1. Evaluate regularly, both in person and in writing
2. Develop a set process and form for evaluation
3. There should be no surprises in the evaluation process
4. Evaluate for the entire period, not just the past two weeks
5. Both the employee and the supervisor should be evaluated

Finally in discipline, the unhappiest part of management, I suggested the following actions:

1. Have a formal discipline process described in your personnel policies
2. Train all of your supervisors annually in how to administer this process
3. If you aren't going to enforce it for everyone, don't have it in your policy
4. Have a feedback loop for your governing volunteers

Good stewards use their resources well, including staff resources. They get the most out of every dollar, every volunteer, every employee. Even if you only have a few staff now, you may well have more next month or next year. Practicing this model of supervision is not just good management and good stewardship, it is the right thing to do. It treats people with respect, while at the same time getting the most out of them to benefit the organization and the people you serve.

Now that you know my theories of overall management and of supervision in particular, it is time to get more technical and to cover other parts of the organization. In the next chapter we'll review finance and its crucial role in making your organization mission-capable.

Chapter Five Checklist

✓ Staff evaluation review

✓ Staff signatures on policies

✓ Delegation training for supervisors

✓ Review of personnel policies

✓ Board reporting on grievances

QUESTIONS FOR DISCUSSION: CHAPTER FIVE

1. Do we really treat our staff members in the way that we would like to be treated? Do we know their opinion on this issue?

2. Do we delegate enough? What are some barriers to more delegation?

3. How do we demonstrate our commitment to innovation?

4. Should we try a two-way evaluation? What problems might this lead to?

5. Can we get our supervisors better trained in our discipline process? Have we avoided disciplining people in the past? Why? What happened?

6

Financial Stewardship

The earth is the Lord's and all it contains, The world, and those who dwell on it. Psalms 24:1–2

PRELUDE

In this chapter you will learn about:

➤ The information you need (and the information you don't need)
➤ Using your volunteers in the financial arena
➤ Budgeting and reporting
➤ Financial controls
➤ A list of key terms and their meaning

We have already discussed two key rules of not-for-profits, whether secular or faith-based. The first rule is: Mission, mission, mission! This means that everything in the organization, its plans, its people, its property, and its priorities must be focused on ways to do more mission more effectively. The second rule, which is the focus of this chapter, is: No money, no mission.

In the following pages we'll look at why it is so important to balance mission with money and give you some tools to make sure that you spend enough time but not too much on this area of management. We'll examine how to use volunteers appropriately in the area of finance, making sure that your volunteers have enough information (but aren't buried in it) to make good financial decisions. Then, we'll look at the best, most efficient, and effective ways to budget and report your financial condition, both inside the organization and to outsiders. We'll also look at the need for good internal financial controls and how to get them developed this fiscal year, not at some far-off point in time. Last, I'll provide you with a list of the most important financial terms and their meaning, translated into clear English from the dreaded language of "accountese."

A SPIRITUAL LOOK AT FINANCIAL MANAGEMENT

Financial issues are an odd contradiction in many faith-based organizations. It has been my experience that in far too many organizations, one extreme or the other takes hold. The first extreme is an organization that is obsessed with its financial issues. They have incredibly detailed financial reports on which staff, committee, and board members spend many hours. Their budgeting process takes a full year to complete, and their financial controls are more rigorous than their bank's. These organizations focus on their financials to an unhealthy degree. In their zeal for control, accountability, and good stewardship, they don't realize that they have become controlled by their finances.

The other extreme is the organization that has very little control over its finances. It has a budget, but only in name. The financial reporting to the board is spotty, inconsistent, and sometimes even inaccurate. The board spends only a few minutes on finances at each meeting, and there is probably no finance committee. There are informal financial policies (or ones that are terribly outdated and usually ignored), and there may or may not be an annual audit.

Do either of these organizations sound even partially familiar? If so, your organization is at risk of not attending to its financial house in the appropriate fashion. As I said earlier, running a faith-based organization is a challenge of balance: balancing need and mission with available resources; balancing controls with initiative; and balancing the very real need for financial oversight and control with the very real fact that there are only 24 hours in a day and that your volunteers and staff have more to do than just count and control the organization's finances. Remember the first rule: "Mission, mission, mission."

In our faiths, we have a lot of guidance about finances and stewardship. In the Bible, the term *steward* originates from that for a household manager or guardian, someone who manages for the owner. Stewards owned nothing, but their reputation depended on the ability to manage wisely and with honesty. The steward served at the pleasure of the owner. *Give me an accounting of your stewardship, for you cannot be my steward any longer.* Luke 16:2–3.

It is the same for you. You are the stewards of God's gifts. You need to manage those gifts with skill and integrity.

We know that there is a tendency to focus on our faith, and our need either to minister to our congregation in places of worship or to help those in need in community service organizations sometimes makes us fall off the balance beam and push for more mission before the money is there. "If it's not in the budget, that's okay," I have heard a hundred boards say.

"This is a real need. God will provide." When I hear this, I am always reminded of my minister friend whom I introduced to you in Chapter Two. He runs a large church, and his response to this is as follows: "I, too, believe that God will provide. But after 20 years in the ministry, I've learned that God often has a different fiscal year than I do."

So how do we balance mission and money? How does your organization raise, budget, use, and account for every dime in the most mission-effective fashion without spending too much time on financial issues at the expense of all the other issues on the organization's agenda? In the following pages I'll show you how to start striking that desirable, if often elusive, balance.

A. THE INFORMATION YOU NEED (AND THE INFORMATION YOU DON'T NEED)

One of the biggest complaints I hear from senior management and governing volunteers in faith-based organizations is about their financial information. They can't understand it. It's too cumbersome. They spend too much time discussing finances at management and board meetings. There is too much information. There is not enough. It seems that everyone is dissatisfied with the way in that their financial information is received and processed.

As I said a bit earlier, most organizations err on one side or another, too much attention to finances (obsessing) or too little (ignoring). But nearly all the organizations I work with are using the wrong information in the wrong format for the task at hand. I am not accusing you, your financial staff, or your auditor of giving inaccurate information, but I suspect that you may not be using the information you do have as efficiently and effectively as you can. There are three keys, discussed below, to increasing your informational effectiveness.

1. Target Your Information to the Reader's Needs

Most organizations have their computers spit out one income and expense statement and one balance sheet each month. Everyone who gets these reports gets the same ones. And therein lies the problem: not everyone in your organization needs to see the same information! Your treasurer and finance committee, for example, need to see very detailed information. Your board may just need summary information for the organization. Staff managers may only need summary information about the entire organization but very detailed numbers for their own areas of responsibility. With today's software and its wondrous reporting capabilities, there is no excuse for only having one report format.

2. Use Your Software to Make the Information as Understandable as Possible

Once you target your different readers' needs, you have the task of making the information understandable. To do this, you again fall back on your software, remembering that some people understand words best, some numbers best, and some pictures best. In Exhibit 6–1, you see the same information presented three different ways in numbers, in words, and in graphical form. The different methods of display will appeal to different readers.

However, increasing understandability goes beyond just using pictures, numbers, or words. It also has a lot to do with making the information useful. To do this you need to remember my main philosophy of financial reporting: *Numbers by themselves are interesting, but numbers in context*

Exhibit 6-1   Second Quarter Financial Report

Income	April	May	June
Weekly Offerings	24,579	26,530	28,140
Pledges	5,000	4,500	5,000
Other gifts	500	0	250
Interest	110	113	117
Day care fees	10,400	9,880	10,920
Total income	40,589	41,023	44,427
Expenses			
Salaries	28,750	28,750	29,613
Fringes	3,450	3,450	3,554
Accounting	0	1,500	0
Depreciation	740	740	740
Insurance	2,450	0	0
Legal	0	0	275
Maintenance	760	0	350
Supplies	650	375	510
Telephone	520	346	671
Transportation	2,510	2,602	2,478
Utilities	540	510	490
Total expenses	40,370	38,273	38,680
Net income (loss)	219	2,750	5,747
Net for quarter			8,716

Exhibit 6-1 (continued) The financial results for the second quarter were excellent. Income exceeded expenses each month, owing to continued strong pledging and a full day care center. Expenses were under budget in each category except maintenance, where a broken water pipe and unanticipated repairs to an air conditioning unit occurred, and supplies.

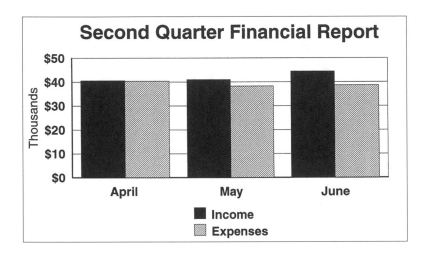

are useful. What do I mean by context? Putting your reports in a format so that the reader can clearly see where your organization is in relation to a benchmark, a budget, or past activity. Let's look at an example. The abbreviated income and expense sheet below in Exhibit 6–2 is fairly typical of many faith-based organizations that I see. It reports income, expenses, net revenue over expense, and the percentage of the year's budget that has been spent.

This is interesting but basically useless information. You don't know if the organization is ahead of or behind its budget, so you have no context in which to frame the information. And the result is that, in an effort to be a good steward, you focus on something, anything, but probably not the important thing. If I am a board or staff member, I read the report and say, "Hmmm. I wonder why we spent so much on transportation? Sounds like a lot of money. I better ask at the next meeting." The transportation line *is* a lot of money, but if it is within budget, there should not be a lot of time, if any, spent on it in a board or staff meeting. But what about the other items? Are they ahead of, behind, or right on the budget? Let's look at a format that tells us.

Exhibit 6-2   Income and Expenses Report

Income	April	YTD	% of Annual Budget	Annual Budget
Weekly Offerings	24,579	101,241	33.2%	305,000
Pledges	5,000	18,500	30.8%	60,000
Other gifts	500	1,950	39.0%	5,000
Interest	110	424	35.3%	1,200
Day care fees	10,400	39,670	33.1%	120,000
Total income	40,589	161,785	32.9%	491,200
Expenses				
Salaries	28,750	115,000	32.9%	350,000
Fringes	3,450	13,800	32.9%	42,000
Accounting	0	250	20.8%	1,200
Depreciation	740	2,960	33.3%	8,880
Insurance	2,450	4,140	63.2%	6,550
Legal	0	150	25.0%	600
Maintenance	760	1,100	45.8%	2,400
Supplies	650	1,646	34.3%	4,800
Telephone	520	2,140	32.4%	6,600
Transportation	2,510	10,240	31.0%	33,000
Utilities	540	2,289	31.8%	7,200
Total expenses	40,370	153,565	33.2%	463,230
Net income (loss)	219	8,220	29.4%	27,970

In Exhibit 6-3, which we will use as the basis of our internal reporting a bit later in the chapter, you see that the same numbers have been put into context. A reader can now evaluate each line item by comparing it with its budgeted amount and even know how much over or under budget the item is in dollars and in percent. Additionally, since some months are atypical, the reader can look at the same display for the year to date, getting a much broader picture of whether the organization is on track.

Now look at *transportation* as a line item. We see that it is not only under budget for the month, but for the year as well. *Supplies* look like a problem this last month, but overall, they are in good shape.

Exhibit 6-3 Income and Expenses (In Context)

	April	Budget for April	Variance	Percent Variance	YTD Actual	YTD Budget	YTD Variance	YTD Percent Variance
Income								
Weekly offerings	24,579	24,000	579	2.4%	101,241	96,000	5,241	5.5%
Pledges	5,000	4,500	500	11.1%	18,500	18,000	500	2.8%
Other gifts	500	450	50	11.1%	1,950	1,800	150	8.3%
Interest	110	100	10	10.0%	424	400	24	6.0%
Day care fees	10,400	10,000	400	4.0%	39,670	40,000	(330)	-0.8%
Total income	40,589	39,050	1,539	3.9%	161,785	156,200	5,585	3.6%
Expenses								
Salaries	28,750	29,000	(250)	-0.9%	115,000	116,000	(1,000)	-0.9%
Fringes	3,450	3,480	(30)	-0.9%	13,800	13,920	(120)	-0.9%
Accounting	0	100	(100)	-100.0%	250	400	(150)	-37.5%
Depreciation	740	740	0	0.0%	2,960	2,960	0	0.0%
Insurance	2,450	2,500	(50)	-2.0%	4,140	4,400	(260)	-5.9%
Legal	0	50	(50)	-100.0%	0	200	(200)	-100.0%
Maintenance	760	200	560	280.0%	1,100	800	300	37.5%
Supplies	650	500	150	30.0%	1,646	2,000	(354)	-17.7%
Telephone	520	550	(30)	-5.5%	2,140	2,200	(60)	-2.7%
Transportation	2,510	2,750	(240)	-8.7%	10,240	11,000	(760)	-6.9%
Utilities	540	600	(60)	-10.0%	2,289	2,400	(111)	-4.6%
Total expenses	40,370	40,470	(100)	-0.2%	153,565	156,280	(2,715)	-1.7%
Net income (loss)	219							

Using this template, readers can simply run their eyes down the column labeled *Variance* for the month and the year to date and immediately focus on where the problems are. I have many clients who use this template and have an agreement that, if a budget item is off by less than 5% in a month and 3% for the year, *it cannot be discussed at the board meeting*. These organizations think of their budget as a contract between staff and board and have developed information that allows them good oversight without obsessing on unimportant issues.

3. Train, Train, Train Your Readers

Can you imagine letting someone just get into a car and drive off without any training (driver's ed)? Or letting a neophyte fly a plane without getting a pilot's license? Or practicing medicine, law, or accounting without the appropriate education? How good would the outcome be without that training or education? Less than stellar, to be sure. So why should we just throw financial statements in front of our staff and volunteers and expect them to "get it" immediately? The answer, of course, is that we shouldn't. Most of your governing volunteers may well work in jobs where they are not expected to see, much less understand, their employer's financials. The same is true for your staff.

☞ **HANDS-ON:** Don't let financial oversight be something that people learn on the job. Invest some time and money and train them in how to read financials, in general at first, and then in how to read and understand your organization's financials in particular. Have someone from the outside, perhaps an instructor from your community college or your auditor, if he or she is a good teacher, present a series of sessions on developing and monitoring budgets, reading the income and expense statement, reading a balance sheet, using financial ratios, and so on. Then have your people apply all of this general knowledge to your organization's reports. Don't do it the other way around—people will focus too much on your organization's numbers and not enough on the overall knowledge that they need.

All strong organizations are constantly investing in their human capital by training, retraining, practicing, and educating. If you do not already have a serious commitment to lifelong organizational learning, this is a great area in which to start. You will see the return on your investment almost immediately.

Beyond these three fundamental ideas for getting more efficiency out of your reporting, let's look at the information that you should be seeing at the staff and/or board level. At some point, in some form, at some level of detail, you should see the following:

• **Cash Flow Projection**

While all of the other information listed below is important, you need to think of cash as your organization's blood; without it you die, and quickly. And, even with the critical importance of cash, most organizations don't have a report that tells their staff or volunteers what their cash status will be in a few weeks or months. Does your organization have a cash flow projection? If not, you need one, and soon. You already have the information and experience to be able to develop one. I'll show you a sample of a cash flow projection later in the chapter, which looks ahead six months, my recommended minimum.

• **Income and Expense**

This report is basically a diary of what happened in your organization during the last reporting period, usually one month. You should see one of these monthly for the organization as a whole and for any programs that you are particularly interested in or responsible for.

• **Balance Sheet**

A balance sheet is another report you should get monthly, and it is closely linked to your income and expense statement. Your balance sheet is a financial snapshot of your organization, and it shows your assets, liabilities, and net worth. Most boards and staff use a balance sheet as the basis for management ratios, preferring the more understandable ratios to the somewhat esoteric balance sheet.

• **Payables**

These are the things your organization owes others. As you look at the balance sheet, the question is: Are our payables growing while revenue is level? (This could mean that you are running out of cash.) Are your payables shrinking rapidly? (This could indicate that your bills are being paid too promptly, which could cause a cash shortage.)

• **Receivables**

Receivables are the things people owe your organization. You will also find these on the balance sheet, and questions similar to those for payables should be answered. Are receivables growing faster than income? If so, it may indicate that no one is paying attention to collections or that the quality of what you are doing is slipping. Are receivables dropping rapidly? That could mean that you won't have much actual cash income in future months.

• **Nonfinancial Indicators**

In addition to the indicators of financial well-being that I have listed above, there are always some nonfinancial indicators that you should look at regularly, which can immediately have impact on your finances. For example, occupancy, new members, staff turnover, patient days, attendance at worship services or in Sunday school, and number of repeat customers are numbers that, while not being counted in currency, do have an impact on your finances. Which indicators are best for you will depend on your organization. But find them, and then set a benchmark against which to monitor them.

Remember to show each and every one of these reports *in context*. Without context, the information loses value, and reading it becomes a fruitless expenditure of time. We'll talk more about this idea in the section entitled Internal Reporting later in this chapter. But no matter how you report, remember to see the crucial information, cast off the unimportant data, and focus on setting goals and budgets and then monitoring how your organization is performing.

B. USING YOUR VOLUNTEERS IN THE FINANCIAL ARENA

Much of the theory of checks and balances in a not-for-profit comes to rest in the financial arena. You need to have volunteer oversight of the budgeting, income, expenditures, and financial controls in your organization. This system of checks and balances is there for the protection of the organization, the community, the board, *and* the staff. If done appropriately, it works. But too often, as I outlined in the introduction, it doesn't. Organizations either get obsessed with their finances or they don't spend enough time on them.

Why do these extremes occur? In my experience, for a variety of reasons, but the most common are poor preparation and poor use of the organization's governing volunteers. I want you to get the most out of your financial volunteers, so let's review the key volunteer players and the essential parts of maximizing their usefulness.

1. The Finance Committee

While all of your board needs to see financials, and while they need to review and approve budgets and financial reports, you need to have a group of volunteers whose focus is on your finances. This is usually called the finance committee, and I recommend that this group be responsible for the month-to-month detail work on budgets, cash flow, long-term capital planning, and any needed debt. For most organizations, whether places of worship or community service–oriented, the finance committee will meet monthly, even if the board meets only quarterly. If your organization has particular financial problems, the meetings will be more frequent.

The key task for the finance committee is to give the board members confidence that good, prudent financial oversight and planning are going on. Boards, as I tried to emphasize in Chapter Four, have a lot more on their plate than just money. At the same time, financial responsibilities are among the most pressing and visible for a board. Board members want to feel secure that there is good oversight, but they also know that all the board members cannot spend all of their time on just numbers. Thus, the finance committee.

Finance committee members need to regularly go into greater detail than the board does. That's the reason why later in this chapter I'll show you some different reporting templates for different people in your organization. For now, though, let's review what the finance committee should be responsible for:

At monthly meetings
- Review current financial statements (versus budgets) and cash flow projections
- Review current bank balances and investments
- Develop a report for the next board meeting

Annually
- Develop an organizational budget (and recommend it to the board)
- Develop updated Five-year projected capital spending plan
- Review organizational debt structure and recommend any needed changes to board
- Meet with auditor to review audit findings and management letter

Every 24 months
- Review and amend financial policies as necessary and recommend to the board
- Review and amend bidding and conflict-of-interest policies as necessary
- Recommend to the board other policies that may be needed

I strongly suggest that your finance committee consist of members of your board. But, as with other committees, consider having nonboard members on the committee with particular expertise that the committee needs, such as banking, accounting, or finance. The chair of the committee should be the treasurer, who is the subject of our next discussion.

2. The Treasurer
Every faith-based organization needs at least one governing volunteer who truly, deeply, and fluently *understands* how the finances of the orga-

nization work. This is no mean feat and in many organizations, particularly those with government funding, the reporting systems are so unlike those of the for-profit sector that it may take many months or even years for this understanding to be achieved. But you need such a person, because the board, the staff, and the finance committee need to know that such a volunteer is in place to provide an expert check and balance. In most organizations this person is the treasurer. I cannot overemphasize the importance of a treasurer who is truly fluent in the finances and not merely a banker or a certified public accountant (CPA) Just having financial training is not adequate for this task. The person must invest the time and effort to really grasp the financial issues, "to be able to visualize the cash flow," as one treasurer whom I know describes it.

The treasurer should be regularly in touch with the head financial staff person in your organization, and should have the following responsibilities:

- Sign checks requiring two signatures
- Review the financial statements, balance sheet, and cash flow prior to finance committee meetings
- Review the checking reconciliation statement monthly
- Plan the agendas for finance committee meetings
- Lead the finance committee meetings
- Be the volunteer liaison on financial issues with outside organizations such as banks, funders, auditors, and United Way

These are not small tasks, and the learning curve may be both steep and long for many volunteers. As a result, someone who is good as treasurer often gets corralled into becoming treasurer for life, which isn't fair to the volunteer or beneficial to the organization in the long run. The organization becomes too dependent on one volunteer, and since no one else has the same knowledge, it's easiest just to stick with the current occupant of the office. But what if the treasurer becomes ill, dies, or moves away for family or work reasons? Then what?

☞ **HANDS-ON:** Grow a replacement, starting right away. Many boards have a hierarchy of succession; the vice president knows that he or she will succeed to the presidency in one or two years and thus can focus on the skills needed to do that job. Do the same thing for your treasurer. Find a volunteer who is willing to be treasurer, but in a year or two. Make that person vice-chairman of the finance committee for that period, giving him or her time to learn what is needed to do the job well, and giving the current treasurer some light at the end of the tunnel. You'll find that people are more willing to serve if they know two things that this suggestion includes, that they'll have time to get up to speed and that their obligation is time-limited.

3. Outside Advisors

You may well want to have some outside advisors who assist you in your financial considerations, your planning, and your budgeting. Some will be paid, such as your auditor. Some will have a vested interest but will not be paid directly by you, such as your banker. And some will just be volunteering their time for you. That's fine, if they deliver. My experience is that, *in most cases,* you get what you pay for. I strongly urge you not to let a volunteer do your audit or your legal work. It is much, much easier to hold someone accountable if you pay them, and the work is much more likely to get done on time.

❏ **For Example:** During my service on many boards, I have seen too many organizations count on board member Joe (a lawyer) or Mary (a CPA) to draw up a certain document (a trust, a financial policy, a collection letter) and have the issue wind up in limbo, as the volunteer in question doesn't get to the job, goes on vacation, has other crises, and so on. Their fellow board members are extremely hesitant to come down on Joe or Mary, since "we're not paying for their work."

4. Train, Train, Train

Here is where you can make an impressive return on investment—training your staff and board members in how to read the financials, in where your income comes from, where it goes, and why it is so important to save, plan, budget, and consider the future, not just the present. I have already outlined a HANDS-ON in this area for you, but I want to repeat here that there is no substitute for knowledge in this area: *Wise men store up knowledge, but with the mouth of the foolish, ruin is at hand.* Proverbs 10:14. *There is no greater wealth than wisdom; no greater poverty than ignorance; no greater heritage than culture.* Islam (Shiite). Nahjul Balagha, Saying 52.

Spend the money and the time. It will be a terrific investment.

5. Get the Right Volunteers

In his wonderful book, *Leading Without Power,* Max DePree observes that not-for-profits often make a key mistake with their volunteers: "mistaking enthusiasm for competence." I love the phrase, not only because it is accurate and succinct, but because it so perfectly describes my experiences with so many not-for-profits. They will put any willing warm body in any job, and don't have the heart to tell a dedicated volunteer that they are not suited for a particular task, even when the volunteer is causing more harm than good. Don't do that in finance, please. Be selective in filling all your volunteer jobs, but most careful in this area. Get volunteers who bring some financial knowledge, and some that bring good common sense, to the table. Train them, put them on the finance committee, and try to keep them there for two or three years.

C. BUDGETING AND REPORTING

Now to budgeting and reporting. These tasks are the core of good stewardship: understanding your resources, how much you have, how much you need, and where the difference between the two will come from. Planning how you will spend those resources, assures that your mission priorities are optimally realized. And then, during the fiscal year, monitoring the achievement of your budget to ensure that you are on track, not overspending, and are accommodating to the ever-changing environment in which your organization operates.

Many people think that budgeting results in an inflexible organization: "We are stuck with our budget and can't deviate!" Nothing could be further from the truth for a well-run organization. Budgets are plans, and like all plans (strategic, marketing, building, etc.), they should focus your organization's resources and give you an operating framework. Like all plans, budgets allow the board to delegate the implementation of its policies and priorities to the staff. But as the year unfolds, changes may need to be made in the budget, to accommodate situations that could not be foreseen during what for many organizations is a long budget development process.

❏ **FOR EXAMPLE:** A small faith-based community service organization in the Southeast had a history of setting its budget and hitting both the income and expense sides of the ledger every year. The board and staff were justifiably proud of their results, and the organization had grown, pretty much according to plan during the past five years. In the fiscal year in question, the organization had budgeted $220,000 for its highest-priority service, teen pregnancy prevention counseling. They planned to pay for this service in two ways, half from service fees, half from their aggressive fund-raising program. Half-way through the year they were surprised, even astonished, to get a $120,000 bequest from a local family. This represented an amount equal to their entire annual fund raising goal, and during the first six months of the year, they had already raised $64,000, just a little ahead of their budget in that area.

The budgeting dilemma: What to do with the unexpected gift. Should they simply put it aside for future needs, spend it on more counseling immediately, forgo any fees for the rest of the year, or put it to some other use? They could have said, "We'll just live within our budget, and not be flexible with this unplanned income." But they didn't. They decided to put most of the bequest ($100,000) in a restricted fund as the beginning of an endowment, and the remaining $20,000 was put into the current year's budget to offer free counseling to clients who were in dire need.

❑ **FOR EXAMPLE:** A church in the Midwest ran a free lunch soup kitchen in its basement. During the year in question, it had budgeted $440,000 for this purpose, with 30 percent to be provided by the congregation, 30 percent by fund raising in the community, and 40 percent by a local community foundation, which had been providing a grant for the past 10 years. Three months into the fiscal year, the foundation notified the church that, because of a change in the foundation's priorities, the grant would be ended at the completion of the foundation's fiscal year, which was just three months away. This meant that the church would be $88,000 short in income during the current fiscal year—a huge amount for this organization and one that they didn't think they could make up in local donations.

Their dilemma? Should they go with their budget and continue with the program in the hope of finding a new benefactor, knowing that they would use up most of their savings, or should they cut back immediately and perhaps permanently until they can find the funds? In short, go with the budget or adapt to the new, unpredictable circumstances? As in the preceding example, they split the difference. They closed one day a week of the six that they were open, with the understanding that if the program could not make ends meet by the end of the fiscal year from increased donations or grants, they would cut back further in the following year's budget. They gave the staff and community time to adapt and adjust, using a portion of their hard-won savings directly on mission, but at the same time cut some of their costs right away.

Changing your budget in midyear is not an admission of a previous failure to budget correctly. Rather, it should be an acknowledgment that your organization does not exist in a static, predictable world. Obviously, if you are amending your budget every two weeks throughout the year, you have lost the point of the exercise: focus and discipline. But don't feel that your budget puts you in chains. It shouldn't.

1. Internal Budgeting

At their core, budgets should be thought of as contracts between your board and your staff. Once they are adopted, if the staff are hitting their budget targets or coming reasonably close, the board should not take an extended amount of time questioning or asking for excessive details on income or expenditures. As I showed you earlier and will repeat just below, if you do good reporting of the numbers in the context of the budget and if the board and staff agree that the budget is a contract, you can focus on the important, big picture things rather than hashing around in the small details—ones that you considered at length during the budgeting process.

I strongly believe in a very inclusive budget process, one where staff and board help set the budget, fully discuss its relationship to the organization's mission, and then move forward. I'm also an advocate of complete disclosure of financials during the year to let everyone monitor and be involved in the implementation of the budget. More on that in the next section. For the budgeting process, though, it means the sequence discussed below.

Staff should draft the initial budget. I urge you to consider a process where all staff have input into the budget process. If your organization is small, have an all-staff meeting to review and discuss the budget and its implications before the finance committee sees the first draft. If the staff and organization are large, give people input into the budgets for their areas of responsibility or work, and then also let them see the entire organization's budget for the year. You may have to have a number of staff meetings for this. Listen to your staff's suggestions, ideas, and reactions. If their perspective justifies a redrawing of the budget, do it! Let them be involved not only in the development of the budget but also in its implementation.

Review the draft with the finance committee. After the staff have done their best, let the volunteer specialists look at the budget. This committee meeting should have a detailed look at what the budget is, why the numbers are what they are, how it compares with the previous year's, and how it relates to your strategic plan, your mission, and your faith. However the committee amends the budget, it then goes to the next level of review.

Have the board review and adopt the budget. The treasurer should present the budget to the board as a committee recommendation, complete with rationales for income and expenditures and for how the budget relates to the mission, the strategic plan, and the sponsoring faith. The board should have studied the numbers before the meeting and should ask questions, make any changes it sees fit, and then adopt the budget by motion and vote.

Monitor the budget's implementation. Monthly, the finance committee should review the financial activity of the organization in relation to the budget and should report to the board at its regular meeting. Remember, if income and expenditures are within a reasonable distance of the budget, the volunteers should not question the little stuff. Monitoring is good oversight; hassling is not.

2. Reporting Inside the Organization
This is an area where most organizations can get *so much* more benefit than they get currently by just following a few simple rules.

Get people the information that they need, when they need it, in the form that they need it. As I pointed out above, there is no excuse for not pushing your software to the limit (or getting new software) to give targeted reports to people who need them, in the simplest, most effective manner possible. We'll look at some sample reporting templates in a page or so; but suffice it to say here that you need to have more than just one income and expense report and a balance sheet every month.

The more financial information people have about your organization, the better. There are two ways to look at financial information. The first is: "Knowledge is power; the more knowledge I keep to myself, the more powerful I am." This is the traditional view of financial reporting: keep the distribution of the information very, very limited. The second way to look at it is this: "Knowledge is power; if I let everyone have the knowledge, we all get powerful together." This is the way I want you to go. Let everyone (that's right, *every* staff member and *every* board member) have extensive financial and nonfinancial indicator reports monthly. Let them become part of the financial team. Increase their understanding of your organization's finances and they will be more invested, more a part of the team. But, *don't do this* unless you read and remember the final rule.

A little knowledge is a dangerous thing. This means train, train, train. You can't reasonably expect your staff not to lynch you if you show them a balance sheet or income and expense statement without first putting it into perspective through extensive training. Imagine them looking at the balance sheet and seeing a line for "Cash and Securities" that is $35,500. In your organization that may be a tiny amount of money, but to you and me as individuals and to your staff people it is a *lot* of cash. They will wonder why, "with all that money just lying around" you couldn't approve their additional budget request, their cost-of-living raise, and so on. Until they understand about the need for cash reserves, current ratios, and debt ratings, this will appear to be a case of Midas (you) keeping piles of gold in your office. Let them have the financial information, but only after they are trained and ready.

3. Sample Reporting Templates

Below you will find a series of sample reports that you can adapt to your particular situation. They are the embodiment of the rules of reporting that we discussed above.

Income and expense. In Exhibit 6-4 you see that the organization has had a pretty good month, and that we are using the same template that we saw earlier. Look at how easy it is to see what, if any, lines are out of budget. Just run your eye down the "variance" columns for the month and year-to-date. How much better is this than wondering about and discussing at length every single number?

Cash flow. I told you earlier that cash is blood. Here is how to find out whether or not you are going to be in good shape or not. The cash flow projection in Exhibit 6–5 is shown for six months out into the future. Remember that this is cash, so we don't show depreciation, we have debt service, and, all the numbers are shown for the month in which the money will actually be received or the bill actually paid. That is why there are exact numbers in the first month, and rounder projections in the later months. At the bottom of the projection is a summary that shows how much cash the church had on hand at the beginning of the month, what was received and disbursed, and at the very bottom the all important line "Ending Cash." If this number becomes too small, is falling rapidly month to month, or is negative, you need to figure out what you are going to do, and quickly.

Nonfinancial indicators. In addition to financial information, you may also want to have reports of some key nonfinancial indicators. For a place of worship, those might be the ones shown below in Exhibit 6-6. Note that this church has a day care facility, and the occupancy of that operation is crucial. Also note that all the indicators are shown in context, with com-

Exhibit 6-4 April Financial Report

	April	Budget for April	Variance	Percent Variance	YTD Actual	YTD Budget	YTD Variance	YTD Percent Variance
Income								
Weekly offerings	24,579	24,000	579	2.4%	101,241	96,000	5,241	5.5%
Pledges	5,000	4,500	500	11.1%	18,500	18,000	500	2.8%
Other gifts	500	450	50	11.1%	1,950	1,800	150	8.3%
Interest	110	100	10	10.0%	424	400	24	6.0%
Day care fees	10,400	10,000	400	4.0%	39,670	40,000	(330)	−0.8%
Total Income	40,589	39,050	1,539	3.9%	161,785	156,200	5,585	3.6%
Expenses								
Salaries	28,750	29,000	(250)	−0.9%	115,000	116,000	(1,000)	−0.9%
Fringes	3,450	3,480	(30)	−0.9%	13,800	13,920	(120)	−0.9%
Accounting	0	100	(100)	−100.0%	250	400	(150)	−37.5%
Depreciation	740	740	0	0.0%	2,960	2,960	0	0.0%
Insurance	2,450	2,500	(50)	−2.0%	4,140	4,400	(260)	−5.9%
Legal	0	50	(50)	−100.0%	0	200	(200)	−100.0%
Maintenance	760	200	560	280.0%	1,100	800	300	37.5%
Supplies	650	500	150	30.0%	1,646	2,000	(354)	−17.7%
Telephone	520	550	(30)	−5.5%	2,140	2,200	(60)	−2.7%
Transportation	2,510	2,750	(240)	−8.7%	10,240	11,000	(760)	−6.9%
Utilities	540	600	(60)	−10.0%	2,289	2,400	(111)	−4.6%
Total Expenses	40,370	40,470	(100)	−0.2%	153,565	156,280	(2,715)	−1.7%
Net Income (loss)	219	(1,420)	1,639	4.2%	8,220	(80)	8,300	5.3%

Exhibit 6-5   Cash Flow Projection May–October

	May	June	July	August	September	October
Receipts						
Weekly offerings	24,579	26,530	24,000	24,000	24,000	24,000
Pledges	5,000	4,500	4,500	4,500	4,500	4,500
Other gifts	500	150	450	450	450	450
Interest	110	113	119	120	122	125
Day care fees	10,400	9,880	9,500	9,500	9,500	9,500
Total Receipts	40,589	41,173	38,569	38,570	38,572	38,575
Disbursements						
Salaries	28,750	28,750	29,000	29,000	29,000	29,000
Fringes	3,450	3,450	3,480	3,480	3,480	3,480
Accounting	0	1,500	100	100	450	100
Debt service	656	656	656	656	656	656
Insurance	2,450	0	0	1,250	0	0
Legal	0	0	50	650	50	50
Maintenance	760	0	200	200	200	200
Supplies	650	375	500	595	500	500
Telephone	520	346	550	550	550	550
Transportation	2,510	2,602	2,750	2,750	2,750	2,750
Utilities	540	510	600	600	600	600
Total Disbursements	40,286	38,189	37,886	39,831	38,236	37,886
Cash Flow	303	2,984	683	(1,261)	336	689
Starting Cash	12,342	12,645	15,629	16,312	15,051	15,387
Receipts	40,589	41,173	38,569	38,570	38,572	38,575
Disbursements	40,286	38,189	37,886	39,831	38,236	37,886
Ending Cash	**12,645**	**15,629**	**16,312**	**15,051**	**15,387**	**16,076**

Exhibit 6-6   Nonfinancial Indicators

	April	March	Six Month Average	Goal
New visitors	44	36	38	50
Repeat visitors	76	66	71	85
New members	12	7	11	10
Day care occupancy	94.0%	91.0%	90.0%	90.0%
% Day care members	50.0%	55.0%	48.0%	50.0%

parative figures for the previous months, a prior six-month average, and a goal provided to aid in analysis.

Now, what about reporting differently to different groups? The finance committee might well see all the numbers shown in Exhibits 6–4 and 6–5, but does the board really need to see that detail if it has an excellent finance committee? Perhaps not; in this case the sample board report shown in Exhibit 6–7 might be sufficient. Note that only the summary numbers are included, along with a pictorial representation of the ending cash status.

What about the pastor of this church? What would he or she want to see? Perhaps the report shown in Exhibit 6–8, with summary numbers and the key nonfinancial indicators. Understand that this exhibit is a sample, just an idea of what this pastor might want. In your organization, ask people what they want and give it to them as best you can.

D. FINANCIAL CONTROLS

All faith-based organizations, large or small, young or old, need financial controls. Remember how I told you in Chapter Two that your organization is held to a higher standard? It is, and as a good steward you will want to have controls in place that are designed to prevent abuses of your financial systems. I know all too many organizations, particularly places of worship, that do not "bother" with such controls, eschewing the investment of time that it takes to develop and then enforce controls. They do so at their own peril.

1. The Need for Controls

If you are on the staff or board of a community service organization, your funding probably comes at least partly from government, foundations, or the United Way. In that event you will almost certainly have the basic set of controls you need because your funders require it. If you are a small or midsized place of worship, you may not have as extensive a set of controls as you should. Remember this: Good stewards try to prevent bad things from happening. Controls help in that preventive effort. What if something untoward does happen; someone embezzles, funds are lost, and you didn't have any controls in place? How will the reputation of your organization fare? Again the Proverbs tell us: *A good name is to be more desired than great riches. Favor is better than silver and gold* (22:1). If your organization gets the reputation (name) of not taking care of its finances, the silver and gold (in the form of donations, tithes, contracts, and grants) will surely *not* follow.

Exhibit 6-7 Board of Directors Summary Report April

Income and Expenses	April	Budget for April	Variance	Percent Variance	YTD Actual	YTD Budget	YTD Variance	YTD Percent Variance
Income	40,589	39,050	1,539	3.9%	161,785	156,200	5,585	3.6%
Expenses	40,370	40,470	(100)	-0.2%	153,565	156,280	(2,715)	-1.7%
Net income	219	(1,420)	1,639	4.2%	8,220	(80)	8,300	5.3%

Cash Flow Projection	May	June	July	August	September	October
Starting cash	12,342	12,645	15,629	16,312	15,051	15,387
Receipts	40,589	41,173	38,569	38,570	38,572	38,575
Disbursements	40,286	38,189	37,886	39,831	38,236	37,886
Ending cash	12,645	15,629	16,312	15,051	15,387	16,076

Exhibit 6-8 Pastor's Report

	April	Budget for April	Variance	Percent Variance	YTD Actual	YTD Budget	YTD Variance	YTD Percent Variance
Income	40,589	39,050	1,539	3.9%	161,785	156,200	5,585	3.6%
Expenses	40,370	40,470	(100)	-0.2%	153,565	156,280	(2,715)	-1.7%
Net income	219	(1,420)	1,639	4.2%	8,220	(80)	8,300	5.3%

Cash Flow Projection	May	June	July	August	September	October
Starting cash	12,342	12,645	15,629	16,312	15,051	15,387
Receipts	40,589	41,173	38,569	38,570	38,572	38,575
Disbursements	40,286	38,189	37,886	39,831	38,236	37,886
Ending cash	12,645	15,629	16,312	15,051	15,387	16,076

	April	March	6 Month Avg	Goal
New visitors	44	36	38	50
Repeat visitors	76	66	71	85
New members	12	7	11	10
Day care occupancy	94.0%	91.0%	90.0%	90.0%
% day care members	50.0%	55.0%	48.0%	50.0%
New pledges	4	2	3	5

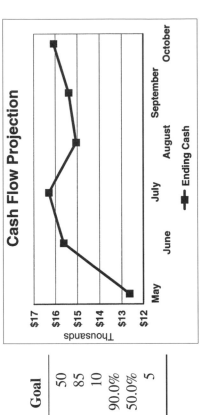

Cash Flow Projection

For many readers controls will already be in place. You will already have financial policies, prudent controls on cash, and an annual audit. Even if you are in this position, don't forget to review and update your control documents at least every 24 months. But, to make sure, let's review the controls you need and then a control development process.

☞ **HANDS-ON:** On all of your policies and controls, you should have two notations on the cover page: the date of adoption of the policy and the date that the policy is due for review. Thus, you might see this on the financial policies of your organization:

Adopted by the Board of Directors June 5, 2000.
Due for revision NO LATER THAN May 31, 2002.

A lot of organizations have the first line on their policies. Add the second one as well. This will help you get the revisions done in a reasonable amount of time.

2. The Controls You Need

The following is a minimal list of controls that you need to have in place. Your auditor and banker can help you further define these and answer the questions that I have provided for your consideration.

Audit. Absolutely get an audit every year. It is the best preventive measure and check and balance available. Make sure that you also get a management letter, in which the auditor will detail what improvements in controls are recommended.

Cash. Who may and who may not receive the cash that comes in to your organization? Who counts it, deposits it, and is responsible for its safe keeping?

Check Signature. How many signatures need to be on checks? Dual signatures on all checks or just on checks over a certain amount? Don't count on your bank to enforce this—it won't. If you want a two-signature rule, someone on the board will need to look at the actual checks each month.

Check Reconciliation. What is the procedure for reconciling the checking account? Who checks the reconciliation? Does the same person who opens the cash and makes the deposits reconcile the checking?

Reimbursement. Who on the staff and board can be reimbursed for what expenses? Do they have to provide receipts? How quickly are they reimbursed? Can regularly traveling staff get advances or use corporate credit cards?

These are just the most common control issues. Get an auditor and a banker and make up your own list of what you need to develop and what you need to update.

3. Conflict of Interest

This is an important area, particularly with an increasingly predatory press outside your door waiting for you to make a misstep. And, in this era of two-income households, you need to have conflict-of-interest policies not only for your board of directors but also for your staff. Conflict-of-interest policies should clearly delineate what is and is not acceptable within the organization in terms of board members and their families (and relatives of staff) contracting with the organization. For example, may a board member also sell the organization insurance or put a new roof on a building? May a print shop owned by the son of the assistant minister provide printing services? What limits are allowable?

I'm not going to tell you what is right and wrong here, because three things will do that for you. First, the regulations of your funders or sponsoring faith may already define this for you, and you will need to look no further. But if they don't, the second and third limits will, namely, the size of your community and community standards. Size is important, since in a small town it is very likely that your board members or staff relatives may be among very few choices you have for good services or products. Community standards will be an issue as well. In some communities, particularly those where there has been a recent scandal, conflict-of-interest policies will probably preclude even the slightest business relationship between your organization and volunteers. In others a more relaxed standard will be prevalent.

However, even though you have to decide what is right for your organization in terms of this issue, I strongly urge you to follow this advice: If any board member or staff relative is allowed by your policy to contract with the organization, *you must have a formal bidding process for the work, and you must make the board member go through the process in the same way as any outside bidder.* The worst thing that can happen to you is to give work to an "insider" and have the outsider who did not get the job claim loudly (and in the newspaper) that the bid was rigged. Have a bid process and make everyone play fair. (As an aside, I think that a bid process is smart for most contacts over a certain size, as well as for your big contracts such as banking, insurance, and the like every few years.) And, you do have the IRS to contend with. Insider conflicts can lead to intermediate sanctions, or worse, revocation of your tax-exempt status.

Conflict of interest is one of those allegedly little things that can sneak up on you and bite hard if you don't pay attention. Get a policy and enforce it.

4. A Control Development Process

Developing and updating your controls is not all that difficult. It does take time and a belief that the resulting work will improve your effectiveness and reduce the likelihood of some financial misstep. Here is how to get it done.

Don't reinvent the wheel. You have many peer organizations. What do they do in this area? Ask them, your state or national association, or your sponsoring faith for examples of good policies. Don't just copy what others are doing— make it work for your organization in your community.

Use your advisers. I've already suggested using your auditor and banker. Other advisors might include a local consultant to not-for-profits, a technical assistance person from your trade association or sponsoring faith, or even someone from your local chamber of commerce.

Float all your drafts. What this means is to let all the staff and the board see the drafts of your policies *before* they are fully discussed in a formal meeting. You will get more ownership and some great ideas from people early in the process. I also find it helpful to send drafts to advisers and any funders as well, for early review.

Revise and adopt. Once you have all your input, have the finance committee recommend the policy to the board, which should review it and adopt it with any changes board members consider necessary.

Train, train, train. Now that you have done all this work, don't forget the last step—training people in the policy and what it means. Sit down with staff, go through the words, but also discuss what the words mean to everyone. What does the reimbursement policy mean about traveling? What does the conflict-of-interest policy mean about board members contracting with the organization? Be specific, and take any and all questions.

One last time—controls are a crucial part of good stewardship. Don't scrimp in this area.

E. LIST OF KEY TERMS AND THEIR MEANING

I have been to many, many board meetings at which it was obvious that the members did not have a basic understanding of accounting and used financial terms loosely, even inaccurately. I have been told many times by board members that their input into financial issues was restrained by the fact that they didn't understand the language of financial reporting. Earlier, I noted that you need to train your volunteers in how your financials are developed, how to read them, and what they mean. Later I noted that you need to develop reporting systems that get the correct information to the right people in language and formats that are both appropriate to their level of review and understandable.

Critical to both those important tasks is defining the terms that you use. I strongly recommend that you provide your board with a list of financial terms and their meaning *in the context of your organization.* For example, the word *income* can very well mean two things. It can mean the money your organization takes in from contracts, donations, and fees. It can also mean specifically to the IRS, the profits of your organization, as defined in the Unrelated Business Income Tax regulation. All this can be very confusing to a new or even an experienced governing volunteer, so develop a list like the one below, provide it to your board during their training, and then suggest that they add it to the board manual that we discussed in Chapter Four. (*Note:* Where one defined term is used in the description of another term below, it is shown in italics.)

1. Accrual Accounting

The most common method of accounting in not-for-profits and is often required by outside funders. Accrual recognizes income when earned and expenses when obligated, even though the organization may not receive the cash or pay the bill until a later accounting period. If your financial reports include the term *depreciation,* you are almost certainly on an accrual accounting system. Even though many staff and board members would like to rename this "cruel" accounting because of its complexity, it is really the best representation of your organization's financial history.

2. Assets

These are things you possess, own, or are owed. Your organization's assets are shown on your *balance sheet.* Examples of assets would be buildings, vehicles, cash and securities, and accounts *receivable* (the money you are owed for prior work). Assets such as buildings, equipment, and vehicles are usually shown with their accumulated *depreciation* subtracted, giving a net value. Assets come in "current" and "fixed" varieties. A *current asset* is one that can be quickly and easily turned into cash within the coming twelve months. Thus cash, securities that can be sold quickly, and collectible *receivables* would be "current," while buildings, multiyear certificates of deposit, and large equipment would be considered "fixed". Most not-for-profits, secular and faith-based, have the vast majority of their assets in the fixed category, usually buildings. This is fine, but not very liquid if you have a short-term cash need.

3. Balance Sheet

A completely different report from your income and expense statement, the *balance sheet* is a financial snapshot of your organization as it was at the end of the previous reporting period (midnight on the last day of the previous month or year). It lists your *assets,* your *liabilities,* and your organization's net worth (sometimes called a *fund balance).* Balance sheets do give you a summary of your organization's financial condition, but they do not tell you whether you are ahead of or behind your budget. To make the reading and understanding of balance sheets easier, I recommend the use of *financial ratios,* discussed below.

4. Cash Accounting

Cash accounting records income as it is received and expenses as they are paid. It is much more like your personal checkbook. Usually only small not-for-profits that don't get any outside governmental or foundation funds use cash accounting. The benefit of cash accounting is that it is simple and is a method of reporting that a lay person can understand. The downside is that it shows income (and expenses) often bunched up, making monthly reporting and its attendant review by your volunteer board very difficult. It is hard to get a good handle on your organization's performance with cash accounting. If you are unsure of which kind of accounting your organization uses, talk to your accountant.

5. Cash Flow

Cash flow is just what it says, the flows of cash both in and out of your organization. You have already heard me characterize cash as your organization's blood, something without which the organization dies, and quickly. Thus it is imperative that the staff and governing volunteers monitor cash flow, making sure that receivables don't get too old, that payables get paid on time, and that cash projections are made to allow for any short- or long-term borrowing that may be needed.

6. Depreciation

This is a method of spreading out the expense of high-cost items over a long period of time. For example, your organization buys a van to transport people for $18,000. Since you will be using the van for a long time (three years is generally standard), you show an expense of $500 each month ($18,000 divided by 36) for three years. At the same time, you are showing this slow and steady expense on your income and expense statement, you would show the vehicle as an asset on your balance sheet in the amount of $18,000, with a figure on the next line labeled "Less accumulated depreciation," which would grow every month by your $500 expense.

While it may sound confusing, depreciation is a more accurate and realistic way of showing expenses. Just remember that it is a noncash expense—all the cash went out when you bought the van. The risk with depreciation is that people see it as a way to book an expense without expending the cash. Prudent financial stewards set aside the amount of monthly depreciation in their savings, so that when the item in question, in this example the van, wears out, they have the cash to replace it without borrowing. This is called funding your depreciation.

7. Development

For not-for-profits this means fund raising and doesn't necessarily have a thing to do with real estate! If you see this line item on your income or expense statement, it means that your organization has an active program of soliciting donations, gifts, bequests, or tithes.

8. Financial Ratios

Ratios are a real Godsend for a volunteer or staff person who wants to simplify financial monitoring tasks and still have a good handle on what is happening. Ratios simplify financial oversight by doing the complex arithmetic for you and allowing your time to be spent reviewing information that is easier to understand.

❑ **FOR EXAMPLE:** One of the most common ratios is called the *current ratio,* and it is an indicator of whether or not your organization has sufficient cash and securities to meet its current obligations (usually over the next 30 days). Obviously, knowing whether your organization has adequate cash is important, but how do you figure this out from your income and expense statement or your balance sheet? You can't, at least not without a lot of calculation. You can, however, find out quickly from a cash flow projection, which is why I am so strong an advocate of those projections, as you read earlier. But even then, you have to do some looking. Thus the current ratio, which is calculated by going to your balance sheet and dividing *current assets* by *current liabilities.* Since you want more assets than liabilities (so that you can pay off the liabilities), you want the ratio to be more than 1.0. But it also can be too high, indicating that you are hoarding cash and not reinvesting it in mission. Additionally, you can track your current ratio over time, noting, for example, that this month it is 1.65, and that is the highest for the past 10 months.

There are hundreds of ratios, and the ones that are appropriate for you and the benchmarks (minimums and maximums) that you should use are things that I cannot tell you; they are unique to your organization. Get help from your accountant, banker, and peer organizations (faith-based organizations that do the same thing you do), and set your own.

9. Fiscal Year

Here is another concept developed expressly to confuse volunteers and staff who do not come from a financial background. Your organization's *fiscal year* is the twelve-month period defined by its budget. For faith-based organizations that get a great deal of their funding from a government source, the fiscal year and the calendar year may well not be the same. For reasons known only to God, the federal fiscal year starts on October 1, and most states' fiscal years start on July 1. If you hear the term *calendar fiscal,* that means your fiscal year is the same as the calendar, from January 1 to December 31.

10. Fund Balance

This item is the "bottom line" for the organization. It is calculated by taking your organization's total assets and subtracting total liabilities. The result is what for-profit entities call your organizational equity or net worth.

11. Income and Expense Report

This report is a diary of what happened during the reporting period (usually one month). It should detail all the income that you have and all the expenses, and show a bottom line that is usually referred to as *net revenues over expenses.* As I told you earlier, this report, like all others, needs to be put into the context of your budget or benchmarks.

12. Liabilities

These are the flip side of *assets:* things you owe people, debts you have incurred, or other obligations you have. They are also found on your *balance sheet* and, like assets, come in two varieties, current and long-term. Examples of liabilities would be accounts payable, contract advances, debt, and fringe benefits withheld for later payment.

13. Payables

A subcomponent of *liabilities, payables* are the funds you owe for products or services that have been provided to your organization. For example, your food kitchen may order a month's of supply canned goods at a time, and then your organization may take a month to pay the bill. Until the bill is paid, the amount is shown as a payable. As you observe this amount over time, watch for any rapid growth. It may be a sign of financial problems—not enough cash to pay your bills on time.

14. Profit

First, I know that your faith-based organization is a not-for-profit organization. But making a profit is just fine, as long as you plow that profit back into your mission. On your income and expense statement, you will hardly ever see the word *profit* because everyone seems to be ashamed of the word. You will see terms such as *net revenues over expenses* and even the pejorative *excess revenues* (if any of your funds are truly excess, please send them directly to me) instead of the word *profit*. But they all mean the same thing; that your organization brought in more money last month or year than it spent. This is nearly always a good thing and certainly not something to be ashamed of.

15. Receivables

Receivables are monies that people owe your organization. They may be bills you have sent out and not yet collected, they may be loans your organization has made to other organizations or individuals, and in some limited cases, they may be pledges of funds that donors have made to you. If your *balance sheet* shows a line for receivables, you know that you are on an *accrual* accounting basis. Having people owe you money is just fine and for many faith-based organizations, a fact of life. However, collecting that money is even better. Make sure that your receivables line does not grow faster than your organizational income in percentage.

16. Restricted Funds

A *restricted fund* is just what its name implies, a sum of money that can be used only for certain, or restricted, purposes. The restrictions on the funds may have been placed there by a donor who, for example, might want her donation only used for a certain program or ministry. Or they may have been imposed by the board of directors to reserve funds for future use or to protect them from certain government or foundation funders, who still feel that any money a not-for-profit has should be completely used up before any additional funds are provided to the organization. In any event, if your organization has restricted funds, you will see the amount reported on your *balance sheet* under *Assets*. If you have a restricted fund, ask about its genesis and its covenants.

POSTLUDE

Faith and finance do mix. Money and mission are closely related in your organization. As you learned in this chapter, the challenge is balancing the two to the best effect. We first went over the need for good stewardship. Then we went over the information you really need to see, and ways to make it more efficient and effective. Remember that this information included:

Cash flow projection

Income and expense

Balance sheet

Payables

Receivables

Nonfinancial indicators

Then we went over the ways to use your volunteers in the financial arena, including some job descriptions for your finance committee, treasurer, assistant treasurer, and outside advisors. We turned next to budgeting, looking at the process and how you can make it more inclusive and more effective. Remember that a budget should be a contract between staff and board. If the staff is on budget, the board should leave them alone!

Next we covered the all important area of financial controls, why you need them, which ones you need, the all-important conflict-of-interest policy, and how to develop the controls. We ended the chapter with some definitions of regularly used financial terminology to help you find your way through the confusing semantics that seem to come with your monthly reports.

I cannot overemphasize the importance of good financial stewardship in a faith-based organization. But at the same time, I can't remind you too many times that you also have other responsibilities, whether you are staff or board. Your work goes beyond just numbers—it goes to mission and keeping the faith. To do that, as a staff or board leader, you need to have critical leadership skills. That's the subject of our next chapter.

Chapter Six Checklist

✓ Reporting template that includes budget

✓ Financial benchmarks

✓ Control review

✓ Nonfinancial performance indicators

✓ Assistant treasurer

✓ Board and staff financial training

QUESTIONS FOR DISCUSSION: CHAPTER SIX

1. Can we get more out of our financial reports? Do we need a software upgrade to do it?

2. Can we integrate the reporting template into our reporting system? What percentages should we employ to reduce extensive budget discussion at board meetings?

3. Should our budgeting process be rethought?

4. Are our stewardship energies being well spent? Are we focused on the mission and our faith or just on the dollars? Or, are we too focused on mission and not remembering our financial stewardship responsibilities?

5. What benchmarks should we use in the financial area? How do we get started in this important area?

6. What controls do we need? How out of date are our policies? How soon can we get them up to date?

7

Leadership in a Faith-Based Organization

When [Jesus] had washed their feet, and taken his garments, and resumed his place, he said to them, "Do you know what I have done to you? You call me Teacher and Lord; and you are right, for so I am. If I then, your Lord and Teacher, have washed your feet, you also ought to wash one another's feet. For I have given you an example, that you also should do as I have done to you. Truly, truly, I say to you, a servant is not greater than his master; nor is he who is sent greater than he who sent him. If you know these things, blessed are you if you do them." John 13.12-17

Scripture credits with performance not him who begins a task, but him who completes it. Talmud, Sota 13b

Whoever does not have a guide, Satan is his guide. Hadith

PRELUDE

In this chapter you will learn about crucial leadership skills:

➤ Motivation
➤ Innovation
➤ Communications
➤ Flexibility
➤ Lifetime learning

We've already talked about management of staff and recruitment and retention of governing volunteers. So what's the big deal about leadership? Why spend time on something that, to many readers, comes naturally?

Because the attainment and retention of leadership skills *that are put into practice* are so important, and, unfortunately, so rare. Faith-based organizations need leaders, people who will stand up, set the organizational course (sometimes after resetting the organizational compass), and persevere, as a result of their belief both in their faith and in the mission of the organization. Beyond that, these people have the capacity to bring others along with them.

General Normal Schwartzkopf, the Allied leader in the Gulf War has said that, "Leadership is getting people to *willingly* do something they would not normally do." Certainly that is true in the military; most people do not normally risk their lives. But in your organization it is true as well. You need leaders to make the hard choices, to see the big picture, to set the vision, and then to make sure everyone else agrees to or at least acquiesces in those decisions.

There are at least 100 good books on leadership available as of this writing. *On Being A Servant Leader,* by Robert Greenleaf and *Leading Without Power,* by Max DePree are two of my favorites, and I'm sure that you will have your own. As one of the essential leadership skills I will review is lifelong learning, I urge you to continue to study in this area. But in the context of faith-based management, I want to take the next few pages to show you the skills that I have found are essential to leaders, how to acquire them, and how to put them into practice. These essential skills are:

- Ability to motivate
- Ability to innovate
- Ability to communicate
- Flexibility
- Belief in the value of lifelong learning

You and your fellow leaders need to attain and then practice each of these skills. For most of us, this is just plain work. We often refer to someone as a "natural leader". That is wonderful for these people and for any organization that they work with, but the vast majority of us have to learn our leadership skills, get over a barrier or two, such as a fear of speaking in public or making people angry, and then develop the discipline of leadership. Although it may sound funny, practicing leadership skills is just as much a discipline as exercise, eating healthy food, daily prayer, or any other regular task that is not an autonomic response (breathing, for example).

Being a leader of a faith-based organization is also a chance to evidence your faith. You will see in a few pages that I emphasize leading by example, and what better example do we have than the icons of our faiths? Also, by associating yourself with the organization, you endorse your sponsoring faith in the community and are held to its standards and tenets, *even if you are of a different faith.* In a faith-based organization, your faith and your management and leadership skills form a complex partnership. One depends on and influences the other.

So let's look at each of my leadership skills in sequence and in detail.

A. MOTIVATION

Motivation was intentionally placed first in my list, since it really pre-empts all the others. Remember that I told you earlier that leaders have to make decisions and then be able to bring others along with them. He or she can do that because they motivated their followers to do so.

Our holy texts are filled with stories of people who led, who persevered, who motivated their followers to do extraordinary things, take huge risks, and accomplish great tasks. Moses, Abraham, Jesus, and Muhammad, while icons of their respective faiths, were also extraordinary leaders, who had the ability to say unpopular things, espouse heretical ideas, and make others follow them to the ends of the earth. Other, more contemporary men of faith who were also superb leaders include Brigham Young, Mohandas Gandhi, and Dr. Martin Luther King.

So how do you motivate your fellow staff and volunteers to come along with you? How do you keep their spirits up when times are tough? How do you get them to make sacrifices for your organization that they otherwise would not make? By putting into practice the following four parts of motivation.

1. Lead by Faith, Mission, and Personal Values

The most succinct way to put this is: *Walk the talk.* People have to trust their leaders, and one of the most important keys to that trust is seeing someone who not only believes in the faith and subscribes to the mission but who puts those beliefs into action. If you are asking people to contribute to a capital fund drive, let your contribution be first. If you are asking them to study your holy texts or your board handouts before the meetings make sure you do as well. If you are asking them to put in extra hours, be there with them. If you have an organizational dress code, follow it to the letter.

If you are all words and no actions, you not only won't motivate people, you will do something much worse, namely build a level of cynicism in the organization that will reduce the amount of energy, effort, and willingness to sacrifice among staff and volunteers. So, mean what you say, say what you mean, and consider every action you take through the lens of your faith, your mission, and your personal values.

❏ **For Example:** A faith-based community service organization that I worked with was run by an energetic, intelligent, and compelling leader, its executive director. On my first site visit to the organization, this minister turned manager (whom we will call Larry) drove me around the small community where the organization provided services, extolling the wonderful work his staff did, showing me how they were hands-on in the community, and waxing poetic about how they were all about faith in action. Larry talked about how much he went to bat for his staff, how he got them the things that they needed, and how his staff obviously was pleased, as evidenced by low employee turnover.

Then I talked to the staff. They also were proud of the work they were doing and believed that they were putting their faith to the test every day on the street. We talked about the best and worst things in the organization, and the positives were pretty standard: the rewards of the work, the people on the team, helping people in need. The negatives? Larry. "Larry?" I asked. "Tell me more." "Well," one staff person put it, "Larry talks a great line. He is a gifted preacher and can talk the varnish off a door. But he isn't a very compelling boss. He's a lot more interested in himself than in the agency, the people we serve, or the staff." "Why do you say that?" I asked. "Ask him about his deal with the board" was the reply.

It turned out that Larry had feathered his nest in a big way. The organization had grown rapidly because of an increase in state funding for services for which there was no competition in this small community; Larry's organization was the only choice the state had. Larry used this growth to talk his board into a big, big compensation increase (over 90 percent) for himself, including a car and housing allowance, and the hiring of his wife and brother. Plus a very sweet retirement deal. This was at the same time that he was recommending that staff pay increases be held to the statewide average, 3.5 percent. Larry argued that staff turnover was low and so the organization didn't need to raise salaries much. Of course the real reason that turnover was low was that this was an isolated rural community, where the staff didn't have many choices.

You can guess what the staff thought of Larry, who went around town telling people how much he did for the community, his staff, and the people that the organization served. They saw him as the hypocrite he was and didn't trust much that came out of his mouth. As one staff person put it, "When Larry says the sun is out, I go to the window to check."

Think about your words and actions. Your staff, your volunteers, and your community are listening and paying attention. Walk the talk.

2. Care about Your People—and Let Them Know

During World War II, my father was in an engineering company serving in the European theater of operations. About five months after D-Day, his unit was attached to Patton's Third Army, which was then sweeping across France but would later be tested as no other army had when it had to disengage from one battle and march 100 miles in the dead of winter, with no rest or hot food, to relieve the American troops trapped in Bastogne during the Battle of the Bulge. On one of the very few occasions on which Dad and I talked about his wartime experiences, I asked him how he felt to be assigned to Patton when the general had been getting so much bad press. Dad's answer was simple: "The guys loved Patton. He wanted to win the war and go home. So did we. He was doing something about it. And, he cared about us. He always told us in officers' meetings that the point of war was not to die for your country but to make the other guy die for his. We liked that." Dad never saw the movie *Patton* in which George C. Scott made just that statement in the opening scene, but I have always remembered his stories of Patton visiting troops, eating their C rations, sometimes sleeping with them on the ground. He cared for them, they knew it, and it motivated them to do amazing things.

What about you? Do your people know that you care for them, that you are trying to get them the things that they need to do their jobs? Do they know that you care about their families, their hobbies, their interests? Do they see you as someone who listens, or just as a figurehead that they view at a distance? And, as you answer these questions, ask yourself this: How do you know how they feel? Have you asked them?

Do you say "please" and "thank you" to your staff every day? Do you remember the names of children, spouses, favorite sports teams, health and family issues? Do you tell them that you appreciate them regularly? Do you pitch in on mundane tasks when there is a tight deadline? Do you ever return to the line of service to work a shift and keep current on how it's going at the point of service delivery?

Think about those questions and then perhaps, make some changes in your daily routine. I don't doubt for a minute that you care about your staff and volunteers. But don't assume that they know that unless you actively, regularly, and visibly tell them by *showing them*.

3. Focus on Your Mission—Tell Your People Over and Over

Your faith is a terrific motivator. So is your mission. Remember to use these resources to your organization's benefit as much as you can. I've already suggested that you have copies of your mission statement on the table at staff and board meetings, as well as on your walls, in your published materials, and even on your business cards. However, in motivating people, you need to take the use of your mission a step further to really get all the benefit out of it that you can.

❏ **FOR EXAMPLE:** I know of many places of worship which list the names of new members as they join the congregation and which keep track of total new members each month or each year. By celebrating the success of bringing people to the faith and by putting a name (and sometimes a face) on the success, the organization focuses on what the mission is all about.

☞ **HANDS-ON:** Celebrate. It's just that simple. We seem to spend time in meetings talking about what we will be doing (planning) or about what we can't do (complaining). Sometimes we even look back on our actions (reviewing) and then say, in essence: That's fine, but what have you done for me lately? This is a mistake. Take the time to celebrate the outcomes of your mission. Your organization is full of hundreds of wonderful people stories, stories about people who have been positively affected by your organization, by your mission. Take five minutes in each staff meeting to tell one of those stories (without violating confidentiality, of course), and make sure that you draw a short and straight line between the good outcome and the fact that to your mission, your faith, and your organization were what caused this good thing to happen. Over time, let all your staff contribute stories to this celebration. Make celebrating part of managing. It will help motivate people and keep them focused on the point—the mission.

Beyond celebrating, use the mission as a rationale for all of your tasks and keep bringing it up with staff: We're doing this because it makes us more mission-capable, we're doing that because it gets more mission out the door. The mission should always be a partner in decisions and in discussions. It will help focus you, motivate you, and keep you on track. Never forget and never let your staff forget that your mission does result in helping real people, your friends and neighbors, every day. Don't lose sight of that.

4. Get Involvement at Every Level

One of the most important parts of leadership may be contrary to your preconceived notion of a decisive, action-oriented leader. It is maximizing the involvement of the people you are leading in the deliberations and decisions of the organization. You already know that I am a huge proponent of constantly training your staff and volunteers. Now put that training into action by letting your staff and volunteers make many of the decisions on their own, particularly by letting them help you make the big ones. People are more motivated when they have a stake in an issue, when they are included in the process, when they have what we commonly call *ownership*. Leadership is not about saying "Do this, do that, now do that over." Rather it requires the leader set the direction for the organization, tell people the desired outcome and the reason why (the mission), and then letting them make many of the hundreds of small decisions that will get the organization to the larger goal. We've already talked about delegation. Involvement includes delegation, but goes beyond it to make people feel that they are part of the solution.

☞ **HANDS-ON:** For all of your staff committees, even the *ad hoc* ones, appoint representatives from throughout the organization, not just the senior management team. I see so many places of worship and community service organizations that have five to seven senior managers who make up the management council, the finance committee, the marketing committee, the quality assurance team, the annual meeting team, and so on. Spread out a bit, and let mid-managers and line staff in on the issues. Not only will this broaden the perspective of the group, but it is a terrific staff development tool, growing your next generation of leaders from within.

If you are the senior staff member for the organization or even for a large department within your organization, you will still need to make some of the key decisions by yourself. But I recommend doing that only after you get input from a larger group. Don't, however, make the mistake that so many faith-based organizations make, namely, going for consensus on everything. In *Leading Without Power,* Max DePree argues eloquently against this habit of not-for-profits, noting that waiting for a consensus to develop can waste crucial time and energy. DePree suggests that we should work for *agreement, not consensus.* I agree.

☞ **HANDS-ON:** Here's how you implement this excellent idea. Let's say you have an issue that you need to make a decision about. Don't just decide on your own. Lay out the issue to the appropriate staff or volunteer group and ask them to give you their perspective on the pros and cons of the various options your organization has. Listen to the discussion carefully, and when it is over, thank people and either tell them of your decision then or let them know that you will be making the decision soon. When you announce the direction in which your organization is going, people will have had input and now they have a choice, to agree with your choice and stay, or not to agree and go. I know that this sounds cold-hearted, but it is the truth. There are some decisions that have to be made alone, by the leader. Involving people in your deliberations will make your decision easier for them to accept, as they will have had input, but waiting for a complete consensus is not only frustrating and time-consuming, but often impossible. Go for agreement.

You know you cannot pay your staff enough. Thus you have to use every tool in your toolkit to motivate them to do their job every day with skill, compassion, and enthusiasm. A tough, but essential part of leadership.

B. INNOVATION

The second leadership skill that is essential is innovation. It may sound contradictory that faith-based organizations, particularly places of worship, whose liturgy is so steeped in tradition, need to innovate constantly. But they do, and leaders like you need to light the candle of innovation to show others the way. Just as in motivation, this is a balancing act. You want to be faithful to the traditions of your organization, to the value structure and accomplishments that brought you to this place and time, but you also need to consider and often embrace ways to make your organization better. As I said in Chapter Three, don't subscribe to the self-limiting perspective of "But we've always done it that way."

❑ **FOR EXAMPLE:** A Boy Scout troop was growing rapidly. A new scoutmaster had been in place for two years, and the troop had grown from 20 to over 55 boys, with a concomitant rise in the number of adult leaders. The troop was very active, with over 15 weekend camping trips per year, plus a week at the district summer camp. A group of older boys went to the Philmont Ranch every two years, and others went on rock climbing expeditions, to the Boundary Waters, and on other special trips.

The treasurer for the troop had been in his job for nearly 15 years. He had set in place a system in which each boy would bring $1 to each weekly meeting as dues. For the first 12 or 13 years that dues system, plus some other fund raisers, was enough to buy equipment and provide for other troop expenses. But now, with such growth, the financial needs had risen. At the same time, the scouts, like all other children of the 90's, had many activities such as sports, music, and school activities that meant that their attendance at meetings was often sporadic, and thus they weren't there to give dues each week. Income from dues was falling dramatically, and the troop council examined the issue. Monthly dues were considered, but it was decided that all the same problems would crop up. A suggestion was made for annual dues, with a statement simply being mailed to the parents of each scout. Everyone liked this idea except *the treasurer,* who advocated solving the problem by just reminding the boys each week that they owed money. The treasurer was also sure that parents would resent getting a bill, and that some wouldn't be able to pay the $52 annual fee at once. However, the council pressed on, and went to parents of the scouts to ask their opinion. Unanimously, they *loved* the idea. They were thrilled with the troop and the good it was doing for their sons. They never quite had understood about dues, and someone (Mom, Dad, or scout) was often forgetting to bring the dues. When a scout missed a meeting, no one could remember how much the family owed. All the parents wanted to help and wanted to pay their fair share, and the annual fee was an easy and quick solution.

Note that the scout troop leadership was innovative, even in the face of opposition from a traditionalist. And note that the innovation was not a huge one, just a small improvement in the overall organization.

Leaders need to consider ideas for innovation openly, fairly, and regularly. They also need to be seen developing new and improved ways to do things themselves. Let's look at some specific things you can do in your organization to help it innovate and ways that you can be a leader in this essential area.

1. Stretch Regularly

As we get older, we lose our flexibility. This is true of us as individuals, and it is also true in organizations. New organizations have very few restraints (or obligations) and can be much more flexible than older organizations with buildings, mortgages, traditions, and so on. To retain our organizational flexibility we need to stretch, and stretch regularly. What I mean by this is to try to make small, regular changes in the way that we do things, so that we don't forget *how* to try new things. Hold meetings in different rooms or at different times occasionally. At least get people to sit in different places (our minister tries this at church all the time, with limited success). Be spontaneous—call out for pizza one lunchtime and sit around talking for a half hour. Be silly—buy a set of humorous (but appropriate) Post-it notes and use them throughout the office. Be innovative—try a method of service that another organization has found to work. Whatever small change it may be, try it to avoid the worst outcome, "doing the same old same-old." If your organization loses its capacity to change and to innovate, it will not be able to accommodate to the inevitably changing needs and wants of its many constituencies.

How can you stretch yourself, your staff, and your organization today?

2. Take Risks to Enable Innovation

Innovating means taking chances; you are trying something new and, even with your best intentions, it may not work the way you want it to. But we need to take risks to test new ways of doing things, to find out what works and what doesn't. This is called innovation or experimentation, and if you duplicate what works and don't repeat what *doesn't* work, it's even called learning!

Risk is a good thing, in moderation. For your organization, you need to think about how to stretch out in new ways, how to try new things, how to observe and learn from your peer places of worship and community service organizations. The problem is that too many of our faith-based organizations are risk-averse; that is they are afraid that if their ideas don't work they will be branded as failures. And I have to agree that our society is all too focused on placing blame, finding scapegoats, and declaring everything but total victory an utter defeat. But the risks you should be taking with your organization are not for you: they are for the people that your organization serves, for your community, for your faith. Thus you, your staff, and volunteers need to learn how to take prudent risk in pursuit of your mission.

And don't let me even hear you *thinking:* "If we try, we might fail, and then there will be a lot of trouble." If you try to innovate, you are experimenting. No one knows what will happen. You may have done the best analysis, market study, survey, or business plan on the planet, but until you put the new idea into practice and see what actually happens, you don't know. As I said earlier, this is called experimentation, and I hope that you had a chemistry or physics teacher in high school who told you that *there are no failed experiments.* In an experiment, you have a hypothesis, you test it, and it is proved to be valid or invalid. Either way, if you learn, *the experiment succeeds.*

☞ **HANDS-ON:** I have used the term *prudent* or *moderate* risk above. To moderate your risk, you need to learn business planning skills and use them to reduce—but never eliminate—your risk in developing new programs, new ideas, new ways of providing services. Business planning is designed to reduce risk to the extent humanly possible, so take this technique and use it to strengthen your organization.

Remember, innovation leads to improvement in the way we provide our services, deal with our staff and volunteers, or spread our faith. Innovation requires some degree of risk. Start thinking of innovation, along with its inherent risk as a good thing.

3. Improve One Percent Per Day

Earlier, I noted that organizations need to stretch to stay flexible. One way of stretching is to incorporate steady improvements into your thinking and that of your staff and volunteers. Slow, steady improvements also overcome the resistance to change that we so fear as managers. The Japanese have a great outlook on this. They say: Don't attempt 100 percent improvement all at once. Rather, improve 1 percent a day *every* day. This is very, very good advice. You need to be asking yourself, your staff, and your volunteers: What can we do today to make ourselves more efficient? What can we do to add value to our services? What can we do to improve our community image, to make the people who pay us happier, to provide services in a more personal, humane fashion? Look at it this way: With all the things your organization does, with all the interactions with the community and the people you serve that are occurring right now, as you read this, there have to be dozens if not hundreds of small but important ways in which you can improve what you do or how you do it. Make it your goal to end each day with the assurance that somewhere in your organization, things have gotten just a little better.

☞ **HANDS-ON:** Make steady organizational improvement part of every staff meeting. Start asking staff to bring lists of their ideas for small but important improvements. Tell them that there are no improvements that are too small to consider. To butcher the proverb, the long road to excellence starts with but a single step. Talk about the staff's ideas openly and approve those that you can. Here's the good news: Most of these ideas will be low- or no-cost items, at least at first. Make sure that you incorporate the mission into the rationale for improvement: How will this idea improve our mission-capability?

Finally, as you do make steady improvements, keep a journal of them, and every month or quarter, review with the staff all that the organization has done. You will all be surprised how far you have come, and this review keeps you from forgetting that steady small

steps can result in your making remarkable progress on your journey
to regular innovation and high quality.

4. Incorporate Risk and Innovation into Your Value Structure

If you subscribe to my belief that risk and innovation are essential partners in providing excellent service, your leadership must develop ways of
incorporating this belief into your written policies and documents. My
suggestions in this area are to formalize the idea of innovation and risk in
two places—your staff evaluations and your organizational values. Let's
deal with each separately.

Staff evaluations. I assume here that your evaluations have a formal
structure and that you evaluate people on the basis of their performance,
some internal criteria, past goals, and so on. Add to the criteria a question
along the following lines: *What new idea, policy, service, or organizational improvement has [name] been responsible for during the evaluation period?* If you weight certain criteria more than others, consider
weighting the answer to this question fairly heavily, making it a priority.
The idea here is to let all staff members see that you value innovation, and
that if they get on the innovation express, they will be rewarded. *Note:* If
you don't have a formal evaluation process, you need one, and soon!

Organizational values. Beyond your mission and the tenets of your
faith, I believe that your organization needs a statement of values, the
things that you believe in. These values can deal with how you interact
with the people you serve, with your staff people, and with the world at
large. What I am suggesting here is that one of those values should state
your organization's common belief that innovation and change *consistent
with the mission and your faith* are inherently good things. This statement
again underscores your commitment to steady improvement in the way
that you provide services.

❏ FOR EXAMPLE: A parochial high school that I visited was in the throes
of a dilemma. In their curriculum, they emphasized what educators call
"higher-order thinking", encouraging students to solve problems in new
ways, try new methods, and so on. For example, in math if students
solved the problem correctly and showed their work, they received
excellent grades. *How* they solved it was not important, only that they
arrived at the correct solution. This idea of thinking outside the norm
was pounded into the students for four years. Outside the classroom the
administration had developed very strict rules and a very set protocol

for the faculty. At a planning retreat, a student who was on the planning committee, asked the key question, "How come you always want us to be inventive, and you never, ever try anything new? If it's not in the rules and protocols, it doesn't happen." Fortunately, the faculty realized the inconsistency, and began to embrace more innovation and higher-order thinking themselves. It wasn't easy, but it was essential.

5. Keeping Close to Your Values and Your Faith

Just a quick reminder about the bottom line: your values, mission, and your faith. Most change is good, but some is not. That is why just above you see the italicized words in my suggestion about a values statement on innovation. As you evaluate your options in improving your organization, don't get so enamored of trends, technology, or keeping up with your peer organizations that you lose the core sense of what your organization stands for. This is yet another reason to have copies of your mission, values, and the tenets of your faith visible and at hand in staff and board meetings.

❑ **FOR EXAMPLE:** One of the more ubiquitous examples of technology today is the automated phone system. You know the kind; the phone is answered by a machine that says, "Hello, you have reached Evangelical Community Services. Press 1 for a staff directory, press 2 for a listing of services, press 3..." and on and on. Nearly everyone truly despises these systems, yet they are everywhere. In my training sessions on the subject of innovation, I bring this issue up, asking my audience, "Who here likes to call in to one of these systems?" No one *ever* raises a hand. Then I ask, "How many of your organizations have phone systems like this?" Nearly *every* hand goes up! I then ask, "Being frank, now, how many of you had a hand in the decision to buy the system?" Two-thirds to three-quarters of the hands reluctantly go up. And then I say *"Why* did you do this? You despise these machines, yet you made the decision to subject anyone trying to reach you, anyone in need of your services, anyone who is in crisis to this torture of technology. And you did it, if you are like most organizations, to "keep up". But in changing to keep up, you simply angered the people you serve."

All of which is to say *think before you change.* Consider before you commit money, time, and your reputation. Remember that you are, at your core, a faith-based organization. Does this change, this innovation make you more mission-capable? Does it promote your faith? Does the change give evidence to the community that you walk the talk?

There are dozens, hundreds, even thousands of small, steady innovations that you can examine, consider, and adapt to your organization that will make it even better at what it is that you do. Be open to new ideas, new ways of doing things. Be aware of changes in the community and the people whom you serve (which is a large part of the marketing skills that we will discuss in the next chapter), and make sure that you can be flexible enough to meet their needs.

C. COMMUNICATIONS

You can't get anything done inside or outside of your organization without good communications. If you can't transmit your message so that the recipient can understand it, all progress grinds to a halt. We communicate in person, in meetings, in writing, over the phone, by fax, and by e-mail. We send out press releases, newsletters, and annual reports. It sometimes seems as if we are spending 70 percent of our waking hours in meetings, and we are buried in paper—memos, minutes, policies, budgets, handouts, and reports.

And after all that, we still are not happy with our communications. Information gets lost, people are not informed of key decisions, staff and volunteers feel left out "of the loop" on what is going on. Why can't we seem to communicate our intentions, our wishes, our beliefs more clearly?

We can, if we just realize a few things, practice a few simple techniques, and not try to figure out who is wrong in the communications effort. Let's be forgiving and fix the problem, not the blame.

1. It's about Trust

Most tomes on communication are filled with techniques of how to be more successful in getting your message across or of how to write a better memo or promotional piece. To me, that is just technique. There are some fundamental points that come way, way before the examination of your ability to compose a declarative sentence.

First, *successful communication only occurs between people who trust each other.* Put another way, you may be the best writer or the most gifted orator on the planet, you may be an excellent teacher and delegator, but you will not be successful as a communicator if people don't trust what you say to be the truth as you know it. Think about it: We all know people who have lied to us in the past. When these people come up to us and tell us something, our ability to listen to what they are saying is impeded by one part of our brain screaming at us, "Are you really going to believe this? Why? This person is a proven liar! We better check and see if it is true!" And while you are listening to your brain, you aren't listening fully to the person talking to you.

So it all starts with trust, which gets us back to one of the first things we talked about in Chapter Four: You have to treat people the way you want to be treated. You want to be told the truth, so watch what you say to others. You want to be able to depend on people, so be dependable. You want to be listened to, so listen to others. We also talked about this earlier in the context of walking the talk—your faith demands that you tell the truth, every time.

Without trust, communications cannot be effective. Do your staff members trust you? How do you know?

2. It's about Successful Communication

Second, it doesn't matter what you say—what matters is what the other person hears. Now we're really into a crucial issue: The point is the communication, not who said what, or who wasn't listening. Here, you need to give up the "boss" mentality and take on that of the servant leader. Thus the question should be: How can we improve our communications? and not: Why doesn't anybody listen to me?

❑ **FOR EXAMPLE:** All of us have been part of too many frustrating discussions in our own households whose main component is something to the effect of, "I didn't say *that,* what I did say was…" No, I *clearly* remember you saying *exactly* that. Don't try to weasel out of it now." Sound familiar? I'm sure it does. Why is this kind of problem so prevalent? Because none of us really listen all that well; we stop paying attention, we're distracted, bored, tired, angry, or impatient. And when any or all of those things happen, our listening and remembering are affected.

In good communications we have to put into practice what I showed you in Chapter Five, that the people at the line of service are the most important, and that supervision is a support function. How? By realizing that the important thing in communication is whether the information transfer was successful, not whether *you* said it right, or *they* heard it wrong. When communications fail, the organization and the people you serve are injured. Your job as a supervisor is not to go around berating people for not listening, it is to figure out a way to make the communications between you and the people you supervise *successful.*

3. Listen

As leaders, we often think our job is to speak, to direct, to delegate, to tell people what we expect from them. All of that is true, but only part of our task. Communication is not a one-way street. We need to listen well, listen hard, and listen often to our staff, our peers, and our volunteers. Unfortunately, listening is not an inherited skill, but rather one that we need to work at. Too often, even though we are not talking, we are not listening. We are just waiting *our turn to talk*. Or, we are simply daydreaming, thinking about all the work that is piling up while the other person is droning on and on and on and on.

I wish that I had a magic cure that would help the droners cut to the chase and would help the rest of us stay focused on the conversation. I don't, but I know from long experience that when I really open my ears, I find out all kinds of wonderful things. Remember that your staff, peers, and volunteers have important things to tell you. They are closer to the line of service than you are, see things in a different light than you do, and have the best interest of the organization at heart. Listen to what they say, learn from it, and put the best ideas into practice.

4. Communicating Successfully in Person and in Meetings

So, if we communicate so poorly, how do we diagnose why and, more importantly, how do we fix the problem? Well, we have excellent role models out there—it's just that we ignore them.

❏ **FOR EXAMPLE:** Have you ever seen a movie about a ship at sea? The captain says, "Full speed ahead, hard to port!" or something equally nautical, and his *exact* words are repeated by his first mate to the crew members on the engines and on the wheel, and those crew members repeat the *exact* command back to the first mate, who repeats it *again* to the captain. This repetition is done all the time in the air traffic control system, where pilots *must* repeat the instructions they receive from their controller word for word. In both cases, the consequences for not having excellent communications are dire, and so excellent communications are mandatory.

In our place of work, no plane will crash nor ship sink if we mess up a bit in our communications. But that doesn't mean that there are not consequences, even of small miscommunications. If you ask a staff person to get you a budget application "by Tuesday evening" and that person hears. "by Thursday evening" it can be a problem, especially if the overall budget deadline is Wednesday. The communication wasn't really off base: you got the report, and what the staff person heard was was only three letters off (an "e", an "h", and an "r"), but the communication still failed.

So what do we do? We follow the lead of the military and air traffic control without insulting our staff.

☞ **HANDS-ON:** Start by meeting with your staff people and asking them if they are happy with internal communications. I *guarantee* that they will have concerns, complaints, and suggestions about your internal and external communications. Then suggest a change in tactics to improve communications. Tell them that all of you are going to stop placing blame in communications and that you are going to start supportively correcting each other to improve the amount of successful communications that occur. You will do this in two settings, in person and in meetings.

In person: When two staff persons are meeting, at the end of their session each should tell the other what he or she committed to and when. For example, John and Cheryl are talking on a Monday about their workload for the next two weeks. Cheryl asks John to get her his list of supply needs for the following fiscal year by Wednesday. He also offers to get Cheryl a memo to all supply vendors asking for a discount at the same time. John needs a few things from Cheryl, as well. He asks for a rough budget allowance figure for supplies by the next fiscal year and a decision on whether to hire a new staff person by Thursday. The two discuss some other matters and at the end of the meeting the conversation goes like this:

Cheryl: Okay, John, let's check ourselves. I agreed to get you the budget for supplies by Tuesday afternoon and the decision on the new hire by Thursday at closing time.

John: Sorry, Cheryl, I thought I asked for the budget amount by Tuesday *morning,* not afternoon.

Cheryl: That's fine, and you may very well have asked for that.

John: I agreed to get the list of supply needs and the memo asking for vendor discounts to you by Wednesday at closing time. Anything else?

Cheryl: Nope that's it.

See what happened? There was a small correction that avoided a big problem, and it was done supportively—not fixing the blame, just correcting the problem.

In meetings: At the end of the meeting, go around the room asking each person to list what they agreed to do and by when. Have the rest of the people in the meeting sign off on what each person says. The format is essentially the same as the conversation above, just with more people. But, if anyone makes fun of anyone else or says something like: "You always get it wrong!," this system will *not* work.

From long experience, I can tell you not only that this kind of check and balance works, but also that a number of other things happen. People start paying more attention and everyone will be *appalled,* and I do mean appalled, at how much miscommunication there is inside the organization.

You will find in your first few meetings that 30 to 50 percent of things will have to be corrected, and you will never get to zero percent. The best you can do is probably 15 to 20 percent that will need correction. Don't be frustrated by that percentage. Just be happy that you are catching it early!

☞ HANDS-ON: If you are nervous about speaking to large groups of people, take a public speaking course or join Toastmasters. Part of a faith-based leader's job is to convey the plans, vision, and mission of the organization to others, often in groups or at large meetings. You want to be comfortable and competent in such settings, so get some training. You will also find that the techniques you use in front of 100 people also have application to one or two people.

Leaders need to be able to communicate successfully. Practice your skills of speaking, listening, and writing. Communicate in the way that best suits the listener and practice the check and balance method, and you will improve your communications skills immeasurably.

D. FLEXIBILITY

Don't you wish your joints were as flexible as they were when you were a child? Me too. But age inevitably brings less flexibility in our bodies, our philosophies, and our organizations. A new start-up faith-based organization is very flexible. It isn't tied down to traditions, to buildings, to debt. As it grows and matures, it becomes more and more rigid, more and more limited in its options and therefore less and less capable of innovating and adapting to an ever-changing world, unless its leaders keep it flexible by their attitude, by stretching the organization, and by developing a method of management that enables that flexibility by allowing for change. Flexibility is an essential partner of the skill of innovation that we talked about earlier, but it has its own place in your leadership skill set.

1. Your Attitude

First things first. You attitude or, to put it another way, the way you walk the talk on this one, will speak volumes on this subject and influence your staff's behavior a great deal. Thus, a bit of self-examination is in order. When staff come to you with an idea, do you listen or dismiss it (even if only in your mind) out of hand? Are you a creature of rigid habits, always arriving at work at exactly the same time, having lunch at the same place, driving the same route to and from home? When was the last time you tried a new breakfast cereal, a new restaurant, a new magazine? When was the last time you sat in a different seat in your church or synagogue? Once you've decided on something, is that *it,* or are you open to suggestions, to midcourse corrections?

If your answers to these questions are not very compelling, your staff probably doesn't see you as very flexible, either. And it is important to your organization for you to be flexible in your thoughts, actions, and words, *within limits.*

❏ **FOR EXAMPLE:** My wife and I view ourselves as flexible *to a point* in our child rearing and in setting limits. Our kids know that they can come to us and ask for a loosening of a certain rule (bedtime, curfew, allowable movies, etc.) And, there have been many occasions when these discussions have resulted in our changing our minds, if the kids didn't whine and if they had thought out their rationales and presented them calmly. However, we have certain things that are non-negotiable, that are core values for our family, and on which we simply do not give an inch. Telling the truth, violence against each other, playing one parent off against the other are examples of these fixed values.

❏ **FOR EXAMPLE:** You have certain limits proscribed by your personal faith. These can not only guide you, but your entire organization. As always, fall back on the foundation of faith to help you set those limits.

In your organization and in your own leadership style you need to have certain limits beyond which you will not venture, certain lines you won't cross. Just don't draw the lines so close to yourself that you can't maneuver.

2. Stretching the Organization

I know what you are thinking. We're already stretched to the limit! Now he wants us to stretch more? That's not the kind of stretching I'm talking about. I mean stretching that keeps you flexible, that keeps your organization limber. Remember the percent per day improvement we discussed in the section on innovation? It has application here as well. Push your people to try new things.

☞ **HANDS-ON:** This takes steady, regular leadership. Try one or more of these ideas to foster a culture that is flexible.

- Take your staff people to lunch, and as a learning experience, have everyone order something new off of the menu. Talk about what they liked and didn't like.

- Have everyone in your management team take a different route to work one day a week, and don't fuss at them if they are late. Ask them what they saw that was new, interesting, or fun. If a new route was stressful, ask why. What could have relieved the stress? (usually the answer is "a navigator," which supports my philosophy of going through change with people, which I will discuss in a few pages).

- If you are a business suit and dress organization, try a casual day. If you are a casual organization, have a day for wearing coats and ties or business suits or dresses. Talk about what was good and bad about the change.

- Have your management team or board members sit at different places at their meetings (you, too!). Talk about what they notice about each other, about the room, and about the meeting from a different perspective.

- If your organization is a place of worship, change the order of worship, have a service outdoors, have an outside speaker, or change the order or type of music.

Try these and any other methods you can think of to keep yourself, your staff, and your governing volunteers comfortable with the new, the different, the changed. If they are not immediately uncomfortable with something new, they will be able to more fairly judge its use, application, and appropriateness to your organization. But if they never, ever do anything differently, they will not be able to judge new ideas objectively.

3. More Flexible Change Management

In my opinion, one of the worst management "truths" of recent years is the common "knowledge" that people resist change. I couldn't disagree more. In my view *poorly led people resist change,* and *well led people not only accept change but may even embrace it.* To keep your organization flexible, you must lower the resistance to change and lead people through it. Remember these techniques as you work in this area.

People are much more likely to go through change with you than for you. Lead from the front in change. Let people know you will be there with them, that you will be supportive, that you will get them the information, equipment, training, encouragement, and support that they need to get the change done. Don't just inflict a change on your staff and leave.

All change is local. No matter what change or new idea you announce and no matter how wonderful your staff and volunteers are, they will, in very short order, reduce the change to this question: How does this affect me? Their concerns will be for their job, their work hours, their dress code, their need for more education, their ability to continue to work on the same team or in the same office, and so on and on. Until you can address these issues and allay their concerns, your team members will understandably not put themselves fully into implementing the change. I know that staff are supposed to be working at your organization for the greater good, but we are all people first. Ignore the local nature of change at your peril.

Change takes time, patience, and support. It really doesn't matter what change you are suggesting—whether it is a new way of filling out a reimbursement form, a new time for worship services, a different way of delivering meals, or a new set of robes for the choir—change is really behavioral change, and that takes time to get used to and to get right. Be patient, coach your people through the change, and be there to support them when they need it.

As a leader you can and must enable your organization to be more flexible, within the limits of your mission, your values, and your faith. Flexibility is a core component of marketing, of meeting the ever-changing set of wants of your constituencies, and of remaining an excellent provider of services. It is a crucial part of your leadership skills.

E. LIFETIME LEARNING

We are told to study, study, and study our Scripture. We are supposed to set aside time each day to read and reflect on our holy writings. Why? Just to take up part of our 24 hours? No, because the more times we read them, the more we learn. Each time we open our Scriptures, we are a different age (even if only one day older) and in a different frame of mind and have more experiences to relate to the text we are considering. Thus, we see it in a different light and learn something different than the last time we read it. Or, a passage that we might have skipped over previously because it meant nothing to us at the time suddenly becomes important.

So, at least in our spiritual lives, we know that constant study and reflection are good. But do we transfer that to our professional lives? For the most part, no. We took a management course back in 1983, so we know about that. We went to a workshop on budgeting five years ago and one about strategic planning the year after that, so we are completely up to speed on those issues. Right? Obviously not.

Proverbs 1:5-6 tells us: *A wise man will hear and increase in learning. A man of understanding will acquire wise counsel, to understand a proverb and a figure, the words of the wise and their riddles.* Verse 7 admonishes us as follows: *Fools despise wisdom and instruction.* The Shiite sect of Islam is taught in Nahjul Balagha, Saying 52: *There is no greater wealth than wisdom; no greater poverty than ignorance; no greater heritage than culture.*

And yet we are hesitant to go back for refresher training, or to take the time and the money to learn something new in any depth. Why? The most common excuse I hear is, "I don't have the time." Of course you do. Remember the rule of 24? You have the time, you just don't choose to *take* the time to invest in learning. Learning more is *part of your job,* not *an addition* to it. Do you consider yourself a professional? I'm sure you do. Other professions (medicine, law, aviation, operation of heavy machinery) require continuing education. So should yours.

Leaders need to be open to counsel and open to ideas and an increase in learning. How can you be flexible and innovative if you are not open to new ideas, not willing to stretch your knowledge, not willing to consider that there may have been advances since you last studied an issue? Successful organizations are always learning, always practicing, always reviewing. And you already have the skills in your organization.

☞ **HANDS-ON:** Where does your organization spend its investment in learning? Take a look and see. Do all of the funds (as they do in many organizations) get spent on the senior management? Review your expenditures on training, conferences, periodicals, books, and the like. Remember to include travel expenses for out-of-town conferences. On whom are your spending the big bucks? If it is primarily on the senior managers, rethinking is in order. And, I will almost guarantee that you need to spend more on training than you currently do as an organization.

☞ **HANDS-ON:** In the quest for an organizational culture that is open to new ideas and values lifelong learning, you need to lead. At a minimum you should:

- Read at least two monthly periodicals related to your field of endeavor
- Read at least one book per year on ways to run your kind of organization more effectively
- Attend 40 hours of training per year of some kind, including refresher courses.

☞ **HANDS-ON:** You need to set a goal for your organization of every staff person getting 40 hours per year of training, continuing education, or practice. This could include workshops at conferences and refresher courses in supervision, delegation, communications, finance, and of course, the actual service provision. It can include live training, distance courses by videotape or satellite, and even conference courses over the World Wide Web.

Of course, all of this costs money and staff time, and here is where you come in. As a leader it is up to you to advocate with the board, the staff, and any outside funders you may have for the allocation of resources to enable continuous learning. I suggest that you view the costs of learning as investments rather than expenditures and try to convince others that this perspective is a valid one.

Without new ideas, organizations stagnate. I've already told you that boards and staffs both need some turnover to bring in new ideas. But the people who are already employed by your organization need to constantly refresh their ideas, add to their wisdom, and accumulate the experiences and perspectives of other professionals.

Leading in this area has its dangers; you may find out that the "trend" is in a method of service delivery that you don't care for, that other organizations are way ahead of you in some areas, which can be frightening and depressing, or that you are temporarily way ahead of other organizations, which can lead to a dangerous feeling of complacency. But lead you must. The organization that stops learning is the organization that stops growing, improving, and providing the best possible service to its constituencies.

Leaders are vital to your organization. Practice the leadership skills we have covered in this chapter, and you too, can be a leader, and in so doing, help your organization in a multitude of ways.

POSTLUDE

As you reflect on leadership, I want you to envision two things that you learned in high school science. One of the basic laws of Newtonian physics is that an object at rest will stay at rest until another force moves it. This resistance to move or to change is called inertia. The other relevant scientific phenomenon, catalysis, is one that you learned about in high school chemistry. A catalyst is something that speeds up a change (in chemistry, a chemical reaction) *without being consumed by the reaction.* In both these parts of the physical world, we know that outside forces are needed to make things happen. In faith-based organizations these forces are our leaders. Leaders give the organization the crucial push to overcome inertia. The vision and energy of leaders often prove to be the catalyst that results in faster, more effective growth and change. Leaders take the initiative, force decisions to be made, and bring others in the organization to their vision of what the organization could be like.

In this chapter we spent time on the all-important issue of leadership. You can have a terrific organizational mission, good staff, excellent volunteers, and a top-notch strategic plan and still not succeed without the leaders to move the organization forward. We saw that the key skills of leaders in faith-based organizations are:

The ability to motivate

The ability to innovate

The ability to communicate

Flexibility

Belief in the value of lifelong learning

I then showed you how to improve your leadership skills in each of these areas. For *Motivation,* we saw that walking the talk, using the mission and your faith, caring about your people, and involving them in many decisions are crucial components. In the area of *Innovation,* we saw that incorporating risk and innovation into the culture, using business skills to minimize risk, and steady one percent per day improvements are the key. In *Communication* we learned that the most important part of the equation is trust and that successful communications go hand in hand with a supervision philosophy that sees management as a support function rather than a fiefdom. In *Flexibility* you saw that regular stretching goes a long way toward keeping you flexible and that flexibility and innovation are closely related. Finally, in *Lifelong learning,* you were shown how to both keep on track for a life of study and how to bring your organization with you on the journey of knowledge.

Leaders and leadership are crucial to your success. Don't just assume that when a person gets a title (executive director, senior pastor, chairperson of the board), that he or she becomes a leader by osmosis. No one does. Even the natural leaders work at their skills, refining and reworking the mix of motivation, innovation, communications, flexibility, and learning both to be the best that they can and to adapt to an ever-changing world.

Speaking of adaptation, that is really the essence of the next chapter, Faith-Based Marketing.

Chapter Seven Checklist

✓ Communications discussion with staff

✓ Plan flexibility exercises

✓ Review my training and reading levels

✓ One percent per day improvement idea discussion

QUESTIONS FOR DISCUSSION: CHAPTER SEVEN

1. Do we as leaders really walk the talk? Are there ways that we can improve putting our words into action?

2. What can we do better to motivate our staff and volunteers? How do we put our faith and our mission more in the center of our motivational efforts?

3. Do we as leaders value lifelong learning? Do we go take the training we require of others? Do we invest in training for ourselves and others?

4. Can we implement the author's suggestions about communications? How will our staff respond?

8

Faith-Based Marketing

*I will extol thee, my God and my King, and bless thy name for
ever and ever. Every day I will bless thee, and praise thy name
for ever and ever. Great is the Lord, and greatly to be praised,
and his greatness is unsearchable.* Psalm 145.1–3

*Call to the way of your Lord with wisdom and kindly exhorta-
tion. Reason with them in the most courteous manner. Your Lord
knows best those who stray from His path and those who are
rightly guided.* Qur'an 16.125

*We are ambassadors for Christ, God making His appeal through
us.* II Corinthians 5.20–6.13

PRELUDE

In this chapter you will learn about:

➤ Marketing as part of faith
➤ The marketing process
➤ Who your markets are
➤ Better marketing materials
➤ Getting the feedback you need

Marketing? In a faith-based organization? How crass, how commercial,
how, well, *secular!* I intend this chapter to show you not only that marketing is appropriate, moral, and ethical but that it is *essential* to a successful faith-based organization. If your organization is a place of
worship, it will help you spread your faith. If you are a community service
organization, it will help you deliver more targeted, more efficient, and
higher-quality services.

Whichever kind of organization you are, you will almost certainly find
that you are already doing much of what I suggest. We will simply show

you how to focus and refine your efforts to get the most mission out of your limited resources. You will spend those resources more effectively and have happier constituencies. Sound good? It will be. Let's get started.

A. CAN MARKETING BE PART OF FAITH?

The simple answer is yes; marketing not only *can* be part of faith, it *always has been.* A key part of marketing is understanding what people want and need and providing that to them in a way to which they will respond. All of the world's major religions have accomplished this; millions of people have responded to the call of the faith. Religion and spirituality meet a core human need and want.

However, the spiritual choices for any individual are vast and varied: Hinduism, Christianity, Judaism, Islam, and Buddhism, just to name a few. Faith is, in short, a competitive marketplace, and within each of the main belief structures are hundreds if not thousands of different choices (sects or denominations), each with its own set of values, liturgy, and requirements of the faithful. The most successful of these many choices are the ones that are most appealing to both new and current believers.

☞ **HANDS-ON:** Look at your own community. Where are people attending services? Which kind of place of worship has grown, which has not over the past 20 years? Is the cause doctrine, location, the spiritual leader of the organization, a change in society? The answer to all of these is yes. The baby boom generation is returning to places of worship in droves. Are they coming to your place of worship? Why or why not?

The immutable law of the numbers is that, in places of worship as well as in community service organizations, people have choices. By applying a few basic principles of marketing to your organization, you can be more sure that people will choose your organization, your faith.

One other point. I earlier described faith as a competitive marketplace, and it is. You compete for members, contributions, volunteer time, good staff. The same goes for those readers who are involved with community service organizations. Many ministers I know prefer to believe that they are not competing with each other, but rather with Satan. Again eschewing the theology, I'll limit my advice to the worldly: You *are* competing, and good marketing allows you to compete successfully.

So, yes, marketing can be, actually *is,* part of faith. Marketing skills are the best single example of business techniques, which, if you are willing to learn them, can be adapted and adopted by you, your staff, and volunteers to do more mission, more efficiently and effectively.

B. WHY GOOD MARKETING IS GOOD MISSION

1. Market? Me?

Do you want to do excellent work? If your organization is focused on community service, do you want it to target its services to meet the greatest community needs? If it is a place of worship, do you want to reach as many people as possible, bringing them to the fold of the faithful? Of course you do. But you still don't want to market? Here's some truth for you—you already are marketing!

❏ FOR EXAMPLE: Just over two years ago, our congregation dedicated a new church building. We had been seven years in the planning, fund raising, and building process, and it was both a relief and celebration to finally move into the new facility.

The first Sunday at the new pulpit our senior minister announced that he was going to begin a series of three sermons entitled "What We Believe." These sermons would remind us all of our belief structure and would also let our visitors understand us better. The minister knew that during the first few Sundays our attendance would be unusually high as friends, relatives, neighbors, and the curious visited the new building. He believed it was a great opportunity to let people know more about us as a congregation.

Was he preaching? Sure. Was he marketing? Absolutely. It's called product definition. Tell people about all the wonderful features of your product or service, and they are more likely to purchase it (or come back to church next Sunday).

❏ FOR EXAMPLE: Do you ever ask your service recipients (or parishioners) whether they are happy with your services? That's surveying. Do you listen and try to improve services? That's market acknowledgment. Do you track where your service recipients come from? Market awareness. Do you try to get people to send or bring other people to you? Working the referral angle. Do you have any written materials to hand to people? Promotion. Do you have public service announcements? Advertising. Have you ever changed any service method, hours of operation, location, or cost in response to a customer's request? Meeting the market's wants.

So, let's agree that you already do quite a bit of marketing and that it helps you to do more mission. Now we need to turn our attention to what the benefits of marketing are and get into some techniques that will help you to "turbocharge" and focus your marketing.

2. The Results of Good Marketing

Even though we agree that you are already doing some marketing, I want you to focus more in this area and to follow a marketing cycle that we'll describe below. I want you to develop a culture of asking your customers what they want, and I want you to have everyone on your marketing team. That's work, and a lot of it. Marketing is not an event, not a one-year quest, not a goal in your strategic plan. It becomes a discipline, part of the organizational culture, part of your tradition. But that takes time, money, and a lot of leadership effort.

So for all this, what do you get? What are the results of doing marketing and doing it well? At least the following things.

A true understanding of your markets. A note here: When I use the word *markets* to refer to groups of people, I am sure that some readers wince. But it is the appropriate term to describe groups of people whom you serve. It doesn't demean them, you, or your organization to think of them in this fashion. They are still people and still deserve to be treated as individuals. Remember, some of the best marketed for-profit organizations in the world focus on people first, their own and their customers. Just because Land's End, Nordstrom, Disney, or Marriott think of you as a market doesn't mean that they don't treat you as if you were the most important person in the world when you interact with them. You can think of the people who interact with your organization as markets *and* as individuals.

In the next section, we'll look at who your markets are and you may be surprised at the listing of all the different groups of people whom you serve. But suffice it to say here that if you do good marketing with the marketing process I recommend, you will, perhaps for the first time, recognize *all* your varied, and sometimes conflicting, markets. That recognition is the first step toward better marketing and service provision.

A constant recognition of what those markets want. Organizations that do marketing well ask constantly. They recognize that the issue is both what people *need* and what they *want*. Asking through focus groups, surveys, and informal interaction allows these organizations to steadily keep their fingers on the pulse of wants that is circulating throughout their various constituencies.

More focused, efficient services. In the for-profit world, if you give people what they want and stop giving them what they don't want, you will be more efficient. In the faith-based world, you need to do your best to give people what they *need* but in the way that they *want* it. If you do that and stop providing services in ways that people no longer want them, you'll be more efficient and more focused.

Happier markets (clients, patients, members, parishioners, students, families, and funders). If you recognize whom you serve, ask them what they want, and give it to them, they will be happier. Why? First, because you asked them; a very simple and very easy thing that we don't do often enough. Second, if you listen and respond, you'll be meeting their expectations, filling a want, and treating their ideas and requests with the respect that they deserve. All of which brings about happiness in these people, above and beyond the good that your services do.

More people to serve. When you go to a restaurant, quick lube shop, retail store, or any place that gives you outstanding service, what do you do? Do you keep the news to yourself? No, you tell people. And then they try the establishment themselves. The same works for your organization. If you make your markets happy, they'll tell people about you, and more people will come. Happy customers make excellent referral sources, and more people in the door mean more services to deliver, resulting in more mission getting done!

A stronger bottom line. On the assumption that growth is a good thing for your organization financially, the more people you serve, the more members you have, the stronger your bottom line. Good marketing will result in more people, bringing in more money to allow you to do more mission.

Sound good? It is. Let's turn to my definition of the marketing cycle to give you a better understanding of the complete marketing process.

C. THE MARKETING PROCESS FOR FAITH-BASED ORGANIZATIONS

Now it's time to get down to specifics: Marketing is not just sales. It's not just promotional materials, advertising, or asking. Marketing, good marketing, *complete* marketing is a combination of all these things plus some others, put in the correct order and then incorporated into an endless cycle that becomes part of your organization's mindset, its culture, its very fabric. Marketing is not an event, it is a process that you *never* complete. Why? Because at its core marketing is a way to respond to changes: changes in your community, changes in the wants and needs of the people you serve, changes in the way you get paid, changes in the way your competition is acting. Since all of these things are constantly in flux, marketing is never complete. It's a process.

The process that I have outlined below works for faith-based organizations. I'm sorry to have to tell you that you can't just do the portions of the cycle that you want to or that look easy or that you already have in place. You need to do them *all*. In brief, the marketing process looks like this:

1. Identify your markets
2. Find out what your markets want
3. Adapt to the markets
4. Look at cost and price
5. Promote the service
6. Get the service delivered
7. Evaluate your efforts

This process works for the organization as a whole and for every single part, program, service, and ministry within it. Let's examine each of these components in greater detail.

1. Identify Your Markets

This sound so basic, and I'm sure that there are readers who are asking, "What's wrong with him? I know whom I work for, my board and the people we serve! That's easy." Not so fast. You are correct, but incomplete. The board and the people you serve are indeed crucial customers, or markets. But you have lots more as well—payers, referral sources, staff, and volunteers—and even the people you serve shouldn't be all grouped together. I'm sure you provide a wide number of services to a variety of demographic groups. Each of those has its own wants and needs. In a few pages, we will spend considerable time identifying your many, many markets. Suffice it to say here that the first step in any marketing effort, for the organization as a whole or as you consider a new or expanded service, is to figure out who your markets are as carefully as possible.

2. Find out What Your Markets Want

Now we come to the essence of marketing. Notice that I didn't say "What your markets need." I used the term *want,* and I used it intentionally. Wants and needs are different things, and it is essential that you understand that difference. All of us *have needs;* all of us *seek wants.* While some people want what they need, all too often that is not the case. And the essential application of marketing for the faith-based organization is to understand this difference and use it to the advantage of the mission: *Give people what they need in a way that they will want it.*

Let me put it another way. I am sure that every reader has a friend, acquaintance, relative, or neighbor who would benefit from adopting your faith. They *need* God. But they won't make that leap of faith, that acceptance of spirituality, that adoption of a creed, until they *want* to.

Needs and wants are not the same, and the problem is that we, as human services people, regardless of whether your organization is a community service organization or a place of worship, focus on needs. We are trained to diagnose *needs,* to do *needs* assessments, to identify and plan a course of correction for community *needs.* But until we recognize that people have needs but act on wants, we can't possibly be optimally effective. We have to find out what people want, and to do that we have to ask. And no, you don't know what they want, even though you might think you do.

The most dangerous sentence you can say in marketing is, "I've been in this business ten (or twenty or thirty) years, and I know what people want." Hear me clearly: *No one knows what people want until one asks.* And what people want changes over time, so you have to ask regularly. Later in this chapter we will devote considerable space to the issue of asking, including a review of how to survey, run focus groups, and conduct valid interviews. However, it is important here to understand that you need to ask to find out what people want.

Let me make another distinction between business marketing and faith-based marketing. You and I both know that many businesses work hard to make us *want* (and thus buy) what we don't really *need.* Chocolate is an excellent example, although I am married to a person who would argue that chocolate is not only a need but a separate food group! But in reality, chocolate is a want. So is a new car every four years, a new toy every week for a child, the latest fashions, and making sure that you see a new movie the first weekend it is out. Business also sells us things we do need such as food and shelter and things that are good for us such as fitness or better-balanced diets. But business, the for-profit world, can and does try to make people want things that they *don't* need.

And here's the difference. You don't. As you practice marketing in a faith-based organization, you only try to make people want things that they *do* need. That is a crucial distinction and one that I want you to keep in mind as we progress through the rest of the marketing process.

3. Adapt to the Markets

The third step is to listen to what people want and give it to them, if you can. This is called adapting to the markets, or listening to your customers.

It is something that successful for-profits, secular not-for-profits, and faith-based organizations are all doing well.

Market adaptation does not have to mean a wholesale change in your faith, your services, or what you believe in. It most often means a different delivery vehicle, location, or method.

❑ **FOR EXAMPLE:** My family and I have vacationed on Squam Lake in New Hampshire since I was about 10 years old. It is a truly beautiful place, the lake where the movie *On Golden Pond* was filmed. People center their activities on and near the lake, and this has resulted in a wonderful place of worship called "Church Island". A not-for-profit formed 40 years ago was deeded a small (10-acre) island, and provides church services on the island each Sunday in July and August. Visiting ministers come to preach, there is a beautiful outdoor sanctuary and a pump organ (powered by a boy or girl pedaling a stationary bicycle), and all the worshipers come by boat. This meets the need and wants of those who live and vacation on the lake to worship conveniently and in a unique, and uniquely lovely, location.

In northern Indiana, a summer church has grown up on a large lake, where during the summer the parishioners come by boat *and stay on their boats during the service.* The minister preaches via a public address system from a boat, everyone sings hymns that are passed out as the worshippers arrive, and an offering is taken. The same thing occurs on the top of the ski slopes of a large, well-known resort in Colorado. People ski up, worship outside, and then ski down the mountain. In each of these examples, the wants of the community have been met by a place of worship in unique ways. More mundane examples include the growth of family activity nights, adult basketball and volleyball leagues, and Saturday evening services in many U.S. communities. People want to have safe family time, and churches (and YMCAs) have responded. People want to be involved in athletics but not on a kill or be killed competitive basis, and some churches and synagogues have responded. Saturday evening services give families flexibility, which, as shown by the growing attendance nationally at these services, they obviously value.

Market adaptation is usually not a huge, seismic change. More often it falls into the category of continuous quality improvement. In Chapter Seven, we talked about the Japanese philosophy of improving by one percent per day. I really like this. Slow, steady improvement means that your organization is always moving, always refreshing itself, always adding value for the people that it serves. It overcomes organizational inertia, reduces resistance to change, and improves quality.

But the direction for such changes should come from the people you serve, your markets. You see, improvements in quality are only improvements if the customer, the market, believes that they are. It does no good to spend time and money on things that you and your staff feel are "improvements" if the people you are trying to serve feel otherwise.

❏ **For Example:** I recently gave a training session on marketing near Detroit and was making this point when a hand went up. The participant told us a story of his brother, an engineer for General Motors (GM) who was constantly frustrated that GM cars were not as highly rated as their subsidiary Saturn's were. "We make much, much better, safer, more fuel efficient cars," the engineer would tell his brother. "Our cars are the best engineered in the world and we spend so much time, energy, and money making them that way. Saturns just can't compare. But people love them. It's just so maddening." The man telling us the story then related how he would try to break the news to his brother that most customers don't care about the engineering, but they do care about Saturn's no hassle, no negotiation purchasing policy. They do care about its great customer service and the friendly showrooms. And thus Saturns sell well, and GM cars sit on the lot.

How did Saturn know that people hated bargaining with the sales staff? They asked. How did they know to hire only the friendliest sales people? They asked the customer what mattered to them.

One other story from the auto industry underscores my comment that most changes are not huge, earth shattering ones. Guess which new feature in cars and trucks has been the most popular since 1990? Air bags? No. Compact disc players? Wrong again. Antilock brakes? Close, but not quite. The answer is *cup holders.* A small, even tiny part of the overall vehicle, but the most popular change in the last decade. What are your organization's cup holders? How can you increase the convenience, helpfulness, or value of your services to your constituency?

4. Look at Cost and Price

Back to money, and you thought we were just talking about marketing! Well, money plays into marketing in a very important way. You have to know the costs of what you are providing so that you can make sure that you price it in such a way as to recover the costs. And, since it is not unusual for people to ask for more than they are willing to pay for, you need to make sure that you provide what you can afford to, and if they are paying directly for services, what they are willing to spend.

I could spend the rest of this book on pricing, but that's not why you bought it. Let me just make two points, ones that are valid and apply whether your not-for-profit is a place of worship or a community service organization.

First, it's *never* about price—it's *always* about *value*. If people value what you do, they will pay for it. Think about the secular world for a moment; if it were always just the lowest price that people went for, we wouldn't have Mercedes-Benz automobiles, first-class airline seats, or huge television screens. As you add value, from the perspective of the people you serve, people are willing to pay more.

❑ **For Example:** A church near my house holds Vacation Bible School (VBS) every year for about 500 kids. It is run in the church on five successive evenings as an evangelistic outreach to the community. There is no fee, and nearly 400 volunteers give generously of their time to make it happen. The total budget for VBS in a recent year was $6,500 for supplies, snacks, materials, and so on, a not insignificant sum. A few years back, the church started providing T-shirts to the volunteers for the cost of the shirt, about $4. The kids, of course, all wanted the shirts, and so the next year they were available for sale, again at cost. About half the kids (or their parents) bought one, Why didn't they price it higher and recoup some of their costs? "That would be unseemly," one top VBS volunteer told me. "Besides, no one would pay much for a simple VBS shirt."

Well, someone did. One volunteer went as an observer to another large VBS operation in another community and came back reporting that not only were they pricing their shirts higher, but that they were selling out at the higher price. This past year the church near me sold their shirts at $9.50 each, and sold one to 90% of the kids enrolled. I was told that many parents, even those with two or three kids enrolled, happily paid for the shirts, noting that VBS was free, and that this was the least that they could do in return. *They knew the church was "making money" on the shirts, and that was an added benefit to them, not a detriment.*

Thus, pricing is part of marketing, and, in this case a higher price led to more demand. Keep it in mind.

My second point about price has much more to do with the philosophy of services and pricing than with marketing. I know that there will be things that you price at or below cost because either the people you serve can't afford to pay more or the people who contract with you (usually the government) won't pay the full cost. And that's part of being a not-for-profit enterprise and certainly part of being a faith-based organization. But in making the decision to do something for less than cost (to have a *loss center* in accounting terms), I want you to make sure you know two things: *what are the real costs, and what is the mission return.* If you decide to provide meals for free, you will certainly lose money. But if the result is a great deal of good mission in a high-priority area for you, that's fine, as long as your organization as a whole makes up the losses elsewhere. In other words, loss centers are fine as long as there are compensating profit centers, such as your development office.

5. Promote the Service

Here we are finally talking about what most people think of as marketing. Brochures, advertisements, sales, public service announcements, videos, web sites, word of mouth, and educational information all fall into this category. You have to tell people about your services for them to know about and hopefully, use them.

We don't have the space to go into depth on all of these ways of promoting your services, but I will spend some time on written materials further on. You want to promote things in a way that meets needs and wants rather than in a way that sells services. Remember, people seek what they want, regardless of what they need.

6. Get the Service Delivered

You have, I am sure, a great set of services or ministries. But if you can't get them to the people you want to serve at a time, place, and in a manner that those people can utilize them, all the work you put into creating the services will be for naught. The sixth step in marketing is figuring out how, where, when, and with whom to provide services. Here, you ask your customers and also observe the best practices of other organizations like yours.

You may provide your services only in your main building and only during traditional office hours, or you may provide them in your main building as well as off-site and in service recipients' homes, on a 24-hour-per-day, 7-day-per-week basis. But however you provide them, you need to constantly monitor the utilization of these services and measure whether the method of service delivery is still wanted, still effective, and still of high quality.

❑ **FOR EXAMPLE:** My sister is a profoundly retarded woman, who lives in a small group home in Connecticut. When she was a child, she resided first in a large state institution (the state of the art in the 1950s), then in a smaller facility still on the state campus, then in a regional center run by the state, and finally in a series of small group homes run by local not-for-profits, one of them a faith-based organization. During these years she grew up, went to work, and in 1982 lost the use of her legs and became much more medically fragile.

Over this one person's lifetime, the method of delivery of education, recreation, employment, and residential services changed repeatedly as her needs changed, but also as the state of the art evolved. If you multiply my sister's tale by hundreds of thousands, you get a small glimpse of the constant adaptations that many not-for-profits have had to make to continue to provide quality services to baby boomers with disabilities. And, the needs of this group will continue to change as they age, retire from work, and become even more medically dependent.

The key is to make sure that the where and how of your delivery of services are still appropriate, and not just to continue doing the same old thing in the same old way.

☞ **HANDS-ON:** Perhaps now would be a good time for a thorough internal review of your services. Are you still providing the same services as you were five years ago, at the same location, at the same times, with the same people? If you are, I suspect you have some adjustments to make.

If your organization is a place of worship, are you still singing exactly the same songs you were ten years ago? News flash: There is wonderful new worship music out there, which if mixed in with the more traditional music, will appeal to the younger population I suspect you would like to attract. How about your service times, your dress code, your location(s)? Is there reason to rethink any or all of those? If you run a community service organization, are your services still the best they can be? Are there improvements in service delivery others have accomplished that you can adopt?

In both cases ask the people you serve. Set up some focus groups (I'll show you how a bit later in this chapter), and ask people how you can improve. I'll bet that there are a bunch of "cupholders" out there for you to consider providing.

7. Evaluate Your Efforts

So how are you doing? Fine? How do you know? Here's an adaptation of my earlier exhortation that no one knows what their markets want until they ask. *No one knows how their efforts in customer service, marketing, or meeting needs and wants are doing until they evaluate.* How do you evaluate? Simple. Find out where you were, figure out where you are going, and then measure how far you got. Okay, so that's too simple. First, what is it that your marketing is trying to accomplish? A variety of things, I'm sure: happier markets, more services delivered, more funds into the organization to do more mission. If you asked your markets early in the process what they want and how happy they are with you, ask again in six months or a year. See how much happier they are. Or, you can look at objective measures. Is membership in your place of worship growing? Remember, people vote with their feet. By how much? How does that compare with other similar churches, temples, or synagogues in your community? Find out where new people come from. Did they hear about you from others that your organization serves, read about you in the paper, see your ad on television, get hold of your marketing material? Once you know this, you can do more of what works and less of what doesn't.

❑ **FOR EXAMPLE:** A faith-based counseling organization in the Southeast focused a great deal of effort toward marketing, surveyed its many markets, and made changes to both its services and marketing materials. It trained all of its staff in better customer service and made them full members of the marketing team. Also, it advertised heavily in the local newspaper, on radio, and on billboards. A year later, as it went through its formal evaluation, the staff and board noted with great satisfaction that things were working; the number of persons seeking services was up by 40 percent (compared with 5 to 9 percent in each of the previous five years). Unsolicited donations were on the rise, and staff turnover was down by 12 percent. Most importantly, the number of people who received more than just two counseling sessions was up by over 145 percent. That meant that the people who tried the service returned consistently.

   While the factual results were above expectations, the staff wanted to know why people were coming in at a faster rate and why they were staying longer. So they set up some focus groups and looked at intake data. At the beginning of their marketing push, they had instituted a system whereby all new patients were asked how they heard about the organization. The data were then collated and kept for later review. When the staff looked at how new patients had heard about the organization, the results looked like this:

Heard about you from another patient	54%
Heard about you from my minister	27%
Heard about you from a family member	7%
Heard about you from a neighbor	4%

Read your ad in the paper	1%
Saw your television ad	0%
Don't know	7%

Then the staff held focus group meetings with patients and asked them why they returned for more counseling and if and why they referred the organization. The results of the focus group interviews were overwhelming. Patients felt well treated by everyone in the organization from the moment they walked in. Repeatedly heard comments included: "Everyone is so nice to me"; "They treat me like a friend, not like a nuisance"; "I always feel welcome and at home."

On reviewing this information, the staff concluded that the money spent on advertising was not cost-effective and that the more customer service training and coaching that they could do, the better. By doing so, they saved considerable amounts of money and focused on what worked.

That's the marketing process, in all its complexity and with all its reward. By using this process, you will get the benefits we talked about earlier in the chapter. However, we should spend a bit more time on some of the key parts: market identification, marketing materials, and asking. In each of these areas there are some simple techniques and rules to follow that will make your efforts more fruitful and more efficient.

D. WHO ARE YOUR MARKETS?

I hope that by now you are becoming comfortable with my use of the word *markets* to describe all of your various constituencies. You have many, many markets, and sometimes the wants of those markets collide. First, though, we need to identify your markets. Because of the vast differences in the markets of a place of worship and a community service organization, I have developed two sample exhibits, one for each type of organization.

For any faith-based organization there are four categories of markets to pay attention to: *internal, service recipients, payers, and referral.* Even though most of us would focus first on the service recipient market as our main customer, all four markets are equally important. You have to have staff and volunteers to do the good works that God has called you to accomplish. To keep staff and volunteers on task and motivated, you have to meet their needs and wants. You have to have money to do your good works, so you have to figure out why people give you money (or contract with you if you are a community service organization) and meet their wants and needs as well. Remember my rule: *No Money, No Mission!* You need people who send you people, your referral markets. What do they want? How can you get it to them? And, of course, you should pay attention to the wants and needs of the people you serve. That's the bottom line of mission for you.

Let's look a little more closely at each kind of organization and its respective market types. Remember that my listings are examples: they are not all-inclusive, and I hope that when you fill out your own market identification template in a few pages you will consider my lists just a starting point.

1. The Markets of a Place of Worship

Exhibit 8-1 shows you an example of the markets of a place of worship. There are the four main categories: internal, service recipient, payer, and referral. Within each category are a list of possible individual markets. *Internal markets* include *Governing volunteers, Employees, other Volunteers, and your Denomination.* We've already talked about why it is so important to keep abreast of the needs and wants of your board, staff, and volunteers, but what about the denomination? For many readers whose place of worship is part of a larger denomination, asking the hierarchy of the faith what they expect from your organization is very smart and often

Exhibit: 8-1   The Markets of a Place of Worship

Internal markets	Governing Volunteers
	Employees
	Other volunteers
	Denomination
Service recipient markets	Congregation
	By age
	By other factors (single, at home mother, etc.)
	By ministry
	Other services
Payer markets	Congregation
	Denomination
	User fees
Referral markets	Congregation
	Family members
	Neighbors
	Denomination

very surprising. You are, after all, a franchise of a larger body, and you have to meet the wants and needs of the denomination to keep your status.

What about *service recipients?* You have many, and I don't know enough about your organization to list them all here. What I've done is given you some breakdown categories to consider.

❏ **FOR EXAMPLE:** Our church has specialized ministries for infants, kids (all ages), teens, singles, the hearing-impaired, seniors, at-home moms, parents, and people (adults and children) involved in a divorce. There are about a dozen individual music ministries, three or four recreational outreach programs, volunteer involvement in community organizations such as Habitat for Humanity and a local homeless shelter, and literally dozens of other opportunities to be involved in the church. Each of these ministries would be a different market with different wants, deserving targeted special attention.

You could also look at the three broader categories of church members, people who attend but are not members, and people in the community who have no church home. There are many ways to look at this issue, but be assured that what the people who utilize our seniors ministry want is not the same as the people in the teen ministry, nor the ministry that deals with the effects of divorce. Different markets, different wants and needs.

I have shown three kinds of *payers,* namely the *congregation*, the *denomination,* and *user fees.* For most congregations, the largest source of income is from tithes, offerings, bequests, and capital donations from the membership. Your organization may also receive funds from your denomination (particularly at start-up or to capitalize a new ministry) and from user fees. User fees are payments that people make for a product or service. On a small scale, a member may pay for a T-shirt with the church name and logo on it. On a larger scale, your organization may provide day care for an hourly, daily, or weekly fee. These would both be examples of user fees.

What all users want is value, as they perceive value. Remember that we talked about that when we looked at pricing earlier. Don't make the mistake of giving people things *you* value unless you are sure that *they* value them as well.

Finally, there are the *referral markets* for a place of worship. These are the people who send you people to minister to. I have listed four kinds in my example: your *congregation, family members, neighbors,* and your *denomination.* Each can send you new prospective members or people to receive other services that you may provide. Each has a different set of wants for you to meet. And each is important if you want to grow and do more mission.

Now let's turn to the markets of our other broad category of faith-based organization.

2. The Markets of a Community Service Organization

Exhibit 8-2 shows a sample of the market breakdown for a community service organization. Again, we have the internal, service recipient, payer, and referral groupings, but within these four large groupings are a different collection of subsets, with the exception of our *internal markets,* which are the same, namely, *governing volunteers, employees, other volunteers,* and any issues with a sponsoring *denomination.* In the area of *service recipient,* I've shown three services, A, B, and C, and within each of those services, two

Exhibit 8-2   The Markets of a Community Service Organization

Internal markets	Governing volunteers
	Employees
	Other volunteers
	Denomination
Service recipient markets	Service A
	Recipient type 1
	Recipient type 2
	Service B
	Recipient type 1
	Recipient type 2
	Service C
	Recipient type 1
	Recipient type 2
Payer markets	Government
	United Way
	Foundations
	Insurers
	Contractors
	User fees
	Denomination
Referral markets	Physicians
	Clerics
	Counselors
	Teachers
	Family members

different recipient types. For example, if one of your services is overnight shelter for the homeless, there are different needs and wants for single men than there are for single moms with children. Or, in grade school, there are different needs and wants by grade, between children and parents, and between special ed and non-special education children. The idea here is to get as targeted as you can in focusing on needs and wants.

The payer markets for a community service organization are really different from those for a place of worship. I have included *government, United Way, foundations, insurers, contractors, user fees, and your sponsoring denomination.* Some or all of these may be payers for your organization and they all have different sets of needs and wants, which are often found in their funding regulations and your contract for services.

☞ **HANDS-ON:** Don't make the mistake of assuming that "government" is one payer. For most organizations it isn't. Your organizations may get funds from different government departments or levels (state, federal, county, local) or different departments within the same government unit. Or you may only get funds from one government department (Child Welfare, for example) but from three different programs, each of which is enabled by different legislation, has different regulations and expectations, and thus is a different market.

The other payer sources require the same caution; they all have their own set of needs and wants. Don't treat them all the same, and don't treat them as a necessary evil—they are anything but that. Funders are far from perfect, but they deserve to be treated as *valued* customers just as anyone else.

☞ **HANDS-ON:** One other hint with the payer (and internal market) of your denomination. If yours is a community service organization, which gets funds from your sponsoring denomination's places of worship, make sure that you spend the time and the energy to keep these people informed about your organization, its growth, and its successes in relation to the faith. Not only do you increase the likelihood that there will be consistent and even growing funds, but these places of worship are outstanding sources of volunteers and community connections, both of which you are sure to need. Personal relations with places of worship are vital; don't assume that they will always be there. You need to pay attention and invest some time.

Referral markets for community service organizations are also different than those for places of worship. This is due to the more regulated and formal relationship that often grows up between the referral source and the community service organization. As examples, I have included *physicians, clerics, counselors, teachers, and family members*. Like all the other markets we have looked at, these have their own wants and needs. But in general, referral sources to community service organizations want two things, almost interchangeably, *capacity* and *quality*. They want capacity of service ("Take my referral now, and get them off my caseload and on to yours!"), and quality of service *from their view of quality*. This means that for some referrers, nothing but cutting-edge, state-of-the-art services will do, and for others, such "trendy" services are too modern, too untraditional. As with all other markets, you have to ask, ask, ask and then listen!

☞ **HANDS-ON:** Now it is your turn. Use the template shown in Exhibit 8-3 to identify your own markets. For payers, look at your organiza-

Exhibit 8-3   Market Identification Template

GROUPING	MARKET	WANTS
Internal:		
Service Recipient:		
Payer:		
Referral:		

tion's income and expense statement. For service recipients, try to think through all the services or ministries you provide and any subgroups of the people you serve within those services or ministries. Make copies of Exhibit 8-3 and then ask your management team and board to fill them in independently. Compare the answers, and you will find that your team is focused in different areas. Make sure that you use this exercise to do two things: find out who your markets are, and reiterate to your staff that all of your markets are important. Also, notice that I have added a column labeled WANTS. Jot down ideas here on what each market really wants from your organization, remembering that you don't really know what they want until you ask! (If you run out of room make up your own form using this as a sample.)

E. GETTING THE FEEDBACK YOU NEED

You already know that the second step in the marketing process is to find out what your many markets want, and that means asking them. Sounds simple, and it is, if you use a few relatively simple techniques. But there is more than just asking. There is tracking, there is follow-up, and there is listening. Let's start with an overall cultural change that needs to happen.

1. A Culture of Asking

Your organization starts by becoming what I call a *culture of asking*. You survey, you organize focus groups, you informally interview. The last thing everyone in the organization should ask everyone outside of the organization every day is: "Is there anything else we can do for you today." Or "Did you get what you needed from us?" The best organizations are always asking and always listening. By doing so, they begin the process of meeting customer wants, of increasing customer satisfaction, and of giving all of their customers more value from the perspective of the customer.

To develop this culture, your people must be trained to understand that good marketing is good mission, that everyone is a market, and to recognize the essential difference between needs and wants. Then get them some training on asking, and as always, lead by example.

Ask, ask, ask, and then listen!

2. Surveys

Surveys are ways to get replicable, statistically defensible data. They also allow for trend analysis; you can ask a set of questions now and again in six weeks or six months and measure the difference. You don't have to pay big bucks for surveys, although for the first one it is smart to get some help in developing the questions and the survey process. You can learn a great deal from regular surveying, and there are some rules for surveys that you should follow.

Have instructions. Unless the survey is going to be administered in person (i.e., read to someone) you need to tell people how to fill out the survey. I like to start all my surveys with a brief thank you, followed by a short explanation of why the survey is being taken. Then put in simple instructions on how to fill out the survey, and end with directions about what to do with the survey (mail, fax, hand in) and by when, if you have a deadline.

Be brief and be focused. The longer the survey, the less likely people are to even start, much less finish it. The rule of thumb I use is that if people *think* that a survey will take longer than *four minutes* to complete, they probably won't do so without some compensation. So be brief, and most importantly, be focused. You have a primary reason for surveying: customer service, the introduction of a new service or ministry, a scheduling poll, or some other important reason. Stick with that reason and don't just throw in every question you've thought of in the past five years for the heck of it.

☞ **HANDS-ON:** There *will* be people (perhaps even your boss or the board president) who tell you something like this: "Since we're going to the expense of the survey, let's ask a couple of questions about... ." I guarantee that this will happen. Resist. The longer the survey, the fewer returns you will get. That makes the additional questions costly, not cost-effective. The less focused your questions are about one subject, the poorer the quality of the data. Be brief and focused.

Limit your identifiers. Identifiers are the things you ask people about themselves: age group, gender, ethnicity, zip code, income bracket. Data dweebs like me love to ask for lots of identifiers, because then we can play with the data, cutting it up into smaller and smaller pieces. Resist people like us. The more identifiers you have, the less response you will get. Why? Two reasons, the first being that the identifier area takes up time, and thus uses up part of your four minutes. The more important reason is that if you are like most organizations, most of your surveying will be on customer satisfaction. With surveys of this kind, you want people to be forthright and frank; if they have a problem, you want to hear it. People will be more likely to be frank if they are anonymous, and the more identifiers you put on the survey, the more people will feel that you will be able to identify them. Your data will suffer as a result.

Only include identifiers that you absolutely need. Ask yourself this: If all the people who respond to the survey are from one category in our identifier, does it matter? Does it matter that I know? For example, if you do a survey of your congregation, and 80 percent of the respondents believe that there is a need for a new women's support group, it would probably be important to know how many of the respondents were female. But if the issue is whether the congregation is satisfied with the senior minister's preaching, gender may not be important enough to take up space, time, and attention.

Be consistent, but not a pest. As I said earlier, surveys allow you to look at trends over time. Are your service recipients in a particular program happier or not as compared with the last three fiscal years? Are people finding out about your place of worship consistently from radio, or more and more from friends and neighbors? Trend analysis is an important management tool, but the key is that if essentially the same questions are repeated time after time, most of us will try to fine-tune the questions to improve them. Be aware that this will skew the validity of the data. And, while you should make use of repeated surveys to measure trends, don't do it so often that you become a pest. I had a client recently who showed me the comments from a survey, one of which was something like, "Great organization, but you survey us all the time. Back off a little." Good advice.

Include closing instructions and a thank you. Even though you put instructions at the beginning of the survey, repeat the ones having to do with returning the survey to you and the deadline. Then remember to thank people for their time!

Get help. At least for your first survey, get some help in the wording and order of the questions and the look of the survey. My recommendation is to develop the survey absolutely as far as you can, and then get what I call a "targeted" volunteer.

☞ **HANDS-ON:** You need an expert, but only for a little while. Find someone in your community (at your bank, utility, large manufacturing firm) who does surveying (we'll call this person Ed) and does it well. Don't go to him, go to his *boss,* whom we will call Megan. Tell Megan where you work, why you want to survey, and that you need Ed for six hours to review and improve your survey. Megan will be so pleased that you aren't asking her for money or recruiting her for the board, that she will almost always agree immediately. Ed will agree, since his boss told him to, and because this will be something new for him. He'll improve your survey and give you many good ideas.

Keep your word, six hours. Don't ask Ed to make a donation, or to serve on your marketing committee, or to join the congregation; 60% of the time, he'll come back on his own.

3. Focus Groups

Focus groups are the other main category of asking, but they are used less often because of their cost. You get terrific information from focus groups, but you have to understand that it is subjective rather than objective and thus not statistically defensible. What you do get from focus groups that you cannot obtain from surveys are reactions, emotions, feelings, and uncategorized responses to questions. As with surveys, there are some rules to follow.

Get a facilitator. Above and beyond all the other suggestions below, get an outside facilitator. Don't assume that you or any staff member or volunteer should do this, even if that person has the skill and experience. Get someone from outside the organization who is both objective and non-threatening to the participants. Again here, you will mostly be dealing with issues surrounding satisfaction or lack of satisfaction with your services or organization, and you want to reduce the barriers to frankness as much as you possibly can. I repeat, get a facilitator.

Be homogenous. Focus groups bear their name for two reasons: they focus on a certain issue, and they comprise a focused group of people. To the extent that you can, be homogenous. For example, if you try to be cost-effective and run one focus group about your organization with the participants representative of your staff, board, funders, and service recipients, guess what? One group will dominate, and you won't get much out of the others. The more that the group members are peers, the better.

Be focused. Just as with the focus in the survey, focus in a focus group. You only have an hour and a half, so key in on the most important things and stay there. If you are having a focus group to get reactions to a proposed new service, don't throw in questions about the organization in general or about community needs or anything else that might tempt you.

Compensate the group members and don't wear them out. I've already warned you that you have about an hour and a half, perhaps two, before you wear your participants out. A good facilitator will know this and guide you to limit your questions, but don't have unrealistic expectations about your participants' endurance. And compensate them in some way, usually food and drink, but perhaps also travel costs, parking, and the like. And definitely send them a letter thanking them for their time and assistance.

Get help. Just as with the survey development, get some help in developing your questions. I would suggest that you work with your facilitator for this task.

4. Informal Asking

Here is where you really have to train and to lead by example. Your staff, as I said earlier, must always be asking, but they also have to be listening and passing on the information that they glean from their questions to the correct person in the organization. But you need to be asking regularly. Questions should include how people found out about your organization, if people are getting what they need from you and your staff, if there are any ways of improving services, if there are other services that your organization can provide, and so on *ad infinitum.* The list is endless, but the key is to have your staff pleasantly asking, focusing on the answers, and most of all, listening!

5. Getting the Information Where It Needs to Be

Now, after you've asked, what do you do? The biggest challenge in any organization is getting the information to the people who need it in a timely fashion. This is why staff meetings were invented. Instead of just having staff meetings be top down (you telling people what to do), have them bottom up, and reserve a part of every meeting for staff to tell you what they are hearing from the people you serve, the people who pay you, your referrers, and your internal markets (staff, board, and volunteers). Not only does this reinforce the need to ask, so that each person has something to report, but when comments on suggestions are repeated to a group, someone may "hear" something that the others wouldn't in a certain comment or suggestion.

Additionally, you should share the results of surveys and focus groups, not only with all of your staff and board but also with the people who participated in the survey or focus group. I call this closing the loop, and it is a surefire way to prove to people that you are listening and to increase participation in future surveys and focus groups.

☞ **HANDS-ON:** Let's say you do a mail survey of 300 people regarding their satisfaction with your organization and 50 respond, a terrific response rate for a mail survey. You find out a number of things from the survey, and they are things you can take care of, fix, or improve, some now and some in future months or years. If you sit on the information, even if you listen to it, you only get half the benefit from it. Go further. Send out a letter to all 300 people (or put an article in your newsletter if all of them receive it), stating that you did the survey, thank the 50 people who responded, and then list what you've learned and *what you have done about what you learned.* If you've already fixed four of the seven key issues brought up in the survey, point that out, noting that you are a responsive organization. Tell the readers what is going to happen in the future with the other findings, and then note that you hope that they will participate in next year's survey. I assure you, more than 50 will respond next year because you closed the loop and gave them feedback.

All of these ways of asking will tell you what people want, and as long as you are listening and are flexible enough to accommodate to the wants of the markets, the asking will have been worth it.

F. YOUR MARKETING MATERIALS

The last key issue in marketing is your materials, which can include brochures, posters, handouts, advertisements, web sites, and even your business cards. If you've identified your markets, asked them what they want, and developed or modified your programs and services to meet those wants, you now need to let them know about your programs in a way that will attract them to come, that is, will make them *want* to participate. How do most organizations do this? By proudly trumpeting their services, telling everyone how comprehensive, spectacular, professional, or exciting their array of services is. On the other hand, how do successful organizations do it? By identifying with their markets and showing them how the organization's services can *solve their problems.*

❑ **FOR EXAMPLE:** Which line do you think will appeal more to teens: "Come to our Terrific Teen Youth Group Sunday at 4:00!" or "Looking for a Place to Have a Great Time with Your Friends? We have it—every Sunday at 4 pm." I saw both of these recently on different church brochures. I had my opinions, but kept them to myself, as I showed both brochure headlines to about 20 teenagers who are friends of my eldest son. By a score of 20-0 the second promotional line won. Why? Because it identifies with the kids' wants and doesn't push the service. As one girl said, "The first line tells you what to do, and what's with the 'Terrific Teen' thing anyway? Sounds like something for a 10-year-old." Those are two excellent points and demonstrate that whoever wrote the first brochure was sure that he or she knew what teens *needed* but never asked, or even thought about, what they *wanted*.

Marketing materials, which are your unsupervised salespersons, need to speak to the reader's problems or wants and then draw a clear and very short line between that problem and the solution your organization offers.

1. Targeting Your Materials

Think back a few pages to the list of markets you read about and then, I hope, filled in on your own. Reflect on those many markets for a moment, considering what your best guess is that they want. Are all the wants the same? Of course not. Your organization has many different groups to appeal to, all of them with unique wants. So how do most not-for-profits, secular or faith-based, respond? With one general, all-purpose brochure, which includes an organizational history, a list of services, and a plea for money. The rationale for this single piece is that it is "a cost-effective overview of the organization." No way. The term *cost-effective* clearly assumes that the result is at least somewhat effective, and this isn't. Think about a general marketing piece, and then think about all of your markets. To which market does that piece appeal? To no one but the senior staff who are under the illusion that they are saving money, when they are really throwing it away.

It's time you recognized that not having specific marketing pieces for specific markets is counterproductive. Today's software and color inkjet printers are so inexpensive that you can't afford not to target your pieces. All of the top five word processing programs have templates that will let you put out great looking materials. You can go to any office superstore and buy paper that has a consistent "look" between letterhead, brochure, business card, and so on. This is *not* expensive. I can't emphasize how important it is to target your materials in today's market. You will be able to identify with your potential customers so much better.

☞ **HANDS-ON:** To what markets might your different materials be targeted? Let me give you some ideas that you can start with. A *community service organization* might have individual pieces for government, insurers, donors (perhaps different for different submarkets), potential and new employees, potential volunteers, referrers, and the major groups of people that you serve. *A place of worship* might have one for prospective members, one for people without a spiritual home, one for various demographic groups (teens, seniors, singles, new parents), and one for particular services that you offer (day care, in home meals, etc.) Think through the most important of these markets and start there. But try, try, try *not* to lump together too many different markets with their different wants.

2. What's in Good Marketing Materials
Let's take a look at some other components of marketing materials, in this case the things you want to include.

Mission, statement of faith. This assumes that your mission statement is brief, but it is important to let people know what you stand for as an organization.

Brevity and focus. Short sentences, bulleted lists, a lot of what's called "white space" are important. Focus on one thing per brochure. If you are describing services, don't ask for money. If you are asking for money, don't spend a lot of time on history. Focus.

Connect problems and solutions. Don't trumpet your wares. Identify with your potential service recipients, donors, or referral sources and show them that you understand their issues and will work to solve their problems.

Appearance. Don't go the low road here. There is no excuse for a brochure that looks as if it were typed by a 1946 vintage typewriter on paper towels. It doesn't make you look cost-efficient, it makes you look chintzy, and if you skimp in this area, the reader will wonder if you skimp in services too. You don't have to have 16-color glossy advertisements, but at least shoot for a professional look.

Credibility. It is fine for you to include how many years you've been in existence or how many people you've helped, but stay away from a year-by-year history of the organization. The sad truth is that no one but the historian cares. A sentence such as "Helping people in Adams County since 1972" may be appropriate. A paragraph on your founding, growth, and trials and tribulations since 1972 is not.

Source for more information. Always include a person to contact for more information. "If you would like more information on how this ministry can help you and your family, call Betty at 555–1100." Be sure to include a person, not just a number. And when Betty changes jobs or leaves the organization, update the materials. The personal contact is so, so important.

3. What's in Bad Marketing Materials

There are, of course, things you want to avoid in your materials. You see them all too often in the printed materials of not-for-profits of all sizes and types. Here they are.

Jargon. I have nothing against oral shorthand, which is what jargon is, if it is used appropriately, which means between professionals to make their communications more accurate and more efficient. Where jargon is *not* needed is in any marketing materials that are *not* targeted at professionals. One of the problems with a general organizational brochure is that since it is trying to appeal to everyone, it includes jargon, which turns most of the readers completely off. Get the jargon out.

Dated materials. Things like photos from the 60's, terminology that is no longer used, references to programs that have been changed. Constantly review your materials and, since it is so inexpensive to change the words, do it!

Lack of focus. One last time, marketing is about focusing on your different markets. Pick a subject for each piece and stick to it. Don't wander off. Stay focused.

Asking for money. Except in a fund-raising piece, never, ever ask for money, membership, or anything else in the financial area. It turns people off, loses the focus on the piece, and takes up space. Develop one or more fund-raising pieces and put your requests there.

History lesson. As I said above, no one cares about your history except the people who lived through it, and they are not the people you are seeking to attract with your marketing materials. With the exception of a credibility line, stay away from your organization's history.

Boring. Use short sentences. Lots of bulleted lists, brief paragraphs, and a graph or two all alleviate boredom. People have very, very short attention spans. Don't give them the chance to change the mental channel on you. Keep your material easy to read, understandable, and relevant.

☞ **HANDS-ON:** So how do you find out what's boring, what is jargon, and, in general what appeals to people? I have a great, free resource for you—high school kids. I use them all the time, and so do many of my clients. Find a group of 14- to 16-year-olds and hand them a draft brochure. Watch them read it. If they ask a question such as "What does this mean?" you are probably using jargon. If you hand them two or three brochures at once and they go to the second one before finishing the first, you just saw boring in action. High schoolers are smart enough to know what they like but not so educated as to understand jargon that may have become second nature to you. And, they are more than willing to tell you where you messed up. Use them. They are terrific at this.

Remember what I said earlier, that your marketing materials are unsupervised salespeople out there. Every time your brochure or informational packet turns someone off or fails to interest someone, it's a lost opportunity, one that you cannot correct because you don't know when or where it is happening. Focus your marketing materials, target them, clean them up, and they will be excellent ambassadors for you in places and at times that you simply cannot be there.

POSTLUDE

In this chapter we studied the issue of faith-based marketing. You learned why marketing is not just a business application but a skill that can be applied both to places of worship and to the delivery of community services. You found that you are already doing marketing in your organization and that doing marketing well has some tangible mission outcomes.

We then moved to the marketing process that I want you to use in your organization. We went through each of the steps in this process, which were:

1. Identify your markets
2. Find out what your markets want
3. Adapt to the markets
4. Look at cost and price
5. Promote the service
6. Get the service delivered
7. Evaluate your efforts

Next we looked at who your markets really are, and you found that you had internal, service recipient, payer, and referral markets, and that within those four broad categories, you had many, many unique and special submarkets, each of whom deserves your attention.

We moved on to asking for feedback, going through the techniques of surveys, focus groups, and interviews, but always remembering that you have to be asking people constantly how your organization is meeting their wants and then carefully listening to their answers.

The last section of the chapter dealt with marketing materials, and I showed you how to spruce yours up, focusing on your target markets. I gave you a list of things to include in your materials and a similar list of things to avoid. Here the essential lesson was to have not just one general marketing piece, but many, each focused on one of your most important service, payer, referral, or internal markets.

> *You are the light of the world. A city set on a hill cannot be hid. Nor do men light a lamp and put it under a bushel, but on a stand, and it gives light to all in the house. Let your light so shine before men, that they may see your good works and give glory to your Father who is in heaven.* Matthew 5.14–16

Your message is needed, indeed commanded. You want your services, your faith to shine like that beacon on the hill. How do you get the message out? Repeat after me: Good marketing is good mission. Repeat after me: Wants and needs are different. Repeat after me: Everyone is on the marketing team. Repeat after me: Everyone deserves to be treated as a customer. If you can hold on to those four critical concepts, your organization can become a turbocharged provider of services in your community. If you forget, ignore or, worst of all, dismiss them as not relevant, inappropriate, or valueless, the people that you serve will suffer.

Good marketing, as I said a number of times earlier, is not an event, it is a process. And it does not just happen; it takes commitment, resources, and planning. So do a lot of other things in your organization, and that is why we will spend our next chapter discussing how and why to plan.

Chapter Eight Checklist

✓ Marketing committee established

✓ Listing of markets

✓ Review of marketing materials

✓ Plans for surveying, asking

QUESTIONS FOR DISCUSSION: CHAPTER EIGHT

1. Who are our markets? How do we know what they want? Should we use the term *markets*, or are we more comfortable with some other term?

2. Do we ask enough? How can we improve in this area? Should we consider surveying? When?

3. How do we treat the people who pay us? Can we improve our attitude? Do we think of everyone as a customer? Is there room for improvement here?

4. How does our marketing material compare with Peter's criteria? Should we schedule a review soon?

9

Vision and Planning

For which of you, desiring to build a tower, does not first sit down and count the cost, whether he has enough to complete it? Otherwise, when he has laid a foundation, and is not able to finish, all who see it begin to mock him, saying, "This man began to build, and was not able to finish." Luke 14.28–31

The superior man does not embark upon any affair until he has carefully planned the start. I Ching 6

Before you climb a tree you must start at the bottom. Buji Proverb (Nigeria)

PRELUDE

In this chapter you will learn about:

➤ What's the point? Where are you going?
➤ The planning process
➤ A planning outline
➤ Capital planning

"Uh-oh. Here is another boring subject—planning. There is something we've never had the time to do. And besides, it takes time away from the delivery of service, and nobody ever reads the plan anyway. Things are changing too fast for the plan to be relevant even in six months. A waste of time and money."

If this sounds like what you were thinking, think again. Here is a real management task, one that can critically affect your organization for the next ten to twenty years. Planning, in all its various forms, is a skill that good managers need to learn and need to practice regularly.

Proverbs 16:9 tells us: *The mind of man plans his way, but the Lord directs his steps.* By planning, we can organize ourselves and better realize what God wants us to do. In this chapter, we'll look at planning in general, then at a planning process, and then at some specific kinds of plans, including outlines for them.

A. WHAT'S THE POINT? WHERE ARE YOU GOING?

We have already talked at length about the special nature of your organization, the combination of faith and mission that makes you so special. We've also discussed your need to be a good steward of the resources with which God has provided you to accomplish that mission and to spread your faith. And we've talked about one kind of planning, budgeting. Deciding beforehand how you will take in and expend funds is a very important component of overall planning.

I believe that good stewardship demands careful planning: assessment of what your community wants and needs, looking at your organizations strengths and weaknesses in meeting those wants and needs, and figuring out how best to focus your resources to get the most mission out the door as soon as possible. I've said for years that if you don't know where you are going, the only way you get there is by accident. What you do is much, much too important to be accidental. So putting some time and effort into developing plans for your organization makes sense, makes good use of your resources, and embodies your responsibilities as a steward.

Another misconception that I need to put to rest is that planning restricts you, that it somehow reduces your options. I've lost track of the number of times people have told me "… if we develop a plan, then we *have* to follow it. What if the situation changes? We're stuck." Well, of *course* the situation will change; it always does. And the idea of planning is not to restrict you but *to focus your organization on what you think is most important.*

Visualize a compass. There are 360 degrees on a compass rose. That means that from any given point, you can choose to go in 360 different directions. Good planning doesn't restrict you to only one choice, or one degree of those 360, but rather says, "We're going to go generally northeast." Thus, as the situation changes, you can deviate a bit in either direction, but your general momentum keeps going forward.

By looking at planning as focusing rather than as a self-imposed straightjacket, you also overcome the perception that planning is only worth the effort during a time when not much is changing. Many administrators tell me that so much is changing in their organization's world that … "by the time we finish the plan, it is already out of date." Certain facts or figures may be overcome by the rush of events, and certainly all of us are amazed by the constant acceleration of the pace of change in our world, but that doesn't get you off the hook of the need and responsibility to plan.

❏ **FOR EXAMPLE:** I've been a sailor all of my life, and in 1985 I earned my private pilot's license. It has always fascinated me that the very different disciplines of sailing and flying have the same rule: Stop paying attention for *three seconds* and you are off course. Planning helps keep you from being distracted, from losing track of your course. Think of trying to navigate a canoe across a calm pond. Pretty straightforward, and you can take the time to look around and enjoy the scenery. But what about a very windy, choppy day? You'd better keep your mind on your task and your eye on where you are going.

You are in choppy seas organizationally, and you and I both know it. Developing a plan helps to remove some of the distractions from your line of sight, so that you can spend your energy keeping your organization on its true course.

By using and reusing the planning process, by developing organizational plans that guide and focus you, you will reap a number of specific benefits. These include:

1. Better and More Effective Services
The planning process will stress the identification of trends, the prediction of future circumstances, and thus the development of services to meet needs that either don't yet exist or don't currently exist in a large enough amount to warrant an allocation of resources. A common expression for this is "getting ahead of the curve."

❏ **FOR EXAMPLE:** A mainstream church had been located in the center of a midwestern community's downtown area for over 100 years. It had made the decision to keep its location in the downtown by expanding its facilities nearly twofold in 1980. But during the 1977 review of its strategic plan, while still deciding to stay in the urban core, it noted that most of the community's growth, including both retail and residential, was on the west side. It knew that people on that side of town would eventually need services and looked for land to purchase or have donated. In 1980, at the same time that construction was going on downtown, a member gave the church 10 acres of farmland, which was over two miles west of the farthest development yet considered. Ten years later, in 1990, by which time the community had grown up around the farmland, the church considered what the best use of that land could be. They built a family life center, with a gym, classrooms, and day care center. Worship services were held in the gym, Sunday school classes in the classrooms, and during the week there were senior meetings, teen meetings, basketball and volleyball leagues and other services that the community wanted. The facility was an immediate hit; many new members joined the congregation, and the church expanded its range of services.

This would not have been possible without the early planning and prediction that had occurred in 1977. By the time the land was surrounded by homes and businesses, it would have been much, much too expensive for the church to buy, and frankly, might well have been too valuable for the member to donate. Good planning keeps you from reacting to and chasing needs. You can predict some needs well in advance and in so doing benefit the community.

2. Coordination of Disparate Activities

Planning lets all of many different activities occur in a more coordinated fashion. By looking at your organization as a whole and then setting goals, you can consider all of the various tasks needed for each goal's implementation and the impact that they will have on the entire organization.

❏ **FOR EXAMPLE:** A community service organization was going through its planning process and foresaw steady growth in the needs and wants of the people in its service area continuing for the next five years. The fastest growth in the services that the organization provided was projected to occur in counseling, residential services for children, training for foster parents, and community-based education on child abuse prevention. Its goal as stated in its five-year plan was: *Grow our service capacity 5 percent per year for the next five years.* Fine. But what were the implications of that laudable goal? First, the residential capacity of the organization would be used up in two years, the rooms for counseling and training of foster parents would be full in three years, and all of the services would require more staff. The administrative and human resources systems (computers, software, and staff) were already maxed out and could not provide much more support without an expansion or updating. The planners also foresaw a need for better communications in the growing organization, with more remote sites where staff would be working. All of this caused them to consider moving to new space or building more space, some immediately, some in four years. The larger building project was needed, and would need a fund drive to pay for 25 percent of the costs. Thus, the staff and board knew that they needed to start laying the groundwork now for a capital campaign in two years so that they would be able to afford a new building in four.

Planning allows this kind of coordination and impact analysis to occur and takes much of the "fire fighting" out of management. And that is nothing if not good stewardship.

3. Less Conflict/More Ownership

How many times have you had to referee when staff people argued over limited resources? Or watched as one part of your organization built up a resentment toward another because the first perceived that the second got whatever it wanted while the first had to make do with leftovers? While competition for resources will occur in organizations where dedicated people believe in the importance of what they do, outright conflict can be lessened by a participatory planning process. Why? Because planning allows people to see their own activities and those of others in the context of the entire organization. It encourages them to participate in decisions that will affect the entire organization, not just their own area of interest. For most people, this results in more ownership, better understanding of how the organization really works, and a more realistic view of their work in the organization. If they choose not to participate, that becomes their problem; you offered them the chance to have their say.

The other thing that planning does is to communicate better what the organization is doing now and where it is going in both the short and the long term. Too often I see organizations in which people complain that they "never know what is going on." If people are part of the planning process or even simply read the draft plan as it is disseminated (more on that in a minute), they will have a much better idea of what is going on both inside and outside the organization where they work or volunteer. Thus, a well-written and focused plan can become an excellent communications tool.

B. THE PLANNING PROCESS

Planning, like marketing, is a process, not an event. You need to learn how to develop the plan, how to use it, and how to revise, update, and modify it as your organization's situation evolves. In this section, we'll show you a planning process that will work for nearly any plan you can think of, whether strategic, marketing, fund-raising, capital, or business development. In each of these cases, some of the particulars will change, but the basic components will stay the same.

One more word before we get into the components of the process. While the results of planning (better organization, more focus, more coordination of activities, and the like) are all important, there is an additional benefit that I didn't list above. It's the process itself, *if you are inclusive.* The planning process gives you an unparalleled opportunity to bring new people into your organizational family and to increase the involvement of those who are already members, staff, or volunteers. Thus, the process itself can become a crucial benefit. And, the best part is that you don't need to have a 10,000-member planning committee! I'll show you how to accomplish this as we walk through the process, but I wanted you to understand this important, and mostly overlooked, benefit of regular, organized planning.

1. Get Ready
First rule: Don't start until you are ready. That sounds simplistic, I know, but let's look at a set of questions for you to consider before you begin the actual planning effort.

1. Do you have an agreed process for the planning, including a deadline, progress points, and areas of assigned responsibility?
2. Have you allocated staff and volunteer time to the planning effort, or are you simply piling it on top of all the other tasks these people have?
3. Do you have the expertise (in house or under contract) to complete any data gathering, statistical or financial analyses, or other specialized tasks that will be needed in the planning process?
4. Do you have sufficient funds set aside for any outside help you may need and for the other expenses associated with planning?
5. Do you have an agreed-upon use of the plan?

Until these things are in place, you really don't want to start. Without a deadline, for example, you'll never get done. If the management team has not allocated the time to get the plan done by the deadline, other so-called priorities will always get in the way. The same is true if you have not allocated enough money to buy any needed expertise. So do your homework and make your preparatory efforts before you start, and you will increase your likelihood of success.

2. Retreat (or Advance)
It always helps to start a major planning effort by stepping back to look at the entire organizational picture in the context of whatever kind of plan you are developing: strategic, marketing, or even new business. And here's the

secret: *You can't do this in an hour and a half meeting.* It really helps to get away from your organization for a set period of time to allow yourself and your planning team to focus on the environment, your goals, your mission, and your faith without the distractions of day-to-day or even month-to-month operational issues. Most people call this getting away a "retreat," although I have a terrific client who terms the time an "Advance"!

Whatever term you use, the idea is to have some concentrated time focusing on your mission, faith, and organizational future. Here are three things that you should try to accomplish at your retreat.

1. *Review your organizational environment.* How will the environment (today and in the future) affect your organization and its programs? What trends will affect you and how? Is demand for your services growing or waning? Is the employment market a buyer's or seller's market? What is going on in the national and local economy? These and other questions like them will get everyone at the retreat on the same page.

2. *Set goals for the plan.* Whatever process you use for goal setting, it is crucial that the initial ideas come out of the retreat. After discussing the goals, have the group either rank or rate them so that the planning committee can put them into a priority order.

3. *Agree on the final planning process.* Although you should have had a draft process in hand as you started the retreat, now is the time to finalize the process, set deadlines and, most importantly, get agreement on who in your organization is responsible for what and when as it regards planning.

This list may seem short, but it can fill up a whole day. Now, to make sure you get more out of your retreat, let's look at some rules about retreats that will help you.

Location: Sorry. You don't have to go to Aspen, Orlando, or Aruba to have a successful retreat! What you do need to do is get away from your place of work to reduce distractions. Try a local hotel meeting room, or if you don't want to pay for a place, perhaps the local Chamber of Commerce or one of your board members has a corporate board room for use. Your local community college, community foundation, or United Way may also have meeting space available. Make sure that the space is comfortable, well lit, and accessible, and that there are adequate rest rooms and parking. Bring food in, and have coffee, tea, water, and soft drinks available.

Note: There is nothing wrong with leaving town for your retreat if you feel that this will help keep people focused. It's just not an absolute requirement.

Participation: For strategic plans, I am a strong advocate of a board and senior staff joint retreat. This may mean up to 30 people, but the cross-fertilization that occurs in a joint session is priceless. Whoever comes, make sure to have them agree that they will not answer the phone or their beepers for the duration of the retreat. The "no phones, no beepers" rule is *really* important because it keeps people focused on the issues. If you allow people to answer to distractions, they will be distracted! For marketing, fund raising, or business plans, have the group of staff and volunteers who are on the appropriate committee attend.

Duration: The cute answer here is, "As long as it takes!," but most retreats need about six to eight hours of working time to really get into the work at hand and have a product to show for it. Meet at the best time for the participants. This may mean on a weekend or an evening and a morning (which is the best timing if you are going out of town). Just make sure that your participants are committed to staying for the *entire* retreat.

Facilitation: I am a very strong advocate of having an *outside* facilitator for your retreat. Such a professional will bring objectivity and a large measure of authority to keep the retreat on track and make people more at ease so that they will participate. Even if you or one of your staff is a skilled and experienced facilitator, you will bring preferences and prejudices to the table, or be perceived by some in the room as having them. So get an outsider.

☞ **HANDS-ON:** It is more important to get a skilled and experienced facilitator than to get someone who has great experience with your kind of organization. You can teach the facilitator about your organization, jargon, and key issues. You can't take someone who may intimately know your faith or organization type and then teach that person how to facilitate in two hours. Obviously, having one person with both qualifications would be great, but if you have to settle for one skill, go for the facilitation.

☞ **HANDS-ON:** Also, make sure that you include some time for prayer and/or meditation of your retreat participants both before and during the retreat. In the materials you send out in advance, ask the participants to think about the goals of your organization and to set some time aside before they arrive to pray about their decisions. And, as the retreat begins and ends, make sure that prayer is part of the process.

Many organizations start with retreats on their first plan but skip them on subsequent revisions, trying to save time and money. Don't make this mistake. Getting away and focusing is no less, and perhaps even more, important in a revision. Take the time to get away.

A quick review. When you leave the retreat the participants should have:

Reviewed the environment, trends, and forecasts that affect the organization

Set goals for the plan

Prioritized those goals

Agreed on a final planning process

3. Gathering Information

Following the retreat, you will begin to do two things nearly simultaneously: gathering information and setting goals and objectives. The information you need will depend on the goals you set at the retreat. You may ask: Shouldn't we have some information *at* the retreat? How else can we knowledgeably set our goals? You *should* have some information at the retreat. Information on your environment, financial situation, utilization or attendance figures, and the like are very appropriate. But I know from facilitating the development of over 150 strategic plans that at the retreat, goals are set that require more information to refine. Thus, after the retreat the information gathering will almost certainly be more time-consuming than before it.

You may have all the information you need internally, or you may need to go outside the organization to do interviews, surveys, focus groups, or pure research. What you do in this area will depend on your goals, as I said, but also on the amount of time you have spent in the planning process and how much money you have set aside for research. Getting information is crucial now. You don't want to set final goals on assumptions, rumors, or beliefs (e.g., "The community is growing in our neighborhood, so let's expand"; "I just know that a day care center would work"; "I'm sure people are reading our billboard, so let's rent a few more") without checking the facts. During this time the staff will also be making estimates of the cost of implementing goals and objectives and barriers to their implementation.

There will also be a fair amount of back and forth between this section and the next, as you get some information, set an objective or two, and raise an issue in committee that requires some more research to finalize. This is unavoidable, healthy, and frustrating at times. Remember that knowledge is power, so go for the information that you can get, but don't perseverate on getting every last detail before you come to a decision.

4. Setting Final Goals and Objectives

At the same time that you are gathering information, your committee should be reviewing the goals set at the retreat, changing them if necessary in light of the information you have gathered, and then setting objectives to get the goal accomplished. This task may take a few weeks or months, depending on how much information you need gathered, how it is acquired, and how often your committee meets.

I think that this would be an excellent place to define goals and objectives. As you probably know, there are many different definitions in the lexicon of planning. Here are mine. We'll look first at my definitions and then at an example of how goals, objectives, and action steps work together.

Goal: A *goal* is a statement of intended long-term outcome. It may or may not be measurable, and while it should be accomplished within the planning horizon (if the plan is a five-year plan, goal implementation should occur within that time frame), it may not have a listed deadline. *Goal Example: Our church will grow to meet the needs of our congregation and the community.*

Objective: An *objective* is a more finite statement of activity intended to accomplish the goal. Goals may have more than one objective, and those objectives may be met simultaneously or sequentially. The sum of the outcomes of all of the objectives should be the accomplishment of the goal. Additionally, objectives must include four crucial components:

1. They must support the implementation of the goal
2. They must have a measurable outcome
3. They must have a deadline
4. They must have a named person or group responsible for their accomplishment

Objective Example: Our church will have recruited 25 new members by the end of the year 2002 (Membership Committee).

Action Step: *Action steps* relate to objectives the same way that objectives relate to goals; they are more finite, short-term activities that together accomplish the objective. Like objectives, action steps need four parts:

1. They must support the implementation of the objective
2. They must have a measurable outcome
3. They must have a deadline
4. They must have a named person or group responsible for their accomplishment

In most cases, action steps are reserved for one-year parts of plans. You usually only see goals and objectives in strategic plans, with the action steps reserved for the annual work plan.

A word about the four parts of an objective and action step. Don't scrimp on these. Having all four parts included dramatically increases the likelihood of implementation. Not having them, particularly the deadline and responsible party, dramatically reduces that likelihood. And, if you can't measure your accomplishment or if the activity doesn't move you toward goal implementation, what good is it? Include all four. It's hard work, but it's worth it.

❏ **FOR EXAMPLE:** Let's look at a goal that could be included in your strategic plan and then at the supporting objectives that might be attached to it.

Goal: The Ecumenical Homeless Shelter will become more market-driven as a way of improving its services.

Objective 1: By April 15, (year), form a marketing committee to address the total spectrum of marketing. This marketing committee will include board members, staff from all levels of the organization, and outside experts. *Responsibility: Board President and Executive Director*

Objective 2: By June 15, (same year), complete a review of all of the key markets of our organization and prioritize their importance to the organization. *Responsibility: Marketing Committee*

Objective 3: By September 15, (same year), ask the key markets (both payer and service) how satisfied they are with our services and how we can improve or add services. *Responsibility: Marketing Committee*

Objective 4: By October 31, (same year), develop a list of core competencies that match the stated needs and wants of our core markets. *Responsibility: Marketing Committee*

Objective 5: By December 1 (same year), the Marketing Committee will have researched any and all competing organizations operating or considering operations within our service area.

Additional objectives would probably be the completion of a marketing plan, the development and revision of marketing materials, the provision of customer service training to staff, and the ongoing asking of markets regarding their wants. They might even include some satisfaction benchmarks and goals. Notice that each objective has all four

components. You know who will do what by when, and you can measure the outcome.

Now let's look at action steps for one of the objectives. Let's use the
asking objective from our example.

Objective 3: By September 15, (same year), ask the key markets, (both
payer and service, what their level of satisfaction with our services is and
how we can improve or add services. *Responsibility: Marketing Committee*
   Action Step: By June 1, identify resources for surveys and focus
   groups, including funds, staff, outside experts. *Responsibility: Director
   of Marketing, Executive Director*
   Action Step: By June 15, identify which groups are to be asked.
   Responsibility: Marketing Committee
   Action Step: By June 20, draft survey questions and focus group questions for review by the Marketing Committee by June 30. *Responsibility: Director of Marketing*
   Action Step: By June 30, assign dates and locations for focus groups,
   as well as mailing and return dates for surveys. *Responsibility: Director of Marketing*
   Action Step: By July 7, find a facilitator for focus groups. *Responsibility: Director of Marketing*

Additional action steps could include securing of focus group sites,
evaluation and write-up of survey and focus group results, and publishing
of findings for all staff to see. Again, all the four elements are present and
you can see how much more finite (and short-term) the activities are.
   Once the goals and objectives are complete, staff can write a full first
draft. I've included some sample outlines in a few pages to ease this task.

5. Getting Outside Comment
Now we come to the single most important part of the planning process,
asking people for their input on the draft plan. Circulate the plan widely.
At least every board member, staff member, and volunteer should receive
it, as should your membership (if you have one), key funders, key lenders,
and any vendors who you think should know about your plans.
   Why do you do this? For two critical reasons. First, you'll nearly
always get excellent suggestions, ideas, and perspectives that you simply
cannot get in a cloistered committee environment. Second, and even more
important, you let people know that you care about their opinion, and you
make them feel more a part of your organization. By letting people in on
your plans, they have a better idea of where they fit, what you have to offer

them, and particularly for staff, a view of the "big picture" that they may never before have been privy to. This is a crucial part of the planning process and one that I strongly urge you not to skip. It takes very little time and very little money, and you get a huge return on the investment.

How do you do this? It's pretty straightforward. Make your list of draft plan recipients, make enough copies of the draft for all of them, and send them the plan, a cover letter explaining why they are getting it, and a simple form that they can mail or fax back to you. On the form ask them to list their three or four favorite goals and their three or four least favorite, and give them space to say why. Ask them for unmet needs in the community and any additional goals or objectives that they would like the committee to consider. Then, give them a deadline of no more than 30 days to get back to you.

☞ **HANDS-ON:** Remember that you do, in fact, have competition. Some things (specific expansion plans, names of potential funders) might, if they are included in a widely distributed plan, be used by your competition to "upstage" you or to cut you out of a great potential market. So *think* before you send out the plan, or send only key portions (the goals and objectives of your marketing plan *without* the complete market analysis, for example.)

Make sure that you clearly state in your cover letter that all the ideas and suggestions will be considered by the committee doing the plan but that there are no guarantees about what will be finally included. You don't want to give people the impression that any or all of their ideas will automatically show up in the final document.

I know that this may sound like an unnecessary delay and expense but believe me, it's not. And, in final proof, let's look again at Proverbs. Chapter 15:22 tells us: *Without consultation, plans are frustrated, but with many counselors, they succeed.* Include people.

6. Final Draft and Adoption

Once you have asked for and hopefully, received comments from interested parties, you should make any needed revisions, have the planning group recommend the document to your governing volunteers, and have the plan adopted. It is important to take this formal step, as it will help you in justifying budget and staffing requests to implement the plan.

7. Implementation and Evaluation

Now comes the tough part. You've got a plan, and a good one. How do you ensure that it doesn't just wind up on your office shelf gathering dust? You want to get the most mission out of all the time, study, and expense that went into the plan. And, you want to be cognizant of where you are in your planning time line, how many of your goals, objectives, and action steps you have achieved, and where you are ahead or behind schedule. To do this you not only need to implement, you need to evaluate. Let's look at both issues, and how they interrelate.

Implementation. Implementation should have been made much, much easier because you included deadlines and responsible agents in your objectives and your action steps. As long as you have done that and have given the people responsible for implementation a chance to review the plan before its adoption, the likelihood of completion is really pretty high. But, it goes even higher if you regularly review your progress and if you hold people accountable for the work that they have agreed to.

☞ **HANDS-ON:** At each staff meeting, or at least monthly, go through the active goals and objectives of the plan. An active item is one that, according to the planning time line, should be in progress. Ask for a brief update on progress and whether the item is ahead of, on, or behind schedule. If an item is behind its time line, ask why, and see if there is a way to get it back on track. A variant of this method is for the people responsible for the active items to simply list in writing prior to the meeting all of their goals and objectives, with a notation of "on schedule," "ahead of schedule," or "behind schedule," and why. This method may well be preferable if you have a large number of active items, a limited meeting time, and other more critical issues to discuss.

☞ **HANDS-ON:** You need to keep your governing volunteers in the loop, as well. At each of their meetings, provide them with a written report of the status of the active items, noting which are on track, ahead, or behind. For any goals, objectives, or action steps that are behind your predicted schedule, make sure to include a rationale and the likelihood that you will get back on track. Sometimes you will be able to, some-times not.

Regular review increases accountability and keeps the plan on track. It also makes everyone more aware of where you are as you go along, which protects you from any surprises at the end of the year or planning cycle. The worst thing you can do is not tell people that you are slowly falling behind and then let them know all the bad news at once. Keep the lines of communication and accountability wide open.

Evaluation. At some point, whether at the end of each year or as you approach the completion of the planning cycle, you need to evaluate your efforts and look for ways to improve your forecasting and planning the next time around.

You already should have objectives and action steps that are measurable; that is, you can quantify whether or not you achieved your desired outcome. As you evaluate your efforts, this will simplify the task; you can then quantify the number of items you achieved easily and with no room for anyone else to second guess.

That's the easy part. The tougher part of evaluation is to figure out *why* you completed one objective and not another. Was the reason your assumptions about the future? Was it the number of resources you committed (or didn't commit)? Was it the timing of the work, or some other totally unpredictable event?

Evaluation of your planning outcomes will help you do better planning next time, and that will not only benefit the organization, but ultimately the people your faith-based entity serves.

8. Start Over

Okay, now you have your plan completed. So take a deep breath, say a little prayer of thanksgiving, and *start over.* "What do you mean, start over? We just finished!" you scream at the page. Sorry, but it's true. You need to start now to prepare for your next big planning push. In the next section, I'll show you my suggestions for planning timelines and horizons, but whether the plan you just completed was strategic, business, marketing, or fund raising, you can begin now to make your next planning cycle easier. Here's how.

First, look at the data that you gathered to complete the plan. Now examine the data that you wished you had but couldn't afford either the time or expense to compile. For any of this information, is there a way to systematize its collection, starting now, so that when you revisit the plan you will have the information on hand, ready to analyze?

Second, look at your planning and work group. Are there other perspectives that you need the next time around? Are there people in the group who really didn't contribute much? The time to make changes is now, right after your plan has been adopted. Once you have your team, consider investing in short training courses for them in goal setting, surveying, committee management, or whatever expertise you feel they need to be better planners.

Finally, look at your budget. You are now, I hope, wedded to the planning process. Can you extend that commitment to include budget allocations for committee training, data gathering, and sufficient staffing to support ongoing planning? I hope so, and the time is now to integrate planning into your budgeting process so that you won't have to run to the board for a special allocation in two or three years.

Planning to plan makes excellent sense. You almost certainly learned from your first planning effort. Put that experience to good use and prepare for your next go at plan development.

9. A Planning Timeline

One of the most common questions I get in my training sessions is: "How often should we rewrite our plans?" It's a valid concern, and you have to balance the desire to look out beyond the next fiscal year with the practical knowledge that things are changing fast enough that it's impossible accurately to predict an environment too far into the future.

My suggestions for planning timelines are shown in Exhibit 9-1. I've provided you with my timelines for strategic, business, marketing, and capital plans. When I use the term *horizon,* I mean the length of time the plan is intended to cover. Thus, a strategic plan that starts in fiscal year 2000 would cover five years: 2000, 2001, 2002, 2003, and 2004. The term *revision* means how frequently you should revise the entire plan. This cycle is shorter than the horizon since the situation will inevitably change. A longer horizon forces you to do what I call *"big think."* The shorter revision cycle allows you to react to unforseen changes.

C. SOME PLANNING OUTLINES

I've included some outlines of plans to get you started or to help you revise and update your plans if you already have them. These are templates, ideas that you can use and improve on. Don't be wedded to them if they don't work for your organization. Rather, use them as a starting point.

Exhibit 9-1   Planning Horizon Recommendations

Plan Type	Horizon	Revision	Comments
Strategic	5 years	3 years	Needs an annual plan with action steps each year
Marketing	5 years	3 years	Needs an annual plan with action steps each year
Capital	3 years	2 years	Use for new business,
Business	3 years	2 years after starting the business	major expansions

For each type of plan, I've included my suggestions on the purpose, horizon (how far ahead the plan should look), and cycle (how regularly the plan should be rewritten), as well as a definition of what the plan should support. Note that the horizon is often longer than the planning cycle. That's intentional—I want you to think of the long term but rewrite regularly enough to keep abreast of current events.

1. Strategic Plan

Purpose: To guide the organization as a whole toward the realization of its mission

The Plan Supports: The mission and tenets of the faith

Planning Horizon: Five years

Planning Cycle: Develop a new strategic plan every three years, with annual components written every twelve months

STRATEGIC PLAN OUTLINE

1. *Executive Summary*
   Key areas of action, priority goals
2. *Introduction to the Plan*
   Why you developed the plan, how it will be used
3. *The Planning Process*
   Who was included, what the process itself entailed
4. *The History of Your Organization*
   No more than two pages on your organizational heritage
5. *The Organization Today*
   A three- to five-page description of your services, clientele, and funders
6. *The World We Will Work In*
   A listing of assumptions about the future environment and how they will affect your organization
7. *Goals and Objectives*
8. *One-Year Plan*
   The priority goals and their objective and action steps for the first year
9. *Time Line*
   A visual representation of the goals, objectives, and action steps. Usually called a Gantt or PERT chart.

10. *Evaluation and Update Methodology*
    How and when you will evaluate progress toward implementation
    and when you will revise the plan

11. *Appendices*
    Minimal supporting information for the plan

2. Marketing Plan

Purpose: To guide the organization as a whole toward the realization
  of its mission

The Plan Supports: The mission and tenets of the faith and the strategic plan

Planning Horizon: Five years

Planning Cycle: Develop a marketing plan every three years, with
  annual components written every twelve months

MARKETING PLAN OUTLINE

1. *Your Mission Statement*

2. *Executive Summary*
   A brief summary of the marketing plan, including a list of your target markets, your core competencies, and how they match up with
   the wants of your markets

3. *Introduction and Purpose of the Plan*
   A rationale for the uses of the plan, may also include a brief recita-
   tion of the planning process and its level of inclusion

4. *Description of the Markets*
   A full description of your major markets, their wants, their numbers, and projected growth or reduction in demand from these
   markets

5. *Description of the Services*
   A description of each of your services, including number of people served, service area or criteria for service, and any accredita-
   tion that these services may have earned

6. *Analysis of Market Wants*
   A review of the surveys, interviews, or focus groups that you conduct to prepare the plan. Should include the wants of the markets
   and how they match up to your core competencies.

7. *Target Markets and Rationale*

Out of all your potential markets, you will choose a few priority targets. Describe them here in more detail, along with your reasoning for their prioritization.

8. *Marketing Goals and Objectives*
The goals, objectives, and (for annual plans) action steps that will result in implementation of your marketing strategies

9. *Appendices*
Minimal supporting information for the plan

3. Business Plan

Purpose: To guide the organization as a whole toward the realization of its mission

The Plan Supports: The mission and tenets of the faith and the strategic plan

Planning Horizon: Three years

Planning Cycle: Develop a business plan for a three-year basis

BUSINESS PLAN OUTLINE

Note to the Reader:

We have not spent any significant time on the idea of business development, but many, many faith-based organizations are developing new businesses or expanding services in a major way. It is not an accident that they are using a business plan format to examine their markets, plan their finances, and in the end, to reduce the risk inherent in any new business to a reasonable level.

I am providing this business plan outline in the hope that it will spark some interest in your organization and that you will consider the issue of growth and development at more length.

1. *Title page identifying the business plan as the property of your organization*
This cover letter includes your name, address, and telephone number and the month and year in which the plan is written or revised. One paragraph states in simple terms to whom the business plan belongs and the limitations on its distribution.

2. *Table of contents*

3. *Summary of the plan*
Should include a brief paragraph about your organization; a four-

line description of the product or service; a four-line description of the market; a brief paragraph on production and one on distribution, if needed; and a short paragraph on financing requirements

4. *Description of your organization and its business with the following subheadings:*
   - The organization
   - The product or service you will provide
   - The target consumer or market for the service
   - The consumer's want for the product or service
   - The overall marketing strategy

5. *Description of the market for your product or service*
   Should include information on the competition and cost price comparisons between competitors and your organization

6. *Marketing plan that includes information on*
   - Markets
   - Customers
   - Competitors
   - The macroenvironment
   - How each of these areas affects the marketing and selling of your product or service
   - Evaluation of potential pitfalls

7. *Financial plan with sources and applications of cash and capital and*
   - An equipment list
   - A balance sheet
   - Break-even analysis
   - Cash flow estimates by month for the first year, by quarter for the second and third years
   - Projected income and expenses for the first three years and notes of explanation for each of the estimates

8. *Goals and objectives with a time line*

9. *Minimal appendix with*
   - Management resumes
   - Survey or focus group data from customers
   - Other pertinent material about your organization and its work

D. CAPITAL PLANNING

There is one more kind of planning to cover, and it is capital planning. I put it here in the planning chapter rather than in the financial chapter because it requires the same disciplines as other kinds of planning do. And it points out, yet again, how integrated and intertwined the various parts of managing your faith-based organization are. Strategic plans lean on marketing plans. Both these kinds of plan have impact on budgeting, staffing, and administration. And on and on in an endless cascade of management issues and challenges.

But capital planning is one kind of planning that most people ignore. I'm not quite sure why, although I theorize that we are so good at budgeting for one year and so tuned to the short term that we don't think beyond it. Well, by now you should be thinking beyond the fiscal year about services, marketing, staffing, and administration. Let's add capital issues to that list.

1. Why Do Capital Planning?

Capital planning has two parts. The first is the examination of the future needs of your faith-based organization to purchase, maintain, repair, or replace buildings, equipment, or vehicles. Your first reaction may be: How in the world should I know when those things will happen? Tell me when stuff will break or wear out and then I'll write the plan! In fact, however, much of this is predictable. You should be able to tell when you need to have your vehicles serviced. The same is true for replacement of your roof or a major overhaul of your heating and air conditioning units. You can walk outside and get a pretty good idea of when your parking lot will need to be repaved, and you can listen to your staff and make plans for a new computer system or upgrade.

You should not wait until something breaks. Nor do you need for something to completely wear out before you realize that you will have to replace it. You should plan for that to occur. If you don't, you will really be behind the ball financially.

The second part of capital planning has to do with the cash you need for your organization to grow. This money is called *working capital*, and it is the cash you need to pay the bills, staff, and so on between the time you provide a service and get paid for it. For example, a street clinic may provide screening for various ailments for free, but it will still incur expenses from the tests, the staff time, and so on. If the state or county funds don't come for 60 days after the tests are administered, the clinic needs working capital to operate in the interim. Now, what would happen if the government funder didn't pay for 90 days? That's right, more working capital would be needed. And if the clinic doubled the number of screening visits it provided?

Again, more working capital required. The need for this cash is real, and if not forecast, it can bankrupt you *even if you are making money.* I'll show you how to predict how much cash you will need in a few pages.

In short, you can run short, *way short,* on funds if you do not do capital planning. So, let's look at a process for this special kind of projection, and then I will show you some examples.

2. A Capital Planning Process

To get this kind of planning done, you will need to spend some time gathering data before you meet with your finance committee, who will probably be in charge of completing the plan. By gathering the important information first, you will save yourself and your volunteers a lot of valuable time.

First, convene a group comprising of your treasurer, accountant, executive director, and finance director. Talk through the following issues:

- How you depreciate items now (what length of time, etc.)
- How soon you will need to replace, repair, or maintain capital items (make a list)
- Which of the items on the list will be expensed in the year that they are incurred, which will be depreciated, and which can or cannot be recovered through your main funders (not an issue for places of worship)

After that meeting, start researching the costs involved for the items on your list. What you will quickly find out is that there is more expense then you can probably afford, and that you will need to start staggering the expenses over a number of years.

☞ **HANDS-ON:** Here's a news flash. You can have all the money you need to repair and replace capital items—all you need to do is "fund" your depreciation. What this means is that each month you set aside the same amount of cash as is expensed under *depreciation* on your income and expense report. Thus, if you show a monthly depreciation of $1,250, you should add that amount of actual cash to a savings or money market account each month. Why? So that when the things you are depreciating (cars, buildings, etc.) wear out, you will have the cash to replace them. Probably not all the cash, as prices do go up, but you'll be a heck of a lot better off than having no cash. Funding depreciation is good management, good stewardship, and very, very logical, but almost no one in the not-for-profit world does it. Why? Because it requires that discipline we talked about in Chapter Six on finance: You've got to learn to save to empower your organization to do more mission later, rather than spend every dime you have now.

Note: Some funders frown on not-for-profits having any savings at all. You don't have the time now to listen to me tell you *all* my feelings about how stupid this is, but suffice it to say that there is a solution. Put your depreciation savings in a restricted account. You'll have to do this by board action, but it protects the money from all but the most carnivorous funding source.

☞ **HANDS-ON:** When purchasing, consider two things, leasing and maintenance agreements. Leasing may or may not be cheaper in the long run than buying. I know we were all told to own, not lease, by our parents. But there are times where leasing allows you to be more flexible, and it certainly costs less cash up front. It's one of those options you have available, so at least consider it.

Maintenance agreements are like repair insurance. You pay a usually small premium now, and the item you are purchasing is covered for a period of time, usually three years, beyond the manufacturer's warranty. Check these out. They can be a terrific deal, but read the fine print carefully.

Now that you have your list of items and the costs you anticipate, you can begin to put the expenses into the years you think you will spend them. Look at the sample in Exhibit 9-2.

Exhibit 9-2   Capital Planning Sample

Item	Est. Cost	FY 2000	FY 2001	FY 2002	FY 2003	FY 2004
Repair roof	45,000	0	45,000	0	0	0
New accessible van	37,500	0	0	37,500	0	0
HVAC rehab	4,500	4,500	0	0	0	0
Replace telephone system	9,750	9,750	0	0	0	0
Repave parking lot	75,500	0	0	0	75,500	0
New computer server/ networking	6,500	2,500	4,000			
TOTALS		16,750	49,000	37,500	75,500	0

You can see that this organization has spread its expense out over four of the five fiscal years (FYs) included in their plan and even split the cost of the computer server over two fiscal years.

Once you have completed this list, you are ready for your next meeting, which should include the initial group with two key additions, your banker and your chief fund raiser. The discussion here should center on where the money will come from to pay for all of these projected expenses. How much will come from prior year profits (or net revenues, if you prefer)? How much from debt? How much from your funded depreciation savings? Will you have to have a specific fund drive for any or all of these items? Are they things people will give money for?

Once you finish the capital items, you need to look at your cash needs arising from growth. All growing organizations need cash, as I told you earlier. How much depends on how much you grow and on how long it takes people to pay you. Let's look at an example of the growth needs for a community service organization, shown in Exhibit 9–3. Remember, this is just the growth needs, not the capital funding we talked about earlier.

This organization has four main programs, and it is growing in three areas, shrinking in one, and starting an entire new program. Note that the residential area is growing this year by $80,000, which, when reimbursed

Exhibit 9-3   Cash Cost of Growth

Programs	Startup Cost	Current Budget	Next Yr. Budget	Days Payable This Yr.	Days Payable Next Yr.	Cash Need
Residential	0	440,000	480,000	95	95	10,959
Day	0	327,500	410,000	56	56	12,658
Outreach	0	457,000	395,000	55	55	(9,342)
Hot Lunch	0	110,000	115,000	45	45	616
Prevention (New)	45,000	0	197,000	0	65	80,082
						94,973

"Day" Calculation
Step 1   410,000 – 327,500 = 82,500   110
Step 2   82,500/365 = 226.03 per day   10,959
Step 3   226.03 × 56 days = 12,658   6,027
                                            17,096

in 95 days, will require $10,959 to afford the growth. Outreach services are declining, which saves some working capital, and the new prevention program will cost cash, not only in start-up but also in working capital. Exhibit 9-3 also shows how to calculate your working capital costs. The key is that growth, or an extension of the time it takes you to get paid, requires a cash investment from you and in the near term. By doing this kind of planning now and every year at budget time, you'll be much less likely to get caught short later on.

3. A Template for Capital Plans
Below are some templates for the information needed in a capital plan. Use it as is, or adapt it to meet your organization's needs. Exhibit 9-4 is for capital planning and Exhibit 9-5 for working capital needs.

Exhibit 9-4 Capital Planning Template						
ITEM	**Est. Cost**	**FY**	**FY**	**FY**	**FY**	**FY**
Buildings						
Machinery						
Vehicles						
Repairs						
Equipment						
Other						
TOTALS		16,750	49,000	37,500	75,500	0

				Days	Days	
Programs	**Startup Cost**	**Current Budget**	**Next Yr. Budget**	**Payable This Yr**	**Payable Next Yr**	**Cash Need**
Existing Programs	0					
	0					
	0					
	0					
Total Existing Programs	0					
New Programs						
	0					

Grand Total

Calculations for growth

    Step 1   Subtract "Next Yr" from "current" budget

    Step 2   Divide by 365

    Step 3   Multiply by days payable

Calculations for increase in days payable

    Step 1   Subtract Days Payable this year from next year

    Step 2   Divide Next Yr. Budget by 365

    Step 3   Multiply by the days difference

Exhibit 9-5   Working Capital Template

POSTLUDE

This has been another chapter full of good stewardship, if not chock full of exciting community service, evangelism, or other direct ways of helping people or bringing them to the faith. Remember, good planning is good stewardship—it helps you find the way to best use the gifts you have to do God's will in an efficient, effective way.

As you went through the chapter, you learned why to plan, and then we walked, step by step, through the planning process. The parts of that process, which work for any kind of plan, were:

1. Get Ready
2. Retreat (or Advance)
3. Gathering Information
4. Setting Goals and Objectives
5. Getting Outside Comment
6. Final Draft and Adoption
7. Implementation and Evaluation
8. Start Over

I have to remind you one last time about the importance of the fifth item on the list. You need to get outside comment and include people in your plans and your organization. Don't skip this part of the process.

I also showed you my suggested time lines for planning, ones that you can refer to as you consider your next plan revision. We then turned to different planning outlines, and I provided you with sample templates for a strategic plan, a marketing plan, and a business plan. You can use these as a foundation from which to build your own plans.

Finally, we looked at the issue of capital planning, forecasting your major expenses for the purchase, repair, or maintenance of property, equipment, and vehicles. I showed you why it is so important to do this planning and provided you with both a case study of a capital plan and some forms and formats with which to develop your own.

So often in our lives, men and women of faith rely on God's great plan, trusting in His wisdom. It comforts us in times of despair or pain, allows us to move on after disappointment or tragedy. We believe that God has a plan for His people. So should we do any less for ours? As you go about planning, remember that you are part of the greater, more wonderful, plan. *The counsel of the Lord stands forever, the plans of His heart from generation to generation. Blessed is the nation whose God is the Lord, the people whom He has chosen for His own inheritance.* Psalms 33:11–12

Chapter Nine Checklist

✓ Strategic plan developed or revised

✓ Marketing plan developed or revised

✓ Capital plan developed or revised

✓ Planning skills in house

QUESTIONS FOR DISCUSSION: CHAPTER NINE

1. Is it time for us to develop or revise our strategic plan? Are we ready to do so?

2. Who should sit on our planning committee? Which board members, staff members, outside experts?

3. What other plans should we regularly develop? Should we write down a schedule for these plans to be completed?

4. What skills do we need to develop in order to do better planning? How can we develop them?

5. Do we agree or disagree that we should be inclusive in our planning, sharing the draft plan widely? Why?

10

Getting the Most From Your Volunteers

Each one, as a good steward of God's different gifts, must use for the good of others the special gift he has received from God. 1 Peter 4:10

All men are responsible for one another. Talmud, Sanhedrin 27b

The best of men are those who are useful to others. Hadith of Bukhari

Be doers of the word, and not hearers only. James 1:22

PRELUDE

In this chapter you will learn about:

- ➤ Your board
- ➤ Outside expert volunteers
- ➤ Other volunteers
- ➤ Recruiting, training, evaluating, and retaining volunteers

More than any other type of not-for-profit, faith-based organizations benefit from, and as a result often depend on, a wealth of volunteers. Motivated by the accelerant of faith, volunteers can burn through huge amounts of work with enthusiasm and gusto, work that without the volunteers either might not be done or would have to be done by paid staff. Volunteers staff reception desks, raise money, gather and prepare food, drive, deliver meals, organize special events, staff gift shops, and perform a thousand other important tasks both for places of worship and for community service organizations.

Places of worship are particularly prone to heavy dependence on volunteers for a number of reasons. The first, of course, is their faith and their desire to put the tenets of that faith into personal action. The second is that, unlike most community service organizations, the funds that run the organization *primarily come out of the volunteers' pockets.* Thus, if it is a choice between hiring a staff person (or temporary office assistant, or fund raiser) and doing it themselves, the governing volunteers will often seek either to do it themselves or to enlist other members rather than requiring everyone to pay more in donations, pledges, and tithes. At the same time, nearly all places of worship are understaffed, the small and medium-size ones particularly so. Therefore, there is neither the time nor the expertise on board to manage volunteers well. This is a problem, especially in organizations where the number of volunteer hours are far greater than the number of paid staff hours each month.

In community service organizations that are faith-based, a different paradox presents itself: The affiliation with a particular faith can be a draw to volunteers of the same faith but a deterrent to those of other faiths. Thus Catholic Charities or Lutheran Social Services may be at a competitive disadvantage to recruit much needed volunteers in communities where they provide service but which do not have a high percentage of Catholic or Lutheran residents.

These considerations are the reason for this chapter, in which we will talk about how to recruit, train, motivate, manage, evaluate, and retain your volunteers. Yes, recruit. Yes, evaluate. Yes, manage. Your volunteers are a resource with which God has provided you. You have to manage volunteers as carefully as you do any other resource, and I'll show you how in the following pages.

But before we get to the specifics, we need to look at two overarching issues in relation to your volunteers. The first has to do with competence, the second with motivation. Both will set the stage for our later discussions of technique, and it is important for you to have this context before we proceed.

Competence. Imagine that you have a job opening for a financial manager, a nurse, or a teacher. How would you go about filling that position? Would you put an ad in the paper that says: "JOB AVAILABLE. Y'ALL COME!"? Of course not. You would develop a job description and a set of minimum qualifications. Then you would advertise those job requirements and qualifications, interview, and check references and any necessary certifications (e.g., for teachers or nurses) before you hired.

Upon hiring, you would give the person an orientation, a copy of your personnel manual, and any other tools they needed to do their job. And then, you would closely monitor the new hire to assure that they were, in fact, doing their job. They would be evaluated and if they were not measuring up, told to improve or leave.

I hope that this sequence resembles what happens with paid staff at your organization. But how much of it relates to your volunteers? Do you develop job descriptions, expectations, or qualifications for volunteers? Are there policies? Do you evaluate them? Have you ever asked a volunteer who obviously was not doing a good job at one task to focus their energy on another task more suited to his or her skills and demeanor?

If the answer is no to any of these questions and certainly if it is no to all of them, you have a problem. You are not taking your volunteer cadre seriously enough, and you may be, as Max Depree wisely notes, "confusing enthusiasm for competence." We are so enamored of people who are willing to give their time that we "don't have the heart..." (a phrase I hear regularly) to tell the volunteers that they aren't doing a good job. And, of course, if the volunteers do a bad job and the staff have to redo everything, what benefit is that to the organization and its mission? None.

So, issue one is this: Just as with staff positions, try your best to match volunteer tasks with volunteer skills. This is, I know, not always possible. You do not have a bottomless pool of volunteers, and they don't possess expertise in everything from architecture to zoology, but try. Don't just fill any job with any willing warm body.

Motivation. I would love to believe that all volunteers come to their tasks with pure hearts and purer motivations to serve. I know from experience that this is not true. I see people on boards all the time who are there because of one particular vested interest rather than the organizational whole, or who are there to be against something rather than for something larger, or whose entire history of interaction seems to be designed to disrupt rather than enable.

In *Letters to the Scattered Pilgrims,* Elizabeth O'Connor writes these wise and obviously experienced words: "*...many of God's flock go about looking at His world through clouded lenses, using church projects to build up wobbly self-esteem, enlisting dependent people to foster their phony selves, passing off a neurotic need for affection as a loving, caring nature, or the compulsion to be ever busy as priestly concern. Such persons have within themselves all kinds of conflict which produce dissension in the groups to which they belong. Their vulnerability, excessive demands, expectations, and criticisms make genuine community impossible.*"

Two comments on what O'Connor says. The first is that your organization wants and needs a sense of community, especially for your volunteers. They come of their own free will, and if they don't feel good about the organization, they are just as free to stay home. Remember my Rule of 24. So, if we need that community, why do we let people such as O'Connor describes into the activities of our organizations? Simply because we are religious organizations and are, by definition, inclusive. We take people at their word that they want to help because as people of God, we want to believe the best of our fellow tenants of the planet. The problem becomes that after we let volunteers in the door, we don't have the framework of expectations, evaluation, or discipline in place with regard to our volunteers to redirect the incompetent or remove the disruptive.

So, let's agree that not everyone comes to the task purely, and examine ways in which we can work with such people within our faith and still to the benefit of our organization, its mission, and the people it serves.

Now that we have set the framework, let's look at some techniques in detail. We'll start with the governing volunteer and move through outside experts and on to other kinds of volunteers. Then we'll spend a fair amount of time on recruitment and retention, motivation, and evaluation.

A. YOUR GOVERNING VOLUNTEERS

Your most visible group of volunteers is, of course, those that govern you. These volunteers have the most responsibility in terms of budget and planning. Even those readers whose organizational governing bodies do not have final authority on hiring and firing have to respond and answer to this group of volunteers to some degree.

In Chapter Four we covered the issue of boards of directors (or boards of governors, or elders, or whatever you may call them). In that chapter we went at length into the tasks of the board, how they differ from the tasks of the staff, and how to recruit, train, and retain governing volunteers. If you want that level of detail and you haven't already read Chapter Four, I advise you to do so now. But I do want to quickly recap two very important points here. The first is that governing volunteers who have final budget and hiring authority, are called *fiduciaries* and thus, unlike all other volunteers, are personally responsible for the actions, plans, outcomes, and activities of the organization. This is a weighty and very real responsibility, and as a result, I feel strongly that these volunteers need to be well trained, well informed and very aware of all that is going on in the organization. It is only fair.

The second thing I want to recap quickly here is the listing of governing responsibilities, as follows:

1. Fulfill the beliefs of the sponsoring faith
2. Fulfill all of the IRS, state, and local not-for-profit reporting requirements
3. Fulfill the responsibilities and contractual obligations of the funders
4. Set policy and establish organizational goals
5. Hire the head staff person, if allowed to do so, and evaluate him or her
6. Help develop, adopt, and monitor budgets
7. Establish personnel and financial policies and ensure their implementation
8. Nominate and elect officers
9. Represent the organization in public
10. Raise money

This is a lot to do, and usually means that your governing volunteers do not need to be asked to do additional volunteer duties on a regular basis. In fact, staff should work to make sure that the governing volunteers do not feel obligated to do all the work of the organization themselves, but get help from other volunteers.

If you want more information on how these tasks should be accomplished, return to Chapter Four. Let's look at some other kinds of volunteers now.

B. OUTSIDE EXPERT VOLUNTEERS

This may be a new category of volunteer for you—outside expert. These are people who have a particular skill, experience level, or reputation who offer those gifts to you for a period of time. Outside experts rarely volunteer on a permanent basis; rather, they come in, fix a problem or provide information and insight, and then leave. These experts are great resources for certain issues. Remember that in Chapter Seven on marketing we discussed targeted volunteers, who came in and reviewed your survey or focus group question? Such a volunteer is an example of an outside expert. And, as you think through the many, many uses of such short-term, high-intensity volunteers, you need to keep in mind a few rules for recruiting such people.

1. Recruit for an Appropriate Problem or Issue
The most important rule in using expert volunteers is to use them for an appropriate task. You don't want to wear out your welcome with the

experts, and you don't want to assign them to such long or involved tasks that they cannot complete the work in this life. In other words, think, and don't get greedy with your experts. Let's look at some good and bad uses of an expert volunteer.

Good uses of expert volunteers

- Review (not development) of a survey instrument or focus group questions
- Website development
- Assessment of options for repair of a major piece of equipment
- Second opinion on an engineering issue
- Review of insurance coverage

Bad uses of expert volunteers

- Developing your personnel policies
- Doing your audit
- Painting your building
- Making major (costly) repairs or renovations
- Developing financial policies
- Reviewing leases or contracts

The main idea is to pick a task that has a short duration, requires specific expertise, and involves no long-term professional liability.

2. Be Completely Forthcoming about the Volunteer's Obligation

Like all of you, I get calls to help on a committee, serve on a board, or work on a project for some worthy organization. I am flattered to be asked and glad to help when I can. Often the request is to do a quick review of a management issue or policy, a piece of marketing material, or some other issue with which I am supposedly familiar. What I want from the organization in these cases is to be told the *entire truth* about my obligation. What will cause me to gracefully (or not so gracefully) withdraw is finding out that I was a victim of "bait and switch," wherein I was only told *part* of the story.

❏ **FOR EXAMPLE:** A few years ago, our church was gearing up for a major capital fund drive. As this project was getting organized, my wife and I were called on to host a gathering of members in our home.

We were told that "all we had to do" was host a two-hour get-together and prepare the food and drink. We would be provided with an agenda for the meeting, and a member of the funding committee would attend, leading the group, showing a videotape, and in general, making sure that things ran smoothly. "That's all?" my wife asked when she took the call. "Yes, that's all," she was assured. With both of us working and the activities of three children to keep up with, that seemed like a reasonable way to help the effort. After all, it really required us to have the house clean and food prepared and to host a two-hour social and educational event. Not a big deal. Right?

Not hardly. A week later we received in the mail a list of the two meetings we were expected to attend to instruct *us* on how to run the meeting at our house, as well as a listing of people to call to provide food and come to our house. We were told that we had to keep track of who signed up for the meeting at our house and submit this once a week to the overall finance committee. We were *not* pleased, but we went ahead and did what we were asked, putting it in the category of "learning experience." Our commitment turned out to require well over 30 hours of work, all of which was, to say the least, not performed joyfully. After the meeting was over, we went to the church leadership to tell them of our unhappiness with the way we had been recruited. And since then, we have, unfortunately, been suspicious any time we are asked to help.

As I write this chapter, the church is starting its newest capital campaign. I know we will be called on to host an evening meeting again. And I know we'll turn it down, which is regrettable. But, fool me once, shame on you; fool me twice, shame on me.

☞ **HANDS-ON:** Treat your expert like the professional he or she is. Put your needs and expectations, as well as the full limit of the work and the duration of the project, in writing. That will force you to really think through all of the needs you have and ensure that your volunteer really knows what he or she is getting into. You don't want the person to go away mad at your organization! *The seal of God is truth.* Talmud, Shabbat 55. *Putting away falsehood, let everyone speak the truth with his neighbor, for we are members one of another.* Ephesians 4.25.

3. Don't Expect to Get a Lot for Nothing

You get what you pay for. In our chapter on the role of governing volunteers, I cautioned you against trying to have board members who were also attorneys or accountants do your audit or legal work. The issue is that you cannot count on even well-intentioned people to put your nonpaying work consistently at the top of their pile. Thus, information or outcomes that you may desperately need can be put on hold indefinitely, perhaps by your volunteer's boss. Or, your volunteer may have an emergency or another crisis to attend to. In this case, it is unlikely that he or she can pass off *pro bono* work on a peer the way that they could hand over a regular, paying contract.

All of which is to caution you to use this volunteer source carefully, for the right task, and for a reasonable length of time.

C. OTHER VOLUNTEERS

You have a variety of other kinds of volunteers to consider utilizing. Let's look at some different subsets and how faith-based organizations use them. This could give you food for thought if you find you need to ramp up your volunteer involvement.

1. Program Volunteers

These volunteers actually do some of the service work of the organization. They could be Sunday school teachers at a church or lay ministers for an outreach ministry. At a community service organization, they might deliver meals, staff a donated goods shop, or read to schoolchildren. Obviously what you need in this area is not only willingness but true skills and, where appropriate, licensing and certification.

2. Administrative Volunteers

These volunteers do a wide variety of secretarial and administrative chores. They may open, sort, collect, or deliver mail, make copies, develop newsletters, collate handouts, make phone calls, answer the phone, perform data entry, file, archive, and do a hundred other of these kinds of tasks. These volunteers also need the skills to do these tasks, and the biggest mistake people make with administrative volunteers is assuming that since the job is simple, they don't need supervision. They do.

❏ **FOR EXAMPLE:** A few weeks before writing this chapter, I was in a faith-based organization's reception area, waiting to meet the executive director. I watched two volunteers in the office area just behind the receptionist struggling with a copier. The volunteers were supposed to make a large number of copies for a meeting later that day, but the copier had run out of paper, and they had not been told how to fill it. I overheard the volunteers say, "I wish Mary had told us how to fill this thing. She won't be back until after the meeting starts. What are we supposed to do?"

A small thing, filling a copier. But a predictable one. Mary had not remembered to show her volunteers how to do a basic part of their job.

3. Fund-Raising Volunteers

These people love to raise money. They may be very good at it, they may not be, but they like it, which is not the case for most people. Here is a classic situation in which you can get into trouble with someone who is enthusiastic but incompetent. What if the volunteers like asking for money, but badger people? What if they ask for money, but don't really know much about what it will be used for? Get them training, and supervise them carefully.

There is no limit to the kind of task in which you can use volunteers, as long as they have the necessary skills and as long as the law or your funders allow noncompensated individuals to perform the task in question. I see many organizations which do not use volunteers enough but even more who don't take the time to match the volunteer to the task and vice versa.

In this area, I go back to the concept of using our gifts from God. Each of us has skills, talents, and abilities that are given to us. This is just as true with your volunteers as it is with your staff. Some of us have the gift of administration, others the gift of listening, or of raising money, or of planning. Just as it is important to match up your staff's skills with the tasks at hand, it is crucial to try to find the right place for your volunteers to shine. For example, it would be pointless to have as your volunteer receptionist a person who, no matter how well-intentioned, came across as gruff and impatient. Nor would it make sense to use an excellent administrator of large projects as a delivery person, or a superb musician in a job that provided no chance to use that skill.

There is another point that I need to make regarding skill/job matching. A friend of mine is a music minister at a huge church. He oversees twelve choirs, a performance orchestra, and two huge presentations at Christmas and Easter. He has, literally, hundreds of volunteers with whom he works. In talking to him he told me that he sees himself at times as the "Minister of Involvement," overseeing a part of the church where people can easily get involved. I thought about that term for quite a while after our conversation, and it reinforced my belief that if you offer people the chance to volunteer, it really is a separate ministry, one in which you feed the volunteer's need to help, to contribute. If that is true, then you need to make that experience as positive as possible, just as you would seek to make a teen welcome in a youth group, or a homeless person welcome at a food pantry. Matching a volunteer's skill with the job is one of the parts of a good experience. Just don't plunk them down anywhere.

What this means, of course, is that you need to know your volunteers, just as I advised you to know your staff. Someone needs to take the time and make the effort to utilize this crucial resource as effectively as possible for the benefit of the organization. Who? And how? That's what's next.

D. RECRUITING, TRAINING, EVALUATING, AND RETAINING VOLUNTEERS

Now we need to look at the most important part of this chapter—how to recruit, train, evaluate, and retain your volunteers. For many organizations all of these tasks may be new. That's right, there are many, many faith-based organizations who practice laissez-faire volunteerism; they let whatever happens happen. They accept the volunteers who walk in the door, send them to their tasks unprepared, take what they get from them without complaint, and if the volunteers leave, well so be it.

This is *not,* to understate, what I want you to do. Let's look at the sequence you need to follow to manage this resource as a good steward.

1. Recruitment

Sorry, you can't just go out and start finding people. The first thing you have to do is figure out which jobs are appropriate for volunteers to do in your organization and which aren't. Here, a funder or a state law or regulation may preclude a noncompensated individual doing a task. You may also have a collective bargaining problem if some of your paid employees are represented by a union. So think this issue through carefully.

☞ **HANDS-ON:** If you are going to have more than just a few volunteers, you are at the point where a staff person needs to be appointed Volunteer Director even if it is just part of his or her job. It will, of course, grow into a full-time position as your use of volunteers expands, but even now you need to have a designated contact for volunteers, someone who gets trained in and keeps up on how to manage this valuable resource.

The reason to do this as a group is to open people's eyes to two things: the potential for using more volunteers, and the hard work and real costs of using them. Too often board members or even some staff view volunteers as a "free" resource. They're not. If they are recruited, trained, supervised, and evaluated correctly, they can be a low-cost resource, but never a free one.

☞ **HANDS-ON:** Bring a group of staff and board together to discuss the best utilization of volunteers. Why do you want to invest in this resource? Is the investment more than the money and time that you save? What has been your good and not so good experience with volunteers before? How do you think that you can do more of the former and less of the latter?

Then, talk through which jobs lend themselves to volunteers. Some jobs will be pretty easy to identify and agree on. Others will be controversial. Don't forget to include a discussion of any current volunteer positions. Are they still valid places for volunteers in today's environment?

☞ **HANDS-ON:** It's time for a field trip. Call five or six peer organizations and talk to them about how they use their volunteers. If possible, go visit them and observe their uses. Call your state or regional association and ask for other organizations that are leaders in volunteer utilization and management. Go visit them, if possible, or at least give them a call. There are a lot of organizations who do the volunteer part of their management array very well. Learn from them.

Once you agree on which jobs you may be able to fill with volunteers, you need to develop descriptions for those jobs. That's right. Even volunteers deserve to have a rough idea of what they are expected to do! These job descriptions should discuss the required capabilities of the person filling the job (e.g., driver's license, ability to work well with seniors, children, or people with disabilities), the hours that are required, and a description of the tasks included in the job. They don't have to be long or fancy, but they do need to be thorough and fair to the volunteer. In addition to your job descriptions, you need a full volunteer manual. We'll talk about that in a few pages.

Now, you are ready to recruit. But from where? There are a few good places to start.

Your membership: If you have a membership, this is the obvious place to begin. Places of worship have a built-in volunteer pool, but my caution to you is to try to avoid having ten volunteers do all the work for a membership of 700. You will almost certainly have some people who are more enthusiastic or who have more available time for you than others, but work to spread the load. Be aware of the time commitment that your workhorses are giving you and be sensitive to it.

Your alumni and their families: If you are a community service organization, one pool of help comes from the people to whom you have already provided service. I see this a great deal in organizations that deal with drug or alcohol abuse or ones that work in child welfare or in disabilities. The people whom you serve or have served (your alumni) and their families are often so grateful for what your organization does that they are happy to help and happy to recruit friends to work with them.

Your current volunteers: No, not to give them even more work but to ask them to bring a friend or a relative to help on a single task or project. For example, one of the community service jobs my father did in the last three years of his life was to deliver food for the local Meals on Wheels provider. When he was asked to help, he said yes, but wanted to bring a friend along for both companionship and navigation. So one volunteer recruited another.

Local business: This is more applicable for a community service organization than for a place of worship, but many private businesses are very interested in establishing partnerships in their community by using their staffs to help local not-for-profits. Talk to your local chamber of commerce to see which businesses are interested, and then network with local business owners and managers to let them know your organization is a potential partner.

Local schools: Again, this is mostly for community service organizations, but hundreds of school districts now require a certain number of hours of community service for high school graduation. This laudable trend can be a real boon to community service organizations that use it wisely.

☞ **HANDS-ON:** Talk to your local school district about their policies and interest in this area. There are some insurance issues to consider, and while the entire district may not participate, some junior high and high schools have community service clubs that are looking for places in which to help. *Hint: Always* require a teacher to accompany the students, at least at first. That way, he or she does the supervision and discipline on site, not you.

2. Training

Why train volunteers? For the same reason that you should train staff; they do their jobs better, and isn't that the idea? For some jobs, the training may take fifteen to twenty minutes, for some the better part of a day or even a week, but you have to tell people what they are expected to do, how to do it, why it is important, what your expectations are of them, and who supervises them. If you don't, even the smallest, shortest volunteer stint can be disastrous.

❑ **FOR EXAMPLE:** This story took place while I was writing this chapter. At noon one day I called my wife at the school where she works to relay some good news about her mother, who was ill at the time. The phone was answered with a pleasant voice: "Lincoln School, good morning!" I identified myself, and asked to speak to my wife who was in the teacher's lounge. "I'm sorry," came the response, "I'm a volunteer, and I'm all alone and I don't know how to do that." I was very surprised, as this had never happened before in the many years that my wife had taught at the school. I suggested that the volunteer just get on the intercom to the teacher's lounge (and I knew that the intercom board was on the wall in front of this person). "I'm sorry, I don't know how to do that, and I'm not supposed to leave the office to go get anyone; I don't have keys to lock up the office. Can I take a message?"

I declined, saying that it was not an emergency and that I would call back later. I wanted no part of leaving a message that my wife might interpret as an emergency regarding her mother. (The idea was to provide my wife with *good* news, not a heart attack!) As I hung up, I wondered what would happen if a parent called with a real emergency, or if the superintendent of schools or the bus company called to say that the busses would be late. Or a thousand other real-time issues. This volunteer, who was very pleasant, was incapable of doing a core part of her job, *because no one had showed her how, no one had trained her*. It wasn't fair to her, to any callers to the school and, potentially, to the students themselves.

The rest of the story is that this school is wonderfully managed, a superb learning environment with (on most days) high morale and commitment to mission. People know what they are supposed to do, whether they are staff or volunteers. I am sure that on this one day, this one person was left "for just a few minutes" on the job. Perhaps there was an emergency. Or perhaps the regular secretary went to the bathroom. Or perhaps the volunteer was left for an hour. But the receptionist is the first point of contact for many of your organizations as well. Do you use volunteers there? Are they well trained?

So train your volunteers, as a group on overall issues and individually in their particular tasks. This requires some thought *before the volunteers arrive*. As an initial, but not all-inclusive, guide, let's look at some possible training topics.

Overall

The mission of the organization

The tenets of the faith

A brief listing of the organization's services

Who supervises volunteers

Hours of operation

Dress code

Volunteer evaluation

Individual

Job description

Job requirements

Hours of expected work

Expected outcomes

Direct supervisor's name and phone number

At the very least, these should be explained to the volunteer orally and in writing. Make sure that you demonstrate as many tasks as possible, which increases learning and retention. Also, have a new volunteer work with and observe a current volunteer if at all possible to increase their learning and overall understanding of the organization's culture.

3. Evaluating

I know that this is a tough one for many staffs and boards of directors. The idea of evaluating someone who is giving his or her time may seem like anathema, but I want you to think of it from the point of view of the people your organization serves. Don't they deserve high-quality services? Of course they do. And don't you evaluate paid staff as part of your effort to keep services of the highest quality? Of course you do. So why shouldn't you do the same with volunteers?

The secret with volunteer evaluation is that it should have two parts. First, is the volunteer well matched with the job? You can try and try to make sure that a particular individual has the skills, demeanor, and work ethic to do a particular task and still find out in the first few weeks that the task at hand is not the one for the volunteer in question. Don't wait. *Move now to a different task.* Talk through your evaluation of the work that the person is doing and suggest another kind of work. If you have ever done this with paid employees who are over their heads, what do they usually tell you? Are they mad? Resentful? Not usually. Most of the time they say thank you because you confirmed what they already knew. The same is true with your volunteers. They want to help, not hurt, the organization and most will willingly move to a different task.

The second part of volunteer evaluation is more straightforward: Are they *doing a good job, promoting the mission, and meeting expectations?*

In short, a regular written and oral evaluation is needed for service volunteers as well as for governing volunteers. It means that you need to state your expectations clearly in orientation and training, and then enforce those expectations just as with paid staff. And, as with staff evaluation, there really shouldn't be any surprises. Your supervisors and/or director of volunteers should be giving volunteers regular feedback, just as your staff supervisors should be giving staff regular praise, criticism, and suggestions on how to do their jobs even better.

One way to ensure that these expectations are clear and to reduce the work load of your volunteer director, is to have a *volunteer manual,* a text that includes all of the various work rules, expectations, lines of reporting, methods of evaluation, and so on. The contents should be very similar to the overall list of training topics that I noted above. This manual should be designed to answer basic questions about the relationship between your organization and the volunteer and to give the volunteer a full-spectrum perspective on the organization and his or her contribution to it.

4. Retaining

Now that you have found your volunteers and trained them, how do we retain them? Just as with our paid employees, we make an investment in orienting and training our volunteers. Therefore, I don't want you to suffer undue turnover in your volunteer cadre. It's expensive, and the quality of work suffers. So how do you keep your volunteers on board? Try these ideas on for size.

Train your paid employees how to work with volunteers. This comes first, since it is the most important task. While some organizations have full-time volunteer coordinators, which is a good thing, not nearly enough invest the small amount of time and money needed to educate *all* of their staff in how to interact with, appreciate, and respect their volunteers. This is important, because your volunteers will interact with more than just their direct staff supervisor or volunteer coordinator. And all it takes is one staff person who is unappreciative, rude, or condescending to put a real damper on a volunteer's enthusiasm for the organization. Remember that I told you everyone is on the marketing team? The same thing applies here—it is in everyone's interest to have happy volunteers, *and it's everyone's job.*

One other crucial point. Your staff will watch and emulate the way that you interact with your volunteers. If you are polite, grateful, and a good listener, your staff will be also. If, however, you are always too rushed to stop and say thanks, if you order volunteers around, or gripe about them behind their backs, that behavior will mushroom. Lead by example.

Say thank you early and often. All of us like to know that our work is appreciated. So, be appreciative. Say thanks to your volunteers, in person, with a personal note, with a volunteer recognition luncheon or dinner, in your newsletter, or in the local paper. If you have an awards program for staff, try to initiate one for your volunteers, as well. You may want a volunteer of the month program, leading up to a volunteer of the year award. Perhaps you could have special reserved parking for your volunteers or a monthly lunch with the head of the staff and board.

Stay close to your volunteers. Just as I urged you to get to know your staff and to be accessible by wandering around, I now strongly suggest that you do that with your volunteers, as well. Not only will you meet some remarkable and wonderful people, but by touching in regularly, you get the opportunity to listen to their unique perspective on the organization. Remember, volunteers look at you and your organization differently from your staff. Use this difference to your benefit; ask about how you can do more for the community, improve services, and make things easier or better for the people you serve, as well as for staff and volunteers. Volunteers have the ability to be more objective than staff, and that objectivity, combined with a real commitment to the organization, can really be of benefit to everyone.

It is not unusual for me to visit a place of worship or a community service organization where some particularly innovative idea or program stands out. When I ask how that innovation or idea came about, I'll more often than not be told, sometimes with a bit of embarrassment, "Well, actually, one of our volunteers suggested that improvement. Our staff never saw the opportunity, but the volunteer did." But in all of these organizations the volunteer was made comfortable with making the suggestion in the first place. The staff treated the volunteers with respect, asked for their input, included them in the review of plans, and let them know that they were part of the team.

☞ **HANDS-ON:** If you have more than twenty volunteers, consider having a quarterly volunteer newsletter, which includes short pieces on new volunteers, ways that volunteers can be of help to the organization, brief informative items on organizational services, a listing of board or committee meeting times (if you have adopted the open meeting policy we discussed in Chapter Four) and other items of volunteer interest. You might also use the newsletter to highlight one or two volunteers a month and to give them feedback on planning processes, results of surveys, and so on. One page, two sides, is about all you'll need, and most word processing programs will drop the text into newsletter format in a heartbeat. An inexpensive and effective communications device.

Look for ways to improve by asking. You need to ask your volunteers regularly about ways that you can improve the volunteer experience. Surveys, focus groups, and informal asking should all be part of this effort. Remember, your volunteers are a key market. Find out what they think of the organization, their part in it, and ways to improve their experience. You don't know what they think until you ask!

As with staff, retention is good to a point. You don't want zero turnover. Some new blood is good in any group. New ideas, new perspectives, and new enthusiasm energize organizations. But on the other hand, losing 50 percent of the volunteers whom you train each year is expensive and disruptive. Work to make your volunteers feel appreciated and part of the team, and you will reduce your volunteer turnover to a reasonable level.

POSTLUDE

Now you know the basics about how to recruit, retain, and motivate your volunteers. In this chapter, we looked at this all-important component of the faith-based organization and the methods and rationales for paying attention to this valuable and often underutilized resource. First, we looked at why your volunteers are so vital to your organization, particularly in a faith-based one. We noted that you, hopefully, pay close attention to your other resources and that you shouldn't just take the volunteer part of your resources for granted. We then got to specifics, reviewing briefly the roles and responsibilities of your governing volunteers.

Next, we examined the issue of using outside expert volunteers—why you would, when you shouldn't, and how to go about finding the right expert for your needs. Then we looked at volunteers in general, including the ways you might use them and how to make sure that they are doing their jobs. Remember, don't mistake enthusiasm for competence! Next, we went on to ways to recruit, motivate, train, and retain volunteers, admonishing you to have high expectations and enforce them, including use of evaluations just as with paid staff.

Volunteers are wonderful people, who can help you accomplish your mission, spread the faith, and make your life easier. They can also be the opposite of all of these things. As a result, it makes sense to pay attention to your volunteer issues, where you use volunteers and how you supervise them. They are a gift, like any other, and need to be used wisely as you go about God's work.

Chapter Ten Checklist

✓ Volunteer policies

✓ Volunteer training schedule

✓ Volunteer evaluation policy

✓ Review of volunteer role in our organization

✓ Train staff in volunteer appreciation

QUESTIONS FOR DISCUSSION: CHAPTER TEN

1. What is the appropriate role for volunteers in our organization? Are we depending on them too much? Not using them enough?

2. Do we need volunteer policies for management? Job descriptions? Expected outcomes? How do we get them?

3. Is it appropriate to turn ineffective volunteers toward another task? To ask them to leave?

4. Are we ready to evaluate our volunteers? Who should do that?

5. Do we need a designated director of volunteers?

11
Final Thoughts

But without Faith it is impossible to please Him; for he who comes to God must believe that He exists and that He is a rewarder of those who search for Him. Hebrews, 11:16

PRELUDE

In this chapter you will learn about:

➤ Holding on to your core spiritual values
➤ Staying motivated year in and year out

You now have read about the core techniques that will help you run your faith-based organization with more effectiveness, more mission outcome. You have learned about why your organization is special and why it is held accountable for that uniqueness. I have given you ideas, examples, and suggestions on how to deal with your staff, what your board should do, how to manage your finances more effectively, how to become a market-driven yet mission-based organization, how to plan for the future, and how to pay appropriate attention to your volunteers. I hope that you have found many ideas to consider and that some have already been put to work.

But nearly all the things I have shown you how to do or exhorted you to try are just techniques and philosophies of management. The bad news is that working on your technique can cause you to take your eye off the long-term organizational ball. You can, to bend another metaphor, focus just on the trees and forget about the forest. In putting too much energy and enthusiasm into the details, you can miss the larger picture.

The larger picture? Your organization and its core spiritual values. In these final few pages, I want to caution you about the times ahead and give you some suggestions about how to not lose the specialness of your organization in the coming months and years. It is easier than you might think to lose your way, and so I want to provide you with a map to help you.

A. HOLDING ON TO YOUR CORE SPIRITUAL VALUES

I don't know your faith. You may be Jewish, Muslim, Christian, Buddhist, Hindu, or of some other belief. But I am sure that you can identify the basic tenets of your faith, those core beliefs and central dogmas of your spiritual self. We've talked throughout this book about the need for your organization to do the same and to regularly remind itself of the tenets of your sponsoring faith in order to ensure that you stay on course. The challenge in an ever-changing world is to help your organization adapt to those changes, to keep up with what people want so that you can continue to do mission effectively, while at the same time not losing the essence of what makes you, your staff, and volunteers special. That is no easy task, and one that can easily result in your being gored by the horns of this dilemma: Do we change and adapt or do we stay the same?

On the one hand, keeping close to your beliefs takes the faith of Abraham, but only combined with the wisdom of Solomon and the foresight of a prophet. And you will often be tempted to stray off course by circumstances, by people of both good and ill intent, and by that scourge of the ages, the deceiver.

❏ **FOR EXAMPLE:** Some change is fine, some a bit too far. And only you and your governing board can decide that. Most readers will have seen the musical *Fiddler on the Roof.* In that wonderful show, the central issue is whether Tevye, the protagonist, can be flexible and change with the times, or whether he will hold on to his traditions. As the show progresses, his dilemmas become more and more serious, and finally he can be pushed no further; what he has been asked to agree to is too far outside his values, his faith, to allow.

❏ **FOR EXAMPLE:** The papers are all too full of stories of ministries and churches that have suffered when their leaders fell victim to deceit, perhaps a sure-fire investment such as Covenant, or to greed, as did Jim Bakker, or to more worldly temptations, as did Jimmy Swaggart.

But it doesn't take a crime or a sin to bring your organization to grief. It just requires your taking your eye off the ball. So what should you do to stay on course? Try the following suggestions.

1. Make Your Mission and the Tenets of Your Faith Visible

We talked about this in earlier chapters, but it is an important part of staying on course. Put copies of your mission and creed on the walls, on your letterhead, on people's bulletin boards, in your newsletter. Have copies of it literally on the table at management, board, and committee meetings. Use it regularly as a benchmark for discussion and a guide for decisions. Will it end all of the dissent in your organization? No, and it shouldn't. What it should do is focus the discussion around options *within the faith* instead of outside it.

2. Make Faith Part of Management and Management an Outflow of Faith

Your faith needs to be part of your everyday conversation, your management framework. In saying this, I mean that your staff and volunteers need to know, and to be reminded that your organization is a devout and spiritual one. I am not saying that you should inject God into every single conversation, but the fact of your faith should be recognizable and evident, hopefully in a manner that both fits your organizational culture and does not make those who don't share your faith (inside or outside of your organization) uncomfortable.

☞ **HANDS-ON:** All the places of worship I have worked with and all the most successful faith-based community service organizations start and end their staff, board, and committee meetings with prayer and often include a short devotion. In organizations whose staff may not all be of the sponsoring faith, devotions from other denominations or beliefs are welcome, but not required to be shared. Thus there are spiritual bookends embracing every meeting, which keep people aware that they are driven by both faith and mission.

3. Ask God for Guidance

I know that there are readers who are tut-tutting that this suggestion should be first. But the first two suggestions had to do with your overall organization. This pertains to you, in your personal decision making. Whether you pray, meditate, fast, or read your sacred texts to gain insight on the correct choices to make, let God work through you by making yourself accessible to His will. After all, Proverbs 3:5-6 admonishes us: *Trust in the Lord with all your heart and lean not on your own understanding; in all your ways acknowledge Him and He will direct your paths.* In the New Testament, the book of James tell us: *If anyone of you lacks wisdom, let him ask God, who gives to everyone without reserve and without reproach, and it will be granted him.* (James 1:5)

4. Have Faith

You are, after all, a leader of a faith-based organization. There will be times of undue stress, even of despair for your own or your organization's ability to succeed in the face of some unusually severe challenge. Then, most of all, you have to use your faith to help you through. And remember the admonition of James to the unfaithful person. This citing immediately follows the scriptural quote above about asking God for wisdom. *But he should ask in faith with never a doubt: for one who doubts resembles a wave of the sea that is driven and tossed by the wind. Let not that man imagine he will receive anything from the Lord; he is a double-minded man, unsteady in all his ways.* (James 1:6-8)

I have given you just four suggestions for holding on to your core spiritual values, but these ideas will be useful in helping you *stay* the course and *on* the course at the same time. As I said in the initial chapters, your faith is a wondrous and wonderful thing, the thing that makes your task and your organization so special. Don't lose that specialness in the rush of day-to-day activities, or in the inevitable changes in the world that you must cope with.

B. STAYING MOTIVATED YEAR IN AND YEAR OUT

Even with all of your faith, there will be times that you, your staff, and your volunteers will despair, become exhausted, and want to slow down, if not stop, for a while. But the people who depend on you to help them are tired, too, and their problems don't wait, they just fester and get worse. So how can you keep yourself and your people motivated over the long run? Here are some things that work.

1. Lead

The best motivator for staff and volunteers is a strong leader, one who shares their values, has a clear idea of where he or she is going, and says, in effect, "Follow me!" This fact is why I exhorted you in the chapter on staff management to walk the talk and why I included an entire chapter just on leadership skills. You need to be visible and committed to the mission, and you must appear confident about the direction of the organization even on days that you are not.

There is no better motivator for staff, and it is part of your job.

2. Celebrate Your Successes

We talked about this a bit in the management chapter and again in the chapter on leadership skills, but it has great application here. Our management and board meetings seem to be filled with discussion about what we've done (our reporting), what we are going to do (planning), and how to deal with crises (what's gone wrong). What hardly ever gets discussed is a huge motivator—what has gone *right*. Your organization is full of wonderful stories of people who have been positively affected by your staff and services. Share just one of those stories at each meeting. It will reenergize your staff and volunteers, while at the same time keeping them focused on the important things in the organization, the outcomes of your mission.

3. Take Time Off
No one is immune to a need to recharge his or her batteries. Force yourself, discipline yourself to take off at least one full week (two is better) and several long (four-day) weekends each year. By taking off I don't mean taking work along or calling in three times a day. Your mind, body, and spirit need a break. Give in to them. You will return refreshed, with a new outlook and ready to face challenges and overcome barriers.

Then, require no less of your staff, particularly your senior managers. Make sure that they spend time away, and that during their vacation they don't sneak in to read their mail or call in for messages. Remind them that you need them rested and healthy. That's what vacations are for.

4. Go Away as a Team
Once a year, take your management team away from the office for a day. Spend part of the day working, planning, and discussing the coming year and how your organization can improve. Spend part of the day socializing together, perhaps over lunch or dinner, with no work allowed. Then spend part of it playing together. Play miniature golf, bowl, go for a hike in a park, or do anything that will let people spend time together and get to know each other better. At the end of the day reconvene for a time of reflection, meditation, devotions, or prayer. This kind of miniretreat can do wonders to bond teams and give them some perspective on their work and their peers.

5. Say Thank You—a Lot
The part of management accomplished by wandering around is touching base with people to talk to them, thank them, and to let them know how much you appreciate their efforts. If you, your management team, and your supervisors all do this, the results can be spectacular.

❏ **FOR EXAMPLE:** Think of some for-profit businesses whose employees always are "on." For me, Disney, Lands' End, Nordstrom, Marriott, and Federal Express leap to mind. And, it should be no surprise that they all have something in common. They tell their employees *every day* how important they are. That's right. Every day for 15 minutes, all of the employees at the Disney theme parks are told that they are important, that they are the crucial link in the customer satisfaction chain, and that their supervisor appreciates them. The same is true at Marriott, Lands' End, and many other highly motivated firms. And they have some of the highest customer satisfaction ratings in the world, because the employees are motivated enough to do their job well, even on days that they might rather just stay in bed with the covers pulled up over their heads.

Such a simple thing, saying "Thank you, we're glad you're here." The trick is in doing it all the time. Try to be more visible, more appreciative, and more attentive to your staff. If they believe your praises are sincere, their motivation and morale will benefit.

6. Spend Time at the Point of Service

Once per month, or once per quarter, spend a shift at the line of service. Get out of your office, away from your meetings, take off your beeper and *serve*—directly, in person, with no management layers, no memos, no appointments between you and the people you are there to help. For nearly every management person I know, this is a tremendous motivator as well as a good reminder of the point of the organization.

There is no one who will tell you that staff motivation is easy, but the organizations that work at it, such as Disney, Marriott, Lands' End, and Nordstrom, benefit from the effort. You can too.

POSTLUDE

In this final chapter, I tried to give you some help in keeping on track and in motivating your staffs. My concern is that in employing the management ideas and techniques that I have given you in the previous ten chapters, you may lose the closeness to your faith and your mission that is so important to you. To avoid that, I suggested the following actions:

1. Make your mission and the tenets of your faith visible
2. Make faith part of management and management an outflow of faith
3. Ask God for guidance
4. Have faith

We then turned to my concern about ways to help you, your staff, and your volunteers stay motivated and focused on the task at hand, in good times and in bad. Here, I suggested the following:

1. Lead
2. Celebrate your successes
3. Take time off
4. Go away as a team
5. Say thank you—a lot
6. Spend time at the point of service

And now, a couple of final thoughts and some good wishes for your journey.

As the leader of a faith-based organization, you have the unique and wonderful opportunity to do the work of your God here and now. Your organization can be a clarion call to your faith, showing by works rather than by words the canon that you and your fellow believers have been drawn to. You have the ability to influence the lives of many people: your staff, your volunteers, the people you serve, their families, and your community. This is a heady responsibility and not one to be taken lightly.

And you haven't taken it lightly, or you wouldn't have read this book. I hope that you have found ideas, thoughts, and suggestions that can help you do your job better, make your organization more mission-capable, and allow others to see the benefits of faith. I also hope that our journey together has just begun and that you will refer back to the text repeatedly as you move forward and that you will continually glean benefit from parts of the book that perhaps do not have any immediate application today, but might well a year or two hence.

My wish for you is that your faith will strengthen your organization and at the same time that working for the organization will strengthen your faith. A belief in God, however you envision Him, whatever you call Him, is a two-way street. You worship, and you receive guidance. You supplicate, and you garner strength. You put your faith into action, and you witness the truth, wisdom, and divine inspiration of your Scriptures come to life. It is, indeed a wondrous thing to see something like that happen in front of you, a joy that only a few are given. You are one of the chosen. Remember that on your hardest days, and rejoice in it.

May your heart be pure and open to the will of God.
May the challenges you face make you stronger and wiser.
May the people you serve rejoice that you are who you are, and do what you do.
And may God be well pleased with your stewardship.

Peter C. Brinckerhoff
August, 1999
Springfield, IL

Chapter Eleven Checklist

✓ Visible mission

✓ Visible tenets of our faith

✓ Devotions at meetings

✓ Regular celebrations

QUESTIONS FOR DISCUSSION: CHAPTER ELEVEN

1. Is our faith visible enough in our organization? Can we make it more visible without making people uncomfortable?

2. What is the best way to display our mission and the tenets of our faith?

3. How much do we actually celebrate our mission? Should we do more? How?

4. What other ways are there to keep ourselves motivated? What have other organizations like ours done?

Resources for Further Study

The following books and workbooks are ones that I recommend for you to use as you continue (or take the first step) on the path of life-long learning that we discussed earlier in the book.

Buchanan, John M., *Becoming Church, Becoming Community*. Louisville: Westminster John Knox Press, 1996

Considine, John J., *Marketing Your Church*. Kansas City: Sheed & Ward, 1995

Jones, Laurie Beth, *Jesus CEO*. New York: Hyperion Press, 1992

Ray, David R., *The Big Small Church Book*. Cleveland: Pilgrim Press, 1992

Rehnborg, Sarah Jane, *The Starter Kit for Mobilizing Ministry*. Tyler, TX: Leadership Network, 1994

Shawchuck, Norman, *Managing the Congregation*. Nashville: Abingdon Press, 1996

Warren, Rick, *The Purpose Driven Church*. Grand Rapids: Zondervan Publishing House, 1995

Wilson, Marlene, *How to Mobilize Church Volunteers*. Minneapolis: Augsburg Publishing House, 1983

Index